D1561861

TIMBERWOLVES
Stalk the NBA
Obsession

TIMBERWOLVES
Stalk the NBA
Obsession

Bill Musselman's relentless quest to beat the best

Bill Heller

Bonus Books, Inc., Chicago

93 92 91 90 89   5 4 3 2 1

Library of Congress Catalog Card Number: 89-85669

International Standard Book Number: 0-929387-05-8

Bonus Books, Inc.
160 East Illinois Street
Chicago, Illinois 60611

Printed in the United States of America

In loving memory of my parents,
Sylvia and Benjamin Heller, and my
Uncle Joe. This one's for you
wherever you are.

Contents

FOREWORD

Last summer while visiting my family in the Twin Cities, my brother Steve and I stopped by the offices of the newest NBA team, the Minnesota Timberwolves. I wanted to check on the season tickets I was getting and on the players the Wolves were going to choose in their first draft. But most of all, I wanted to visit with my old coach and friend, Bill Musselman. We hadn't seen each other since a Lakers game the previous season. A lot had happened in both our lives, so we had a bit of catching up to do.

At the end of our conversation, he surprised me by asking if I would do him the favor of writing the foreword to his life story. I surprised myself by declining the invitation. I was in the midst of therapy for a season-ending back injury, was trying to devote time to my foundation, and had a fast-approaching deadline for a manuscript of my own, *The Complete Baseball Player*, that I was writing for Avon Books. I just didn't think I could take on one more responsibility.

The more I thought about Bill's request, however, the more I realized that I couldn't turn the guy down. And the fact that I had a lot to do made it even more appropriate. The heart of Bill's philosophy when he coached me at the University of Minnesota was what he called the "overload principle." Basically, you worked until you dropped, then you got up and worked some more. That was 15 years ago, and here he was doing it to me again! I called him up a few days later and said I would do it.

One reason I changed my mind was that I felt the public might benefit from seeing Bill Musselman through my eyes. You see, I was there when he first came on the scene in Minnesota. It was a spectacular debut. As an eyewitness, let me introduce you to Bill by recollecting my own introduction to him.

I had come to Minnesota with a scholarship in baseball. In addition, I played on the freshman basketball team. My next two years, however, I was content to play intramural basketball with my brother and a team of friends called the "Soulful Strutters." One day early in my junior year when we were scrimmaging the freshman team, Jimmy Williams, one of the assistant varsity coaches, saw me play and asked me to try out for the varsity. I told him that I'd give it a shot.

I was not only flattered by the invitation, I was also impressed by what I had heard about the new head coach, a fellow named Bill Musselman. He'd caught my attention and a lot of other people's by announcing that he planned on guiding Minnesota to the Big Ten championship that year. He wasn't daunted by the fact that the Gophers hadn't won a basketball title in 37 years. "I don't believe in rebuilding seasons," he said, challenging himself, his team, and his opponents in one swoop.

Preparing to play was as rigorous a regimen as I had ever gone through—mentally and physically. To begin with, here I was, a walk-on from the baseball team, someone who might fight his way into the lineup and take a spot away from one of the "real" basketball players. By that time I had already decided that my future was on the diamond and not the court. I suppose that made me even harder to take for some of the Gopher players who were looking for lots of playing time and an eventual career in the bigs. The Gophers had a half dozen pro prospects on their roster that year. Several went on to play professionally, and one of them, Jim Brewer, became a standout in the NBA.

The players didn't exactly put out the welcome mat for me. In fact, a few of them were downright nasty, and on occasion actually tried to injure me. Under these conditions, every day was a challenge. The more they beat on me, the more I hustled. I kept my concentration and my spirits high until one day for one moment, it all came crashing down. The pressure had finally gotten to me. I threw the ball off the court and fell to my knees in tears. It was all over in seconds and Bill came over to me and told me to go to his office and wait for him.

As I waited, I just knew that this little incident was my ticket off the court, that Coach was coming to tell me to clear out my locker because I hadn't made the team. Well, that wasn't it at all. Bill closed the door behind him and told me that he knew what I had been going through and how hard it was. He then told me he wanted me to keep at it and that he had faith I would prevail. I wasn't so sure at the time, but Bill's talk and his confidence in me were inspirational.

As my first game drew closer, our practices seemed to get even more intense. Coach Musselman stressed tight, in-your-face defense and punishing physical workouts. We'd practice with weight jackets— an extra 20 pounds or more as we ran up and down the court—and whichever team lost ran laps immediately afterwards. We used weighted basketballs to build up our wrist and hand strength. For rebounding and developing the upper body, we had a special instrument of torture, the McCall Rebounder. It was an elevated platform that held a regular or weighted basketball and was rigged with a lever that made the ball that much harder to grab. Fighting this machine almost required a third hand. You didn't even attempt one-handed rebounds.

The result of all this training and conditioning was a pretty tough team justly known as ''Musselman's Musclemen.'' Shortly before the first game, Bill took me aside and told me that I had made the team. That hurdle cleared, other barriers dropped, also. Having seen my intensity and ability, the other players knew I could help the team win and accepted me. Many of them went from being teammates to becoming friends.

We got off to a good start, and in our fifth Big Ten game of the season were looking to upset a team that usually beat us, Ohio State. There was some rough play during a slow first half, but nothing out of the ordinary. The half ended with the teams tied at 23. As we got ready to go into the locker room, the Ohio State center punched our point guard right in the face. Everybody was so stunned that the center was well down the hallway before we could even yell a threat at him. There was some tough banging out there in the second half and some fouls that didn't get called, but things stayed pretty much under control until the last minute of the game. Then the OSU center went down on a foul and all hell broke loose. Soon it was not just players fighting. The fans poured onto the floor and both teams ran to the safety of the locker room.

We lost the game to the Buckeyes and two of our starting players were suspended. In only the fifth game I played, I became a starter, one of the "Iron Five" who would play virtually every second of the rest of the games on our schedule. I won't keep you in suspense. Despite all the setbacks, the Gophers won the Big Ten title by taking the last game of the season, by one point over Purdue. Coach Musselman made good on what many had considered an idle or foolish boast.

A flood of media coverage resulted from the Ohio State game that was far from accurate or fair. Unfortunately, it gave Bill a black eye that has overshadowed his many remarkable accomplishments.

My senior year we stayed close enough in the Big Ten race to almost claim back-to-back titles. We finished second and went on to the National Invitation Tournament at Madison Square Garden.

Following his career at Minnesota, Bill went on to coach the Cleveland Cavaliers. Then he rewrote the record books in the Continental Basketball Association with a 19-game winning streak and four straight titles. Indeed, he set the standard for professional basketball with the highest winning percentage ever recorded in a single season.

Now he's ready to tackle what may be his toughest assignment: to take a brand new expansion team into the competitive stream of the NBA and come out a winner. If anyone can do it, it's Bill Musselman. He's savvy, disciplined, and driven. What he lacks in height, he makes up for in depth. People either love him or hate him, but in my experience, it's hard not to respect him.

When I played for Bill, I didn't always agree with him and sometimes he infuriated me. He could help make you or help break you. If you endured, you had a good chance of being able to survive other challenges to follow. Bill coached me at a formative time in my life and played many different roles for me. He was part teacher, trainer, motivator, confidant, friend, and authority figure...and all coach. Few people have contributed more to the philosophy of my personal and athletic life. What I learned from Bill helped get me drafted in three different sports, and has helped me persevere through 17 years of major league baseball.

So, Muz, keep on keeping on and doing for others what you've done for me. Promise them heaven and give them hell. Share that explosive gamesmanship, the competitive drive, and the work ethic that are the foundation of your success. Challenge them to share the opportunities that you so regularly enjoy. I hope you go on to stand the NBA on its ear. Regardless of what sort of win-loss record you post, you're a winner in my book, and your book is a winner, too. So, fans, kick back and prepare to meet an American original, Bill Musselman.

Dave Winfield
October 1989

Acknowledgments

There wouldn't have been a book without my wife, Anna, who never for a second lost faith in me and my work. Her emotional support was dwarfed only by her physical work: transcribing more than 100 taped interviews into notes; re-typing rough copy into final drafts, and working tirelessly listening to rewrite after rewrite. That she also poured her heart into the growth and care of our baby son, Benjamin, is a testament to her remarkable resolve.

Dave Winfield was asked if he'd do the foreword for a writer he'd just met on the phone. Winfield agreed. His insightful foreword reveals a unique perspective of Bill Musselman and reflects Winfield's commitment to quality. His promptness was incredible.

Larry Donald, Editor of Eastern Basketball and Basketball Times, steered me to Mitch Rogatz at Bonus Books. Rogatz was a tower of support from Day One.

Gary Urcheck sent a carton of newspaper clips which saved weeks if not months of research which would've precluded the completion of *OBSESSION* in time to coincide with the Timberwolves' first season.

Musselman's son, Eric, was extremely cooperative and helpful.

Special thanks to former Wooster High School Basketball Coach

Jim Byrd; my network at Ashland College: former Sports Information Director (SID) Chuck Mistovich, current SID Dr. Al Hall, his assistant Brian Bay, and Athletic Director and Football Coach Dr. Fred Martinelli; Public Relations/SIDs: Tim Bryant (Timberwolves); Steve Snapp (Ohio State); Bob Price (Cavaliers); Brian McIntyre and Terry Lyons (NBA); Bob Peterson (University of Minnesota), and Alan Aldinger (Wittenberg); author Charles Salzberg; Larry Creger of the L.A. Summer League; "Crazy George" Schauer; Eric Swenson; "Seltzer" Ingle, Keith Marder, Maureen Kelly, Bob Gersowitz, Mrs. Ben Berger, Marion McIntosh, Abe Lacheta, Ken Lyons, Barry Ikler, and R. Heller.

Finally, I offer my appreciation to the people who helped shape my career in journalism: Al Hart, Eddie Palladino, John Bonifacio, Dick Clemente, Dr. William Rowley and Paul Simon, an unwavering source of creative inspiration.

Previewing the Timberwolves

A sultry summer night in San Antonio, July 26, 1989, was the setting for the Midwest Revue, a three-night stand for free agents and rookies hoping to make the NBA rosters of San Antonio, Houston, Denver and the Minnesota Timberwolves. The round-robin tournament seemed insignificant to the NBA season three months away, but that didn't lessen the anxiety for two of the principals inside the San Antonio arena. They had little in common except their unbounded appreciation of the moment.

San Antonio's 7-1 center David Robinson, an All-American at the Naval Academy, fidgeted awaiting the jump ball. The first pick of the 1987 college draft had waited two years to play in the NBA because of his post-graduate commitment to the Navy.

Across the court from Robinson, Timberwolves Coach Bill Musselman felt a familiar dryness in his throat, his body's signal that a game he was coaching was about to begin. Musselman's NBA exile had been $3^1/_2$ times as long as Robinson's. He'd been jettisoned from the hapless Cleveland Cavaliers the way one spits out a watermelon seed, except he'd been spat out twice by Cavs owner Ted Stepien, in 1981 and 1982. Musselman's ache to return to the NBA raged inside himself, an obsession to once again belong to the tight-knit fraternity of 27 men in the world who are head coaches in the National Basketball Association.

His journey back had stops at Sarasota, Tampa Bay, Rapid City, S.D., and Albany, N.Y., in the Continental Basketball Association, the poor man's NBA. Four straight CBA championships fueled Musselman's return to the NBA with the Timberwolves, one of two 1989-90 NBA expansion teams. After signing a four-year contract Aug. 23, 1988, Musselman spent the entire 1988-89 season scouting. He hadn't coached a game since April 30, 1988. "I was ready to go," Musselman said. "It'd been a long time."

Musselman savored his moment of return while fans in the Twin Cities of Minnesota celebrated the first breath of life of the Timberwolves 29 years after the Lakers left for L.A.

They weren't disappointed.

San Antonio went with a powerful line-up. Guards Willie Anderson and Vern Maxwell had started much of the previous season for Coach Larry Brown. Then there was Robinson, who signed an eight-year, $26 million contract with the Spurs. "He's going to be a great player," Musselman said.

Musselman didn't have any proven players, let alone a great one. The Timberwolves first three picks of the Expansion Draft, starting power forward Rick Mahorn of the NBA Champion Detroit Pistons, small forward Tyrone Corbin of Phoenix and center Steve Johnson from Portland, weren't on hand. Nor were two of Minnesota's three selections in the NBA College Draft, UCLA point guard Pooh Richardson and Villanova shooting guard Doug West. West had undergone hernia surgery a week earlier.

Of Musselman's 14-man squad in San Antonio, only center/forward Brad Lohaus and forward Shelton Jones, the Timberwolves No. 4 and 6 selections in the Expansion Draft, had played serious minutes the previous season in the NBA. Lohaus was traded in mid-season from the Boston Celtics to the Sacramento Kings. Jones, who signed a two-year contract with the Timberwolves, July 24, played with the Philadelphia 76ers.

A third member of the Timberwolves, Clint Wheeler, split last season in the NBA with Miami and Portland and in the CBA with Rapid City (S.D.), whose General Manager was Musselman's son, Eric.

Joining the trio in San Antonio were rookie center Gary Leonard from Missouri, Minnesota's second pick in the NBA College Draft, and several free agents who had played well during tryout camps in Minneapolis earlier in the summer: Sam Mitchell, Tod Murphy, Jim Thomas, Keith Smart and Mike Whitmarsh. Thomas, Wheeler and yet another prospective Timberwolf, Conner Henry, all played last season for Rapid City. Another CBA refugee was Donald Royal from Cedar Rapids, whose coach, Gary Youmans, played for Bill Musselman at Ashland College and worked with him as the General Manager with Tampa Bay.

Mitchell, a 6-7 forward, and Murphy, a 6-9 center, each played in Europe last season, Mitchell in France and Murphy in Spain. Each had played for Musselman previously in the CBA, Mitchell in Tampa Bay and Murphy in Albany.

Mitchell's dominating presence in three Timberwolves' free-agent camps earned him a two-year contract the day before the Midwest Revue began. "This guy is no border-line player," Musselman said. "He can help us."

He did in San Antonio.

Despite the Spurs' obvious edge in talent and experience, the Timberwolves used Mitchell's 17 points to stay close as a crowd of 2,275 grew antsy waiting for a blowout which never materialized.

Leading 66-65 after three quarters, the Spurs eked out a 90-86 decision.

"We played hard," Musselman said.

Murphy played hard and well enough to stake a claim for a spot on Minnesota's opening-day roster. "Tod Murphy played well," Musselman said. "Robinson didn't score on him for 20 minutes." Murphy's performance in the Revue games led to his signing of a two-year contract in mid-August.

Robinson, who finished with 22 points, six rebounds and five blocked shots, dominated Gary Leonard, who also signed a contract in August. Labeled "a project" in preseason, Leonard did nothing to disprove this assessment with his 10 minute stint that netted no points or rebounds.

Thomas had 18 points, seven rebounds and four assists. Royal scored 15.

To prove the close score wasn't a fluke, the Timberwolves beat Denver, 108-101, and Houston, 104-100 in triple overtime, the next two nights. Mitchell had 23 points in each game and 10 rebounds and three blocked shots vs. Houston. "We gave Sam a contract, and he played well three straight games," Musselman said. "He's an NBA player."

After scoring just 10 points in the first two games, Lohaus uncorked a fine performance against Houston, 23 points and 10 rebounds. Lohaus made a 25-foot, 3-point field goal to tie the score with 17 seconds left in the second OT.

The heroics weren't appreciated by the crowd of 2,153 waiting for the Spurs to square off with Denver. "They just wanted to get us the heck off the court so they could see David Robinson," Lohaus said.

Musselman liked what he saw: "We came here looking for consistency and concentration, and I think, for the most part, we got that for three games in three nights."

Timberwolves' fans got a whiff of success which will be hard to reproduce once the season starts. "It gives us some cautious optimism that we can be competitive this season," Timberwolves President Bob Stein said.

Realism suggests otherwise. Charlotte and Miami, the NBA's expansion teams last season, generated just 20 and 15 wins from an 82-game season. If nothing else, their performances provide a gauge for Minnesota and its expansion cousin, the Orlando Magic.

Desperately, Stein wants to avoid the black hole of the NBA, the one Miami couldn't escape last year when it wrote an ominous first chapter in its franchise history by starting 0-17. "The Midwest Revue went well," Stein said. "We want to go forward from that. What we've seen so far is what we want to see, players who play together and play hard. From a team standpoint, we want people who play hard all the time; people who are intense competitors, have a good knowledge of the game and are unselfish."

Stein isn't concerned about his coach being an intense competitor. Musselman's resume is fat with remnants of intensity strewn throughout his roller-coaster career.

He acknowledged the difficulty of his mission with the Timberwolves: "It's going to be a lot of hard work."

Indiana University Coach Bobby Knight, a long-time friend of Musselman who played against him in high school and coached against him in the Big Ten, said he hopes Timberwolves fans are realistic: "I think it'll be hard for any expansion team trying to get players who'll be around for five years. People have to understand he'll do everything he can, but an expansion franchise is an expansion franchise. If it's hard for Bill to accept, he shouldn't have taken the job. He understands that. I know how he works. He puts a lot of himself into his work."

Knight knows first-hand. He and Musselman made their Big Ten debuts against each other. Musselman's University of Minnesota team won by a point. Musselman's initial Big Ten season ended in a championship, an accomplishment obscured by the most notorious fight in the annals of college basketball, Minnesota vs. Ohio State. "I didn't think he'd get another chance after what happened," Knight said.

Resiliency has always been a Musselman attribute. Controversy has always been a companion. But with the Timberwolves, Musselman starts anew.

Quite understandably, he wanted to shape his new team with players he knew well.

Nobody in pro basketball is better suited to Musselman's system than Sidney Lowe, the point guard who led North Carolina State to the 1983 national championship. Lowe quarterbacked three of Musselman's four consecutive CBA championship teams, two with the Tampa Bay Thrillers and the last one in Albany when Musselman's Patroons produced the best winning percentage (.889; 48-6 regular-season record) in the history of the CBA and the NBA.

After 21 NBA games with Detroit and Atlanta in 1984-85, Lowe returned to the CBA, where he watched many of his teammates get the call to the NBA while he remained behind. "We had all these guys that got called up, and there I was. I played for him for three years," Lowe said. "Maybe 14, 15 guys went up, and I was the starting point guard on all three of those teams."

Ironically, Lowe got back to the NBA after playing for Eric Musselman in the CBA at Rapid City. After Albany traded Lowe to the Thrillers for Kelvin Upshaw in preseason, Lowe sat out much of the 1988-89 season. He joined the Thrillers, Feb. 24; played just 13 games, and was called up to Charlotte, where Lowe, his wife and their son, Sidney Jr., lived.

Lowe not only played for Coach Dick Harter, he played well. His NBA return turned into a special moment. Lowe was given a long standing ovation when he was introduced for his first game with Charlotte against the New York Knicks, March 27. "This is where I played, and I have a lot of friends here, but I didn't expect that," Lowe said.

Three months later, Lowe was asked to do commentary about the NBA College Draft for a Charlotte radio station. "There were more than 15,000 people at a Draft party," Lowe said. When the Tim-

berwolves came to bat with the 10th pick in the first round, NBA
Commissioner David Stern told a national prime-time TV audience,
''Minnesota drafts Jerome 'Pooh' Richardson.''

Lowe remembered his reaction: ''I was a little shocked. I didn't
know if Coach Musselman was planning on having three point guards
or not.'' (Minnesota had already selected point guard David Rivers of
the Lakers with their No. 5 pick in the Expansion Draft.)

Lowe found solace in the words of his coach, Bill Musselman:
''After about half our guys moved up to the NBA, Coach told me about
18 times, 'I don't care where I go. If I go to Timbuktu, I'm going to
take Sidney with me.' ''

Phonetically speaking, Musselman was prescient. Instead of
Timbuktu, Lowe went to the Timberwolves. Minnesota formally bid
for Lowe's services in late July, signing him to an offer sheet. Charlotte had 15 days to match the offer and keep Lowe. Charlotte passed.
Lowe and Musselman were reunited. Lowe was jubilant: ''Charlotte
didn't match it, so I get to go. I'm feeling awfully good.''

Lowe's acquisition gave Musselman peace of mind. Word leaked
out in early August that Pooh Richardson was being courted by Il
Messaggero, the Italian team which pried Danny Ferry, the No. 2 pick
of the NBA Draft, away from the L.A. Clippers. The *Dallas Morning
News* said in a story, Aug. 7, ''The next player with a chance to put a
little lira in his pocket is UCLA guard Pooh Richardson. The same
team that signed Ferry is in the final stages of offering Richardson,
who was taken by Minnesota with the No. 10 pick, a two-year contract.''

Stalled negotiations between Richardson and the Timberwolves
painted a bleak picture, but Richardson signed a four-year contract
with Minnesota, Aug. 31. The Timberwolves also signed Whitmarsh,
a 6-7 forward, and Jim Farmer, a 6-4 guard, and announced Tom Thi-
bodeau, a former assistant at Harvard, as one of Musselman's assistants.

The Italians' woo of Pooh was one of several summer stories affecting Musselman. Musselman's predecessor and succcessor with
the Albany Patroons each signed lucrative contracts, Phil Jackson as
head coach of the Chicago Bulls and George Karl with Real Madrid in
Spain.

Ironically, Minnesota's first home game ever will be Nov. 8
against the Bulls, matching Musselman and Jackson, two former
coaches of the Albany Patroons.

Musselman's delight when the Patroons hired his former assistant, Gerald Oliver, to replace Karl, was tempered with the tragic death of the CBA's 25-year-old Commissioner, Jay Ramsdell, eight days earlier.

Ramsdell was one of the fatalities of the United Airlines flight which crashed in Des Moines, Iowa. Oliver had been best man at Ramsdell's wedding. Ramsdell's emergence as the youngest pro sports commissioner in America mirrored Musselman's rise as the dominant coach of the CBA. Ramsdell was thrilled when the Timberwolves signed Musselman, a measure of prestige and acceptance of the CBA by the NBA.

Back in Minneapolis, season tickets for the Timberwolves reached 14,200 by September 1. "We'll cut it off at 15,000," Stein said.

Further excitement was generated when the Timberwolves announced their first preseason game would be against the Lakers, Oct. 18, in the Hubert H. Humphrey Metrodome, the Timberwolves' home until next season when they move into a multi-million dollar new arena next to Butler Square in downtown Minneapolis.

The new arena's design generated considerable controversy. "If it had been a student project, we probably would have sent it back to the drawing board," Ralph Rapson, former Dean of the University of Minnesota School of Architecture, said April 30. And that was the Timberwolves' second attempt. The original design was tossed when it elicited criticism by local architects.

Nobody criticized the Timberwolves' community involvement in the summer. The Timberwolves staged a series of free clinics for children in July and announced plans for a 3-on-3 basketball tournament to benefit Minnesota Special Olympics. Additionally, the Timberwolves said the preseason game against the Lakers will benefit the 1991 International Special Olympics Games in the Twin Cities.

"Off the court, ideally, we at least want players with no problems," Stein said. "Hopefully, we'll have people who contribute to the community. Rick Mahorn is a good example. He quickly got involved with Special Olympics. When he played for the Bullets (before he was traded to Detroit), he was the chairman of Special Olympics in Washington, D.C."

Of course, Stein doesn't mind having a starter for a championship team now playing for the Timberwolves. "We were surprised to see him out there unprotected," Stein said. "We knew that Detroit was deep with a lot of young players."

Minnesota isn't. That's why Director of Player Personnel Billy McKinney scouted the L.A. Summer Pro League in July and August. "We thought about bringing a team out here, but then we decided our time would be better spent focusing on the guys here and seeing how they stack up against our guys," McKinney said.

One of the guys Musselman wanted, Lakers swingman Tony Campbell, was available as a free agent in the summer. Campbell, though, said the Timberwolves "might not have the money."

For one team or the other, Campbell figures to be in the Metrodome when the Timberwolves and the Lakers clash in preseason.

Just two weeks later, the Timberwolves start the real season, opening Nov. 3 at Seattle.

Lowe was asked how Musselman handled the final weeks before camp opened in October. "He's bonkers," Lowe said. "He's still the same coach. He's still Bill Musselman."

Musselman admitted he couldn't wait: "I'll be ready to go, that's all I've got to say."

—————————————————————— • *1*

Obsession: A Way of Life

The lane was wide open. Nobody was boxing out. Players were slow getting back on defense this late February evening at Siena College outside Albany, New York.

Then again, it was an exhibition game for charity.

Most everybody on the court, the basketball playing members of the New York Giants (Pepper Johnson, Kenny Hill, Tom Flynn, Herb Welch, and ex-Giant Dave Jennings) and the opposing members of a celebrity all-star team, seemed to understand the concept.

Except one.

Flynn rushed over to the celebrities' bench and beseeched their coach: "Get that nut out of there before he kills someone. Doesn't he know this is for fun?"

Nobody on the bench had to ask whom Flynn was talking about. That nut, Bill Musselman, had just shoved Pepper Johnson, a 6-foot-3, 250-pound starting linebacker for the Giants, squarely in the back to get a rebound in the lane. Now that same nut, 47-year-old Bill Musselman, was outsprinting the entire Giants' team, professional athletes 25 to 30 years old, downcourt for an easy deuce.

Bill Musselman plays hard. After the game, he laughed: "Did you see those guys out there? They've got 20 years on me and I was beating them down the floor."

Musselman wasn't exaggerating. While Johnson threw down an astounding array of slam dunks, none of the Giants seemed in quite as good shape as Musselman. Of course, the Giants were playing an entire game with six people. And they had played a game that afternoon.

However, there was something wonderfully revealing seeing Musselman determinedly beat the New York Giants to loose balls and rebounds. And how many 170-pound men in their late 40s would have the guts to shove a Pepper Johnson out of the way? ''That's the only way I know how to play,'' Musselman said. ''It's fun to play that way, with enthusiasm, intensity, and really going after it. That's why I like to play. That's competition. I don't care who I play. The New York Giants, they don't bother me.''

Competition comes only one way to Musselman, never sugar-coated, never for fun: 'Compete with me and you pay the price. Challenge me and I'll beat you. I'll keep beating you, keep pounding you. That's what competition is.'

That's the *only* way it is for Musselman. Who else would call time-out with a 48-point lead and 30 seconds left against one of his best friends? Musselman did it to Charleston coach Gerald Oliver, his former assistant with the San Diego Sails of the ABA and the NBA's Cleveland Cavaliers. ''We weren't executing well,'' explained Musselman, whose Albany Patroons beat Charleston by 49 that night. ''Every second on the floor, you're supposed to play hard. Regardless of the score, regardless of the time of the game. You ask your players to execute every time up and down the floor. Not many coaches do that. If you're up 20 points or more and still demand perfection at that point, it's hard for people to cope with. People aren't used to perfection.''

Basketball teams frequently reflect the nature of their coach. In 1987–88, Albany became the killer shark of the Continental Basketball Association (CBA), not only beating other teams but drinking their blood. Besides winning the CBA championship, the Patroons went 48–6, producing the highest winning percentage (.889) in the history of the CBA—and better than any ever in the NBA. ''I'll make them notice me,'' Musselman said, ''them'' being the powers of the NBA. They had ignored his remarkable achievement of four consecutive CBA championships while sending 22 players from the CBA to the NBA. ''He felt that he won those championships, but nobody took notice,'' his son, Eric, said.

Bill Musselman still hadn't earned his own passage back to the

NBA. He'd yet to gain another chance after his abysmal failure in Cleveland in two seasons (1980–82) with the Cavaliers.

The hurt burned deep inside Musselman. "The drive within me is incredible," he said. "I used to go running, thinking I will push myself relentlessly. I'd be working out thinking this is how hard I'll push to get a damn NBA job. I'll work as hard at coaching as I am pushing myself physically. I will not ever give up."

He couldn't; he was obsessed.

Eric Musselman, general manager of the CBA's Rapid City (South Dakota) Thrillers, called his father "very, very competitive. We stopped playing one-on-one against each other after I beat him one day. There came the point where I got to be a little quicker than he is and a little faster. He just didn't want to play anymore. He wanted to play tennis or something where he could kick my ass.

"It's kind of funny if you ever see the guy playing Pac-Man on the road. He plays Pac-Man all the time, and he gets so intense he won't leave the game until he beats the top score, even if it takes two hours. And that's kind of how he is. It's the same type of thing when he's playing racquetball or tennis.

"I've played doubles with him where he'll be serving and if you screwed up the time before that, on his first serve he'll purposely hit you in the back of the head with the ball. That's just to show you, 'Hey, don't screw up again.' He's just so competitive in anything he does. He doesn't do anything for fun."

Ask Pepper Johnson.

————●

On August 23, 1988, Bill Musselman was named head coach of the Minnesota Timberwolves, one of two expansion teams entering the NBA this season. "We could have made a safer choice, where everyone would have said, 'Yup, that's a great choice,'" Timberwolves President Bob Stein said. "That entered my mind, but I never considered that to be a good reason to make a choice."

Most basketball fans have heard of Musselman, but more people are aware of his notorious reputation than his glittering record, 151–47 in four seasons in the CBA and 192–68 in 10 seasons at Ashland College and the University of Minnesota.

Do a word association test using "Musselman" and the two most frequent responses will be "Cleveland" and "the Minnesota–Ohio State fight."

This will likely change as Musselman's name becomes part of the Minnesota Timberwolves' NBA history. Now, however, people wonder. How did this guy get back to the NBA? Just how did the coach who screwed up in Cleveland, going 26–67 in two seasons and trading away several high draft choices for mediocre players, get another shot?

''When Bill's name came up quite often, initially I tended to dismiss it,'' Stein said. ''On the surface, I wasn't sure he'd fit in with the philosophy of the organization. I was thinking about the things other people had raised as a concern, trading away draft choices for players in Cleveland and the fight in Minnesota. Essentially what happened, though, is I kept hearing a lot about him, both from people who were supporters and people who said we shouldn't hire him. Virtually every conversation from anybody, whether they liked him or not, started out saying he's a hell of a coach. It was either 'He's a hell of a coach but. . .' or, 'He's a hell of a coach and. . .' The more I thought about it, if there's that kind of unanimity about something that critical, that's worth looking into.''

Stein developed interesting insight examining Musselman's most celebrated controversies: ''I saw his concept of appropriate loyalty. He just took the heat. He didn't go back and ever say, 'Well, it was an impossible situation because of this and this and this,' even when it was true. I think of all the times I see someone doing that when they're just making up excuses. And here's a guy who had some situations that I knew were almost impossible, and yet he felt, 'Hey, somebody gave me a chance, and I'm just going to shut my mouth and win my way back to the NBA.' Just gut it out and earn it, and I thought, God, what an unusual amount of character and determination.''

From an early age, Bill Musselman's life was framed by sports; his childhood divided into seasons of basketball, baseball, and football. He played all three in high school in Wooster, Ohio, going head-to-head against two boyhood pals, Bobby Knight from Orrville and Dean Chance from West Salem. ''We played all the time,'' said Chance, a Cy Young Award-winning pitcher. ''Bill's been a friend of mine a long time. Listen, once you're kids and you're friends, you're always friends.''

When Musselman faced Knight on the basketball court, Wooster won all six meetings. Musselman's football team beat Knight, also, taking a 6–0 victory in 1957 when Knight's punt into a wintry wind wound up landing eight yards behind the line of scrimmage. Musselman rushed for 125 yards on 16 carries that cold evening in Orrville.

When trauma terrorized his boyhood world, when he was seven and his mother and father divorced and made him choose which parent he'd live with, Musselman drove himself harder into sports. He found unrestricted joy in pursuing athletic excellence, and he set the standards extremely high. "Bill was really a dedicated kid," said Jim Byrd, Musselman's high school basketball coach.

Musselman saw dedication every day his mother came home from work. "My mother had to work her heart out in a potato chip factory in town," he said. "Yet she managed to keep our house spotless. She used to tell me, 'You get out of life what you put into it.' "

Musselman put everything into coaching after playing football, baseball, and freshman basketball at Wittenberg University in Springfield, Ohio. "I knew I wanted to coach when I was 12 or 13 years old," he said. "I was given the ability to be a coach."

He was 24 when he became head coach at Kent State University High School. Two years later, he was named head coach at Ashland College, just 20 miles from Wooster. "When I was coaching at the age of 24, I thought I could win," Musselman said. "You're always confident when you work hard. I think that I had that ability. God gave me the ability to do that."

At Ashland, Musselman turned a nondescript small college program into a personal showcase. Following a 10–10 debut, his Eagles went 119–20 in five seasons, leading the nation in defense the last four. In 1968–69, they set an NCAA record by allowing 33.9 points a game.

Before they stifled opponents, the Eagles treated SRO crowds of 3,500 to a ballhandling show, an idea Musselman borrowed from his college coach, the legendary Ray Mears.

At Ashland, players spun balls on their fingertips, juggled balls three at a time, and made crowd-pleasing dunks while "Keep the Ball Rollin' " blared on the PA system. The best ballhandler was "Crazy George" Schauer, who later made a career of his basketball wizardry.

Musselman brought show business with him when he moved on to the University of Minnesota. Literally. "Crazy George" transferred from Ashland to Minnesota, where he scored just one basket in three years, but thrilled crowds with his pregame routine. He wasn't a one-act show. Musselman told the story: "This guy comes in my office. He weighed 150 pounds and he's 5-foot-9. He says:

'I can make your club. I can play Big Ten ball.'

'Where'd you play last year?'

'I was in your pep band.'

'How you gonna play Big Ten ball?'

'Come out in the gym.'

"This kid got on a unicycle and asked me to toss him three balls. He juggled three balls right on the unicycle. I says, 'Hey, come up to my office.' He made the club.

"In the middle of the season, a guy walks into my office and says, 'I want to make your ball club.' He had big, thick glasses and was skinny. I said: 'What in the hell are you going to play for us?'

'I can beat out your unicyclist.'

"I thought, This is getting to be a circus. I've got a second-team unicyclist."

But people remember the fight. They see the wildly intense coach still on the sidelines. They see his icy stare and fiery manner, and they think of the night of infamy in Minneapolis.

On January 25, 1972, a match-up of undefeated Big Ten teams, Minnesota and Ohio State, turned into the ugliest brawl in the history of college basketball. With 36 seconds left and Ohio State leading 50–44, Minnesota's Marvin "Corky" Taylor and Ron Behagen went wild, attacking Ohio State center Luke Witte. Then Minnesota fans poured out of the stands and attacked Ohio State players. Representatives of the national media watched in disbelief. Witte and two teammates, Mark Wagar and Mark Minor, were hospitalized.

The brutal moment Taylor kneed Witte in the groin and the ensuing pandemonium were shown on TV newscasts around the nation. A *Sports Illustrated* cover story pointed a national finger of guilt at Musselman, who was blamed for inciting the crowd and his team. He was introduced as a coach who'd win at all costs.

Seventeen years later, Witte said he's worked out his "severe hate."

Then and now, Musselman has denied responsibility for the incident: "There was nothing I could do. People said I showed no remorse. People said I over-motivated the crowd. It's ridiculous. They said the fight happened because of my pregame warm-up. That I over-psyched the crowd, over-hyped it. That had nothing to do with it. My job was to create enthusiasm, get the crowd behind the ball club, and to get people into the stands.

"The fight was the last thing I ever wanted. I didn't want that fight. I didn't want that. I wanted to win a ball game. I didn't care about that other stuff. On the advice of the Big Ten, I was told not to say anything about it. It bothered me more than anyone ever knows because it was the state of Ohio. People don't realize how sensitive I was because I was from Ohio. I have friends and relatives who live there. The reaction to the incident hurt me."

Others had more tangible pain. Witte's vision was impaired. Wagar suffered a concussion. Taylor and Behagen were suspended for the rest of the season by the Big Ten. Musselman won anyway, taking Minnesota to its first outright Big Ten title in 53 years and leading the nation in defense by using an iron-man lineup of five players. One of the five had just joined the team from intramurals. His name was Dave Winfield. "Best rebounder I ever had," Musselman said.

The fight and a separate NCAA investigation of his program that uncovered 128 violations obscured Musselman's considerable accomplishments at Minnesota. He and Knight made their Big Ten debuts against each other in 1972, with the Gophers prevailing 52–51.

Knight, speaking last fall to a group of tire company managers in Minneapolis—with Musselman in attendance—offered his perspective of Musselman's Minnesota days: "When Musselman came here, he brought in trained parrots and unicycles, and it was like damn Ringling Brothers. Basketball was way down the list. And what he did was captivate all of the people that knew absolutely nothing about basketball, and they continued to come to games. And that's why Minnesota has such a really good following to this day."

Other teams Musselman coached didn't have a following. His brief, unsuccessful ABA tenure in 1975–76 began with the San Diego Sails (3–8) and ended with the Virginia Squires (4–22). Both franchises folded.

After working in San Diego installing tennis and racquetball courts, Musselman returned to pro coaching in the short-lived Western Basketball Association. He took the Reno Bighorns to the threshold of a championship in 1979 before losing Games 6 and 7 of the finals to the Tucson Gunners, coached by Herb Brown.

At Reno's first game, Musselman invited Billy Martin to appear. He did, and he subsequently got involved in an incident, punching a reporter after the game. Musselman helped settle the ensuing dispute and has remained Martin's close friend.

Last spring Musselman joined one of his boyhood idols, Whitey Ford, on the dais at a roast of Billy Martin in Las Vegas. "We go way back," Martin said. "He's quite a guy, a real competitor. He wants to win so badly. That's the type of person I like."

Martin said he believes Musselman's dedication will serve him well in his return to the NBA: "He'll do well with the Timberwolves because he's a good coach. He knows how to motivate people."

He also knows how to make people laugh.

Before an Athletics–Padres exhibition game, Musselman donned a Padres uniform and catcher's mask and equipment and walked in uninvited on Martin. "They're all lined up, Rickey Henderson and all those guys," Musselman said. "They just came back in from batting practice. And here's a Padre walking in. They didn't know who the hell I was. And I got my head down...face mask, chest protector, shin guards...nobody said a word. Martin's in a corner with his coaching staff, complaining about not being able to use the designated hitter because they're playing the Padres. I go, 'Mr. Martin, Mr. Martin.' Every step, I got closer to him—I was going to take a bag of marshmallows, but I thought it was a bad idea if he didn't know who it was—I get about three feet away from him. I pull my face mask off. He gets like a stunned look. 'Bill? Bill Musselman? What are you doing? Are you workin' out with the Padres?' "

Fifteen years later, Musselman still laughs after telling the story. Martin recalls his initial reaction before Musselman removed the catcher's mask: "I said, 'Who the hell is this kook?' "

Luke Witte could have said the same thing when Musselman called his house in 1979 to recruit him for Reno. Witte had played three seasons in the NBA and then in Europe, but retired after a severe ankle injury.

"The first time he called me was about 5:30, 6:00 in the morning," Witte said, "So it had to be 2:30, 3:00 out there (in Reno), which didn't surprise me after I thought about it. But obviously I was not awake. And I woke up and I kept saying, 'Who is this?' I thought it was a fraternity brother or something. A friend that would just give me a hard time. And I said, 'Come on. Who is this?' I thought it was a joke, and then, afterward, I say 'Did this really happen? Did the phone ring?' I wasn't sure that it had taken place.

"So a couple days later, my wife Donita says, 'Hey, that guy called again. He was telling me about tennis courts and swimming pools and country clubs and this and that.'

'You've got to be kidding.'

'He talked for like a half hour. I said nothing.'

'Okay, so it's real. It wasn't a dream. Let's collect myself here.'

"So he called back two days later and he says: 'What's your answer? I'd like to have you out here right away. This would be a great publicity hype.'

'Yes, it would. It would be a great publicity hype for you, because it would make me look really stupid and that's what I'd be, going out and playing for you.' "

Witte declined. He said, "I thought it was a joke."

It wasn't.

Musselman is so focused on his obsession to win basketball games, he rarely considers anyone else's perspective. Life, as seen through the eyes of Bill Musselman, is narrow in scope. That's quite evident as he discussed recruiting the one player in America who hated him the most.

"I called him because I thought he was a good basketball player," Musselman said. "I felt he was a good competitor, a good player. Sure, I called him. What do I care? I judge a guy by how he plays basketball. I felt he could help us win. I felt he had a chance to get back in the NBA. I really believe that he could have gotten back in the NBA if he'd have played again and that's why I called him. Hey, I wouldn't have called him if I didn't think he could have dominated our league. I told him I respect him. Something happened that was wrong. It happened. And what's that got to do with it? I thought the guy was a great basketball player, so what did the fight have to do with anything? I thought he had a couple of years left. I'll coach anybody, and I have."

The list is a long one, especially in Cleveland. Musselman was hired, fired, re-hired, and re-fired while losing miserably in the 1980–81 and '81–82 seasons. He was vilified for years following his dismal record. His son, Eric, had hot dogs thrown at him while he was playing for his Cleveland high school basketball and baseball teams.

Bill Musselman's sister Connie remembered the blatant abuse she and her mother encountered in the stands at Cavaliers home games: "It was awful, absolutely awful. We tried to protect our mother from a lot of it for a long time because she couldn't deal with it at all. It was hard enough on the rest of us, but it was really hard on my mother."

Musselman was blamed for trading an ungodly number of future draft choices for players he thought could provide an immediate fix. He was operating, however, on strict win-now orders from owner Ted Stepien, who went through six coaching changes in three seasons before selling the team. The NBA interceded with the new owners, providing extra draft picks for the ones scurrilously traded away.

Many thought Musselman's purge from the NBA would last a lifetime.

Musselman tried to salvage his career in the CBA, landing in Sarasota, Florida, where he promptly got fired again 19 games into the 1983–84 season. He re-entered the CBA a year later with the Tampa Bay Thrillers, fueled with the improbable goal of doing well enough to earn another chance in the NBA.

Three CBA titles weren't enough. Eric wondered if the reality would crush his dad's dream: "After he won the third and he didn't get to the NBA, I said, 'You know, the guy is going to go . . . he's going to go off the deep end. He's not going to make it.' "

But he did. When the Tampa Bay Thrillers relocated in Rapid City, South Dakota, Musselman moved to Albany for the 1987–88 season. He assembled an awesome cast featuring three former first-round NBA draft picks, Michael Brooks, Micheal Ray Richardson, and Tony Campbell; proven CBA stars Lowes Moore, Derrick Rowland, and Kenny Natt; and talented newcomers Scott Roth, Scott Brooks, Tod Murphy, and Rick Carlisle.

Musselman not only predicted success, he talked openly of winning all 54 games, or at least 50. People snickered right up to Albany's 11–0 start. After losing two in a row, the Patroons won a CBA-record 19 straight. Albany finished 48–6; gave Musselman a fourth consecutive championship despite losing four players to the NBA (Campbell, Roth, Michael Brooks, and Carlisle), and set remarkable records for fewest points allowed in a quarter (8), half (26), and game (60).

"I just felt every time my team took the floor, it was going to win," Musselman said. "The worst thing you can do is have players with talent who don't want to compete. The guys I had in Albany took a lot of pride in themselves to win game after game. In the CBA, there aren't a lot of great competitors. A competitor competes whether he's in the NBA, CBA, racquetball, or whatever. Our society doesn't have a lot of great competitors."

How do his players respond? Michael Brooks, voted the CBA's MVP in 1987–88, put it simply: "Winning comes from the top. Coach

Musselman doesn't like to lose. He only knows how to coach one way, and that's hard. A lot of people say, 'How do you play for him?' It's easy. You do your job."

Musselman said, "I'm a mellow person off the court. Since I got the Minnesota job, I've had so many people meet me and say, 'You're just like anybody else. You're normal.' "

Until he steps onto a basketball court.

When professional basketball returned to Minneapolis, where the original Lakers won five titles in six years before moving to L.A., Musselman completed his arduous journey back to the NBA. "So many coaches and players have come up to me and said, 'God, you earned this job; you really paid your dues,' " Musselman said. "The reality has set in. The long struggle is over. I'm back in the NBA."

Boyhood Days

"Everybody wants to know what motivates me," Bill Musselman said. "The intensity level comes from, obviously, something in your background. Athletics has been my whole life. Period. I had no other interest in school, outside of school, but sports."

Wooster, a village of 22,000 in northeastern Ohio, is small compared to Cleveland, 80 miles to the north, yet large by the villages dotting its periphery: Orrville to the east, Fredericksburg and Shreve to the south, West Salem to the west, and Madisonburg and Smithville due north.

Settled in 1807, Wooster sits in the heart of productive farm country yielding wheat, corn, and potatoes. Dairy farms are prominent, but Wooster also has served as a site of manufacturing plants producing a variety of goods: brushes, roller bearings, furniture, aluminum, brass, paper, and rubber products.

Wooster is cited as the home of the first Christmas tree in America. In 1847, a young German immigrant, August Imgard, was disappointed with Americans' celebration of Christmas. He cut down and decorated a spruce tree, which impressed his neighbors enough that they copied the idea. The custom spread quickly through Ohio, then the rest of the United States.

Basketball at Wooster High School began in 1904 without a coach or a home court. The team went 0–8. The 1906 team was deprived of a place to practice when the roller skating rink at the armory closed. The team was disbanded after losing its opener to Dover, according to the Wooster High School *Basketball History*.

On March 17, 1908, Wooster High School organized the Athletic Association "so that the athletic program may be self supporting." That same year, the school board hired Frank Bonham as coach, marking the beginning of an organized basketball program.

Most Wooster students didn't even know what basketball was. Thus, the 1909 annual explained: "Basketball is a game usually played indoors between two teams, the object being for each side to throw a leather sphere inflated with air into a basket and to keep the opponents from doing the same. It often happens that the two teams are so unevenly balanced that a person ignorant of the game never learns the above fact and imagines they are all on the same side. This is the first real attempt at basketball in the high school. And if we consider only the games played with the out of town teams, we cannot call this attempt successful. But by no means should the merits of the game itself be criticized simply by the showing of one team against another.

"This indoor winter sport affords an opportunity for 'Young America' to work off its surplus energy, with which, if any indications in the class room are not misleading, the average youth is certainly blessed. Of course he can chop wood and a thousand other things in which he would be useful as well as ornamental, but is this recreation? The boy must do for his recreation that which he likes or his disposition will sour. And what is more pleasing to behold than a well-muscled youth with an active brain and manners at all times becoming to a gentleman? Now that the boys have this place they can call their own, all should get out and take advantage of the pleasure the game affords."

William Clifford Musselman did, and he hasn't stopped since.

The second of three children, he was born August 13, 1940, in Wooster to Clifford and Bertha Combs Musselman. Their first child, Bob, was two years older. Daughter Connie was born seven years later.

The Musselman heritage traces roots to five different countries in Europe (Germany, Ireland, France, Holland, and England) as well as to America. Bertha Musselman's maternal grandmother was a full-blooded Cherokee Indian. Her maternal grandfather emigrated from England to America. In 1923, when Bertha was five, her father sold his general store in a small town in Kentucky and relocated his family in Ohio.

Bill Musselman's mother worked several years in a potato chip factory. His father was an auto mechanic who raised coon dogs and was an avid hunter. "He had 20 dogs," Musselman said. "He was going to crossbreed a greyhound to a coon dog. Make that coon dog run like hell."

Coon hunting was important to Clifford Musselman, so he shared the experience with his two boys. Bob liked hunting. Bill didn't. "My dad used to take me hunting when I was four or five years old, coon hunting in the middle of the night, like 12 o'clock," Musselman said. "He'd leave me in the middle of the woods by myself. He'd let the dogs go, and they're out looking for a coon up a tree. And when they started barkin', he'd set the ladder down and say, 'Stay by the ladder,' and then he'd take off.

"And the dogs...you'd hear them in the hollow or a valley away. Shit, they'd be a mile away barking. He'd go out after them. I'd be sittin' there with a ladder, one o'clock, two o'clock in the morning. Sittin' by a ladder and I'm saying, 'Oh, man, I hope he comes back.' I hear the dogs barking. My God, it sounded like miles away. Hoot owls hootin' hoo-hoo. And that's why I never hunt. Man, that turned me off. I remember nights he left me out there. I'm sittin' in the middle of the woods by myself, five years old."

Musselman remembers one night he heard too much barking. "I hear a bunch of dogs screaming," he said. "The coon just attacked one of the dogs and stripped the skin right off him."

Musselman remembers more pleasant times with his father, such as when he sang to him or those special moments when they'd play baseball. "My father started hitting fly balls to me when I was six, a ton of them," Musselman said.

He remembers, too, his father's fierce pride in his work. "He worked very hard," Musselman said. "He was one of the top automobile mechanics in the country. He worked on Clark Gable's car. Clark Gable had a car failure, and they called my father in to work on it. He was the head mechanic of a large company."

Musselman remembers another of his dad's attributes, one he describes as intensity. Nights hunting coons were invariably intense. But the separation anxiety Musselman sporadically endured in the woods took a more tangible and frightening turn when he was just seven years old.

"I was out playing ball one day when I heard that my parents had separated," Musselman said. "It had to do with his interest in dogs, being away a lot. I was very devastated at the time, and I was torn between where to go between my father and my mother.

"I went with my father, and my mother was devastated. It was very difficult for me, the decision, because I never thought it would happen. I always wanted to live that down. I didn't know which way to go. I went with my father, and found out how devastated she was, so then my brother stayed with my father and I went with my mother. Then my father was hurt. He didn't speak to me for. . . .

"He said he watched me play high school ball. My senior year, my last game, he came to the house, the first time I'd seen him. He said he'd been watching every game. I thought he had no interest. I never knew what went through his mind. But, when he came that night, I knew that he really cared. My mother, when she came to see me two years ago, it was the first time she ever talked to me about my father. She broke down crying. She said how much she really cared for him. That was the first time she ever expressed it to me. Ever. All the years. . . here I am at my age (46 at the time), and my mother was talking about it for the first time."

Forty years haven't been long enough to erase the hurt in his voice when he talks about it.

Musselman's father died in 1964. His mother had long before married Jimmy Miller, whose 35-year career at the Goodyear plant in Akron once included work on the NASA Lunar Exploratory Module. One of Musselman's two half-brothers, John, played basketball for Bowling Green University and then played professionally in Australia.

"Bill was always sports-minded," Jimmy Miller said of his stepson. "Anything pertaining to sports. And he was good in them."

Musselman called Miller "the nicest guy in the world. My stepfather is so close to me. He treated all of us, my brother, my sister, and me, like we were his kids."

Much earlier in Musselman's life, when he faced the trauma of his parents' split-up, sports went from a hobby to a salvation. "It was my way out," he said. "It was my way of escape. I loved basketball. It was a sport you played by yourself. Nobody else was around."

The playgrounds of Wooster offered Musselman a different world, one much easier to understand than the dissolution of his family. "My whole life was centered on sports," he said. "I'd spend hours at the city parks, the high school fields and Wooster College. I'd do anything to play ball, no matter what time it was. At night, my buddies would drive by and yell, 'Hey, Billy. You want to get a bottle of milk?' They'd go out and party and I wouldn't.''

Musselman just played harder. "I'd practice by the hour," he said. "I'd work out on weights, play basketball, play football, all day long. The city always gave me summer jobs in recreation. My high school coach gave me a key to the lights to the outdoor court."

His mother provided unending encouragement, attending all of Bill's high school games. "It wasn't that I loved the games," she said. "I went because the kids were there, because my children were playing. I knew Bill liked sports. When a kid plays sports, he's got his mind occupied on that. They don't look for something else to do. I never had any trouble with Bill or any of my kids.

"I don't think Bill was really any different than a lot of kids that like sports. He just put more time into it, and he was more dedicated. And he was good at them."

Her support didn't subside when her son went from player to coach. "I went to every game at Ashland," she said. When Musselman moved on to the University of Minnesota and the Cleveland Cavaliers, Bertha Miller had trouble understanding and coping with attacks on her son by the media and fans. "Everybody who writes anything about him always brings up that stinking thing (the Minnesota–Ohio State brawl)," she said. "They get new writers and they got to dig it up. It was over before he even got off his butt. It wasn't his fault. He didn't hit anybody. It'd be different if he'd been guilty of doing something like Woody Hayes of Ohio State clobbering somebody. How many fights have they had on the basketball courts since?

"I get nervous even reading about sports since that stinking thing at Cleveland," she added. "They got bad fans up there, I'll tell you. Ohio has the worst fans in the country. I don't know why they are. Maybe they're that way everywhere. I don't know. When I was in Cleveland, it almost drove me crazy. My children protected me from things in the paper. You get to be 71, you don't want to read things that make you nervous."

She seems confounded by the win-at-any-cost mentality the media frequently attaches to her son: "As far as a coach, he ain't no different than any other coach. They all want to win. I never seen one yet that didn't. He's no different. Only he works harder. That's the whole point. Yeah, he's good, but that's because he puts in more hours.''

Musselman came home for a weekend last April to be enshrined in the Ashland College Hall of Fame. He talked of his mother's devotion: ''Her kids are everything. She's always been like that. Her whole life has been her children, and every one of us knows it. The biggest thing with her was the discipline with every one of us kids. I never crossed her, never once. Nobody did, because we all knew she put us before anything.''

Bertha Miller spent years working in the Frito-Lay potato chip factory just outside Wooster, demonstrating the priorities of her life. When she wasn't working there, she frequently was working in her kitchen, feeding her kids and their friends. Musselman's sister, Connie, said their house was a meeting place for him and his friends: ''They all seemed to congregate there. My mother is just the type of person that the more people, the merrier.''

Musselman labeled his mom ''an incredible woman. If I got home from college at 3:00 in the morning, she'd get up and make a three-course meal. If I brought friends to the house at 5:00 in the morning, she'd get up and cook them breakfast.''

Such late-night encounters were rare. However, somewhere along the line, Musselman set a foundation for the unusual way he lives, requiring only four to five hours of sleep each night. Most friends and acquaintances realize this after their first 2:00 a.m. phone call from him. At every stop of his coaching career, others speak of the double-digit-hour work days that Musselman viewed as routine. He credits the physical regimen he's followed his whole life, one shaped by a daily commitment to exercise and one which precludes smoking and alcohol.

''I tried to get him not to work so hard,'' said Bertha Miller. ''You can't tell him anything different. He just always wanted to do a good job, to do things right.''

His relentless manner has always served Musselman well in athletics. Baseball held a special fascination for Musselman, an affinity cultivated by the allure of a distant relative. Earle B. Combs, a Hall of Famer on probably the greatest baseball team ever, the 1927 New York Yankees, was a fourth cousin of Musselman's maternal grandfather. Baseball was the first organized sport Musselman played.

''My dream was to be a major league baseball player when I was 10 years old,'' he said. ''I always followed baseball. The Indians, the

Yankees. September 12, 1954. Cleveland Stadium, against the New York Yankees. I was there. They had the biggest crowd ever, 80-some thousand."

Connie Musselman vividly recalls her brother's devotion to sports: "Bill would be the one getting up early, drinking all the milk and having his breakfast, and then going out running with weights around his ankles.

"What was really important to him was shooting baskets. He would just go do it by himself and be on the court, and someone would feel sorry for him and turn the lights on. I remember him working out and trying to eat the right things. He would mow the lawn or some- thing. . . anything to stay in shape. Now that I'm older, I can look back and see that it's kind of unusual for someone at a younger age."

So was Musselman's lack of rebellion in his younger days. "The coaches told him that he was supposed to be in by a certain hour, and he always was," Connie said. "I know that his friends and him had a good time, but I don't ever remember him getting in trouble."

Musselman, though, could prove troublesome to anybody he per- ceived as threatening his sister. "My brothers, because they're older and I'm the only girl in the family, have always been concerned about their little sister," Connie said. "If I would be somewhere and a guy would start paying too much attention to me, my brothers would start questioning, 'What's that guy staring at you for?' They'd wonder if he had good intentions. I felt if I ever needed any protection of any kind, I knew my two older brothers would be there for me."

One night they proved it. Musselman was home from college, watching TV with his brother. Connie, 15 at the time, was baby-sitting next door. "It was kind of late at night, and I was laying on the couch," she said. "All of a sudden, I saw two guys peeking in the win- dow at me. It scared me to death."

As best as she could, Connie feigned nonchalance as she worked her way across the room to the phone. She called her mom, who promptly informed the Musselman boys of the situation. "Bill and Bob went chasing those two guys," Connie said. "I remember they didn't have any shoes on, and they went across the gravel driveway, carrying on, screaming at these guys, running in their bare feet. They didn't catch them, but they sure gave those guys a scare."

A quarter of a century later, Musselman smacks his lips and

sighs. "Never caught 'em," he says as if he'd still like one more shot.

He should have caught them. He wasn't even wearing his ankle weights.

An Athlete Emerges

Musselman's boyhood friends included two pals from the neighboring villages of West Salem and Orrville. Their names: Dean Chance and Bobby Knight.

Chance, destined for greatness as the youngest pitcher to win the Cy Young Award, was a year younger than Musselman and Knight. "I played baseball and basketball against them all my life," Chance said.

"Dean, Bobby and I played hoop together in the summer all the time," Musselman said.

Musselman spent plenty of time watching Chance play baseball and treasures an afternoon he got two hits off him. "Two singles against Dean Chance," Musselman said. "What do you think that'd be worth?"

One of Wooster's biggest rivals was Orrville, which featured its own intense competitor, Bobby Knight. "Bobby, you know how he is now?" Chance said. "If he would've had to play for himself, he probably wouldn't have stuck on the team. He had the worst attitude. His whole attitude on everything changed when he went to West Point."

Chance has always been impressed by Musselman's competitiveness and resiliency: "Bill's had his ups and downs. Everybody does in pro sports. It's the man who can keep getting up, the one that doesn't quit, he's a competitor. Criminy sakes alive, he worked for Stepien in Cleveland. Criminy sakes alive, he was terrible.

"Bill's a guy who is a dedicated human being. He strives for excellence. He's very, very intense. And the main thing is he can control people. If he can't control them, he's not going to leave them on the team. You show me any team, whether it's high school, college, or NBA. If the coach don't totally control them, they aren't worth a shit. He may win some games, but they'll never win the title."

Wooster High School didn't win many basketball titles. When Musselman joined the team in 1955, the Generals had produced just four winning seasons in the previous 17 and never won more thàn 14 games in one year.

In Musselman's three seasons, the Generals went 6-12, 10-10, and 14-8, the last with Musselman as captain. In those three years, Musselman and Wooster beat Orrville and Knight 72-47, 53-45, 51-33, 70-43, 72-65, and 57-49. "Musselman and I played against each other all through high school," Knight, looking Musselman straight in the eye, told a group of sales managers last fall in Minneapolis, "and I'm not sure we ever beat the son of a bitch in any sport." Musselman grinned at the recollection.

In their first meeting as seniors, Knight scored 37 and Musselman 27. But the Generals won on Orrville's court 72-65.

Their duels weren't limited to basketball. That same year, Wooster blanked Orrville 6-0 on the gridiron. "Snowstorm that night," Musselman said. "Big rivalry. It's a big game, the last game of the year every year." Musselman, a fullback, rushed for 125 yards. A 32-yard pass from Jim Zurcher to Musselman set up the game's only score.

Knight? They'll forever remember the punt he shanked off the side of his foot against an unfriendly wind. He downed the ball eight yards behind the original line of scrimmage. "I went downfield to catch the punt," Musselman said. "The ball looked like it started off his foot, but all of a sudden it started going back the other way. That's how bad the wind was blowing."

Zurcher, whose family owned "The Treat Shop" ice-cream store in town, was a year behind Musselman in school but started alongside him in basketball and football. He remembers life back then in Wooster: "You'd go down to the local YMCA, or you'd go hang out at the park in the summer. Not real exciting. Back then, we were all pretty straight. We didn't have a lot of the outside influences that kids are exposed to now with drugs and all that type of thing. That wasn't even a part of growing up.''

Sports certainly were. Zurcher watched two of the most celebrated basketball coaches in America play frequently against each other as teenagers, not only in high school competition, but in endless pick-up games. Asked who was more intense, Zurcher said, ''Flip a coin. In all honesty, I think Bobby Knight probably worked a little bit harder in trying to become a basketball player. He would literally go out and shoot baskets for hours upon hours. Bill did that and different things. One summer, he was trying to improve his foul shooting. He went out on the court with the theory that if he had a patch over one eye, he could improve his foul shooting in some fashion.''

Ironically, Musselman and Knight, two coaches from neighboring small towns in Ohio, each won a Big Ten championship for universities in other states. And they made their Big Ten coaching debuts against each other. Musselman won 52–51 in Minnesota. ''It was pretty intense,'' Musselman said. Nearly 20 years after their first Big Ten meeting, Musselman wouldn't provide an answer when asked who was more intense.

Though Musselman left Minnesota for pro basketball while Knight remained at Indiana and won three national championships, their lives have crossed frequently. One encounter came at the Houston airport in 1971. ''He had taken the Indiana job,'' Musselman said. ''I said: 'I think I'm going to Minnesota.'

'You really want to go there? Don't you know, they ski every month up there except for two?'

'Really?'

'Yeah. All but January and February, because it's too cold.' ''

Musselman called Knight's 1988–89 season at Indiana ''one of the greatest coaching jobs of the century. I've watched him for years. He prepares longer and works harder than anybody. When I was at Ashland and we led the nation in defense (for small colleges), Knight's Army team did, too. I think Bobby Knight is the greatest coach the game's ever had. I'm talking about consistency and durability. When it comes to teaching, he's as good as anybody.''

Musselman said he knew he wanted to be a coach when he was in the eighth grade. But first, he had to see how far he could get as a player.

Musselman spent the 1953–54 season on the freshman team coached by Jacques Hetrick, now the director of public relations for

Spaulding Sports Worldwide in Chicopee, Massachusetts. ''I'd probably characterize him as an overachiever,'' Hetrick said. ''He had good basic skills. He could dribble and pass and shoot the ball the proper way, but the basic thing I saw was that he was very competitive, very motivated.''

He had good reason one afternoon. ''We had this drill where we lined up at halfcourt with a partner,'' Musselman said. ''You'd chase your partner, and if you caught him, you'd slap him in the face. Coach would blow the whistle, and you'd reverse.''

Musselman watched in horror one day as an upper-class football player, one Musselman had mouthed off to, came to practice and decided to try Hetrick's slap drill. ''I had called him a name,'' Musselman said. ''He was older than me. He was riding me about something, and I talked back to him. I said, 'I don't care how big you are.' And that's the guy who walked in the gym one day. Coach said to step in and do the drill. I said, 'Oh my God, that's the guy.' He was 6–2, 220 pounds. He caught me once and hit me in the face, and I back-pedaled as fast as I could.''

He left practice a little red-faced that afternoon.

In 1955, sophomore guard Bill Musselman made his varsity high school debut for new Coach Jim Byrd. Wooster lost to Canton South by the inglorious score of 88–44. The Generals then rebounded to hammer Orrville 72–47 as Musselman began an assault on the Wooster record books.

He completed his prep career as the school's No. 2 all-time scorer with 534 points, 62 less than Bill Schrieber. Subsequently, both were overtaken by players on teams which had one or two more games each season. Still, Musselman was No. 9 on the Wooster list as late as 1973.

He did it with an unorthodox shot. He held the ball with his right hand flat, elbow jutting out, and left hand on the side of the ball, which was positioned well above his head and just slightly in front of his body. ''Bill put the ball on the back of his hand,'' Byrd said. ''He shot more from the palm than he did from his fingertips.''

After scoring 28 in a 73–66 win against Canton Lehman's Polar Bears, Musselman was described as ''the hard-jawed General'' in the local paper. Canton Lehman was chaffed at for ''permitting Musselman to move to his right and shoot.''

It wasn't easy preventing Musselman from shooting. ''Bill was a gunner," Byrd said. "He shot about every time he got the ball. At times, we had to try to keep the ball away from him."

One time in Musselman's senior year, Byrd actually tried. "We had a kid by the name of Spider Konkle," Byrd said. "He was about 6–7. One game, he came over to the bench and threw his jersey down and said, 'I quit. You know I've been out there almost three whole quarters and I've never touched the ball. The ball comes into Musselman. He brings the ball down the floor, and that's it. I've had enough.'

" 'Why don't you guard him?' Byrd told Konkle. 'When he comes down the floor, you get on him and take the ball away from him.' "

So, with Wooster holding a comfortable lead, Konkle did. "Bill, he didn't know what to say," Byrd said. "He just looked up and kind of laughed. We called time out to get him off the floor, and I said, 'Bill, you get the point?' He said he did."

Byrd's initial impression of Musselman hasn't changed much: "He was a very quiet kid. He was shy in high school. His whole life revolved around athletics. Even as a junior high kid, he would shovel off the snow in his driveway to play basketball.

"Bill was only an average athlete, but he had such dedication that he became outstanding. I think it taught me that ability is only a small part of the game and that with dedication you can reach your goals."

Under Musselman's senior picture in the 1958 Wooster yearbook is an inscription: "They that run fast, stumble." Musselman explained its significance: "I always researched, checked, and double-checked everything I ever did. Slow and deliberate. I didn't just take off and do things in a hurry. I was always calculating."

Byrd speaks about Musselman with affection nurtured by a long-standing relationship. "He always wanted to talk basketball," Byrd said. "Even when he was maligned with the Cavaliers, I think still, deep down, coaching was all he wanted in life. I think he'd coach a seventh-grade girls' team if he had no one else to coach."

On one visit home, Musselman, fresh out of college, told Byrd of his ambitions in coaching:

'Coach, I'm going to be one of the outstanding coaches in the country.'

'Well, Bill, that's a lofty goal. I think we all, somewhere along the line, think of that. It would be nice.'

'I'll be there. You just wait and see.'

4

Wittenberg and Beyond

After graduating from Wooster, Musselman narrowed his college choices to Wittenberg in Springfield, Ohio, a two-hour drive, and Dartmouth in distant New Hampshire. He picked Wittenberg, which offered him a scholarship for football and baseball. "I thought I could play three sports there," Musselman said. "All my friends went there."

He played one season of freshman basketball. Musselman, destined to be a brillant defensive coach, was the same guy who never met a shot he didn't like. And take. He sealed his varsity fate one afternoon in tryouts when he launched several long-range bombs to the consternation of Wittenberg Coach Ray Mears.

Mears, however, already knew about Musselman. "I got to know Bill in a little different way than you'd think," Mears said. "I also coached football, and Bill was an offensive guard. I worked with the line a lot. He wasn't big. But he was tough, one of the toughest guys I've ever been around. And he could open a hole."

Musselman played four seasons of football and baseball at Wittenberg. His exploits in football earned him a nickname, "Scrap Iron," because of his unrelenting manner. "They asked me to move, as a sophomore, to the offensive line. No technique. Just told me to come over and play the line on offense and linebacker on defense," he said.

''They used to have a drill where I'd have to trap 270-pound guys, and I weighed 175 pounds. I pulled down the line of scrimmage one-on-one with the whole team watching. That's why I do one-on-one drills in basketball. I do it with the whole team watching. I don't do it with guys passing off because, when everybody watches you, you can't duck or hide.''

Musselman's playing career at Wittenberg continued in football and baseball, but the foundation in basketball he received from Mears has lasted a lifetime. Specifically, Musselman learned the intricate defensive maneuverings of the match-up zone, one he modified to lead the nation in defense when he coached at Ashland and Minnesota. ''Coach Mears was a brilliant tactician,'' Musselman said. ''Hardworking, constantly working. He was such a perfectionist, one of the greatest coaches ever.''

Mears was 121–23 at Wittenberg and then 278–112 at Tennessee, where he coached one of the highest-scoring combinations in college basketball history, the Bernie and Ernie show. Bernard King was one of the NBA's top scorers in the '80s; Ernie Grunfeld played for three seasons with King for the New York Knicks.

Musselman's affection for his other coaches at Wittenberg, Edwards in football and Dr. Howard ''Red'' Maurer in baseball, is unrestrained: ''I received a classic education in the ways you can be a successful coach. I had unbelievable, unbelievable coaching in college.

''Bill Edwards was the last collegiate player to play without a helmet,'' Musselman said, his voice flush with the mere thought of such daring. ''He was a master psychologist. I loved the guy; he cared for his people. He persuaded us to win for him, for the man he was. Matter of fact, I didn't like contact when I arrived at Wittenberg, but he taught me to like it.''

Maurer had a different approach in baseball. ''He kept everything light,'' Musselman said. ''He emphasized winning while having fun. Before each game, we'd hold our bats to our shoulders as if they were rifles. And we'd hum the national anthem.''

From football, Musselman learned techniques which would influence his methodology of coaching: ''I think football coaches are all good teachers because they deal with so many players. They've got to teach the fundamentals and break them down. They work hard at it. I think I learned a lot from football: teaching a stance; teaching body control; arranging a notebook; how to break down and review plays, and how to show players their mistakes on film.''

Musselman was an eager apprentice, and one who rarely socialized. Playing three sports left him little free time. "All I did was work and play sports," he said. "My freshman year, I didn't date at all until the last two weeks."

One date, set up by a friend, Al Hunter, was with Kristine Koch. The date led Musselman to marriage.

Another date almost killed him. Continuing a dangerous habit of confronting large people, he got fed up with the remarks of another football player who didn't like Musselman's choice of friends. "This guy—he was 6–2, about 240 pounds—got upset with me for who I was running around with," Musselman said. "I run around with whoever I want to. Al was a black kid on campus who introduced me to my wife. He was a good friend of mine. I always sat and talked with him. Then this guy made fun of me."

He didn't stop.

"I just got sick and tired of the guy riding my fanny about who I was hanging out with," Musselman said. "The guy really had made remarks, and I had just let them go. I wasn't going to take it anymore. I said, 'If you don't like it, you know what you can do about it.' I got to the point where I said I didn't care what he did.

"It was a Friday night, and he made some remarks again. There was this little hollow back of campus. I said, 'Let's go. Nobody'll know but you and I.' We went down there, and we start screaming. Finally, I looked at him and said, 'You may beat the hell out of me, but you know one thing. You're going to have to put me away, because I'm never going to quit. You may beat the hell out of me, but you're not going to look pretty either.'

"He turned and stared at me. Then he turned and walked away. I psyched him out. He was huge, man. He was huge. At the moment we quit, I said, 'Thank God.'"

Chalk one up for mind games, a tool Musselman would use many times in coaching.

Another lesson in college wasn't as subtle. Musselman was a catcher in baseball. "In one game, a guy tried to knock me over at home plate," he said. "I saw him coming. He was going to knock me for a loop. I saw him and did a little dip. It was me or him. He was going to bowl me over at home plate. They carried him away. Broke his collarbone."

Just as he held his ground that afternoon, Musselman dug in and didn't flinch when life knocked him down. He got up again. His resiliency is borne from his ultimate belief in himself and the work ethic drilled into him every time he saw his mother return from work after a shift at the Frito-Lay factory.

Believe in yourself, work relentlessly, and fulfill your potential regardless of the obstacles. It's the only road Musselman has ever traveled.

Musselman studied biology but majored in health and physical education at Wittenberg. He then earned his master's degree at Kent State University, where he was a graduate assistant coach in football and a voluntary assistant in basketball. His roommate at Kent State, Larry Carra, said Musselman's two loves that year were Kris Koch and sports. "He was really smitten with Kris," Carra said. "She was pretty, a real nice girl. She wasn't the kind that would go out and let her hair down.

"Her family didn't really want her to get married. They were pretty well-to-do, and Bill was this crazy basketball coach."

Carra recalled the night Musselman phoned and told him of his divorce: "I don't really know what happened between them, but I do think Bill was just too much into sports, too much into basketball. He'd go out and buy three or four newspapers from different places. He'd throw them all away except the sports pages. He was a real nut about that." Years later, the Ohio newspapers Musselman cherished would tear him to shreds.

In 1963, Musselman became the head coach at Kent State University High School. He was 23. Musselman went 14–5, and his Statesmen were conference co-champions.

Kevin Wilson, a sophomore guard who was second on the team in scoring, would witness Musselman's development as a coach, playing four years for him at Ashland and serving four more as his assistant at Minnesota.

Wilson described Musselman's lone season of coaching high school basketball:

"He was fresh out of Wittenberg, real young and very energetic, very eager to go. He'd just come from Ray Mears' program, and he was really ready to get into coaching. Our offense was very basic, slowed down and patterned. On defense, we used the match-up zone Bill learned from Ray Mears."

Wilson learned of Musselman's passion for the game. "My freshman year in high school, I was a marginal JV player," Wilson said. "I wasn't real serious about it, but somehow the JV coach knew Bill and earmarked me as a guy who's going to be a comer. Bill got a hold of me that summer, and I worked out in a real hot, sweaty gym with him about everyday. I used to do all the ballhandling drills that Bill became real famous for. Bill got me convinced to be really serious about basketball.''

Wilson made All-Conference as a sophomore. The following season, after Musselman had left to become an assistant at Ashland, Wilson was All-State. He was later reunited with Musselman at Ashland, and became a Small College All-American.

''I went to Ashland pretty much because Bill was there,'' Wilson said. ''Bill was intense, very dedicated to the game. He was a very good teacher and motivator. It was the most important thing in his life.''

5

Heady Times at Ashland

In 1964, Fred Martinelli, head football coach at Ashland College, decided to take a leave of absence to pursue his doctorate at Ohio State. Columbus is only 80 miles south of Ashland, so Martinelli could return weekly on Saturdays to keep tabs on his football program.

"We had to get a person to handle my football recruiting and help the basketball coach, Bob Stokes," Martinelli recalled. "I told the president of the school, Dr. Glenn Clayton (now a president emeritus), I'd go on the leave if we could find someone to do my duties. We had some alums in the Kent State area, and they recommended Bill to us."

In 1964, there was no aid for college athletes at Ashland. There was also no divisional separation of collegiate sports. Rather than the current set-up begun by the NCAA in 1973—Division I for major programs, Division II for programs offering limited athletic support, and Division III which allows no athletic scholarships—there were two classifications: university (major college) and collegiate (small college).

Ashland was clearly the latter. Basketball games were played at the local high school. The program was, in a word, innocuous. Then Bill Musselman arrived in 1964.

"Bill came across as very intense, well-organized, and extremely knowledgeable about football and basketball," Martinelli said. "He had a sense of direction which was extraordinary for a person his age (23). He wanted to be a college coach. A lot of people at that age aren't really certain what they want to do."

Martinelli penciled in his leave of absence to begin in January 1965. In the months between Musselman's arrival and Martinelli's planned departure, Martinelli became increasingly impressed with the fiery, young assistant coach.

"He began as an assistant in football and basketball," Martinelli said. "He did all the recruiting. He really did an extraordinary job of selecting good talent."

In August 1965, the fascinating tapestry woven by timing, opportunity, and ability dealt Musselman a chance he could scarcely have imagined as he turned 24 years old. Basketball coach Stokes was offered a job at his alma mater, Muskingham College. Ashland suddenly had an opening, an extremely late one from the perspective of a coach intent on recruiting his own players. Ashland also had a hungry young assistant with a chance to jump-start his promising coaching career. "Bob recommended him because he had done a good job in basketball. I think it would've been difficult to bring in an outside person, it being so late," Martinelli said.

With the team and recruits Stokes left him, Musselman fashioned a 10–10 season in 1965–66. If there was any hint of the immense success that would soon follow Musselman, it appeared in the Eagles' final game of the season, a 116–69 blowout of Cleveland State. Musselman's Ashland teams wouldn't allow that many points in a game in the ensuing four seasons. Five of his six teams at Ashland led the country in defense.

While allowing opponents fewer and fewer points, Ashland gave its fans more and more of a pregame show. Musselman gleaned a routine from three sources: the Silver Basketeers, a group of grade schoolers in Dover, Ohio, who mimicked the Harlem Globetrotters; Ray Mears, his coach at Wittenberg, and Jim Byrd, his high school coach.

"My roommate was from Dover, Ohio," Musselman said. "He took me home, and I watched the Silver Basketeers practice. They traveled all over the world performing at halftime of college games. They even made a movie with Jerry Lewis years ago."

Mears also influenced Musselman with his Globetrotter-like warm-ups. When Mears moved from Wittenberg to Tennessee, he took the pregame show with him. "We tried to fire up the crowd," Mears said. "Entertain them and get them ready for the ball game so they'd be ready for us. It helped our kids concentrate because they didn't want to look bad. Bill picked it up, and he did it at Ashland."

With zest. Ashland's players would spin balls on their fingertips, juggle three balls at once, and wind balls around their necks, behind their backs, and through their legs before passing to a teammate for a driving dunk. Overflow crowds of more than 3,500 would rock the gymnasium, clapping, stomping, and singing to the tunes of "Keep the Ball Rollin'," "Higher and Higher," and "Sweet Georgia Brown." Opposing coaches fretted that their players would stop warm-ups to watch.

Showing absolutely no hint of humility, Musselman described the routine as "an incredible show of entertainment. The fans just went berserk." Musselman has been and will be called many things. Choreographer isn't one of them.

"It was a big part of what Ashland College was about at that time," said Roger Lyons, who played on Musselman's final team at Ashland and returned to be the Eagles' head coach from 1986 to 1989. "Every home game was a sellout. The pregame warm-up was something that people really enjoyed. I enjoyed it, too, as a player, because it was something out of the ordinary. We worked hard at it. We practiced it every day. We had a set routine of music that we would go through, and Bill was very insistent that we get it right and that it look good."

Martinelli said the routines were done "well and in good taste. Bill felt it was important. That was an era when athletes were supposed to be straight. It was looked at in some wonderment and with some question. Sometimes our opponents felt a little intimidated, but it was used to get our student body behind the team. I thought the things Bill did got his own kids and our crowd going."

Martinelli feels the success of Musselman's basketball program was a direct factor in a dramatic increase in enrollment at Ashland. "We grew from about 700 or 750 students to 2,000 by 1972 or '73," he said. "I think our athletic program helped us attract a good student-athlete to our campus. The year 1967 seemed to be a big turnaround in our athletic program. I doubt if a small college had all the success we had. Since 1967, our school has had over 350 All-Americans."

In 1967, Ashland opened a new facility for basketball on campus,

Charles Kates Gymnasium. That same year the school also made a commitment to offer grants-in-aid for athletes. Martinelli, who has coached football at Ashland for 30 years, called the time from '67 to '73 "our golden era."

Clayton, Ashland's president at the time, said Musselman "was what we needed. He built a basketball tradition that had not existed previously. He was so successful, people still talk about it. They remember the Bill Musselman era."

Although Musselman developed a close relationship with Clayton, the man he felt the most for was Bob Bronson. When Musselman arrived, illness had already forced Bronson to relinquish his duties as head football coach to become athletic director. "I was loyal to Bob Bronson," Musselman said. "He hired me, then passed away. He was like a father to me. The guy puts his arm around me, and he's a great speaker, and he says, 'Young man, I'm giving you a chance at a young age. I believe in you.' You're going to walk through a wall for a guy who does that.

"When he was replaced, it hurt me. Nothing against Fred Martinelli. I was an assistant football coach for Fred, and I enjoyed working with him. I learned a lot about coaching. But I wasn't as close to him. I went to the president when I wanted something. The president told me I had an open door to him."

And a phone still on the hook at 2:00 in the morning. "That happened several times," Clayton said. "A college president is on call at all times. He's supposed to be accessible. He's on 24 hours call."

One evening—or early morning—Musselman called Clayton insistent the Eagles could beat the University of Iowa. "He called me," Clayton said. "It was the middle of the night. He had it all worked out. Even though Iowa was pretty strong, he thought we could beat them."

Clayton invited Musselman to his house that night. Musselman got his game with Iowa the following season. Ashland lost 82-56, but the Eagles didn't lose too many others in 1970-71, capping Musselman's outstanding tenure with a 25-3 record. He was 119-20 his final five seasons. Not bad for a young coach who had survived a rocky start (4-7) to finish 10-10 his first year.

Gary Youmans, who would later work with Musselman and coach against him in the CBA, had never heard of Ashland when Musselman started recruiting him out of Ferrum Junior College in Virginia in 1968. The 6-7 Youmans had been All-State in basketball and football at

North Syracuse (New York) High School. Youmans then enrolled at Ferrum, hoping to go on to the University of Virginia.

He didn't have the grades, but he did possess sufficient talent to entice Musselman, whose tracking system somehow found Youmans after his outstanding schoolboy career and two seasons at Ferrum.

"He just continued to call," Youmans said. "He did a great job of recruiting me. He'd had a pretty good team there the year before, and he just sold me on coming there. He was really positive about what he was doing and very aggressive. I mean, he'd call me every day, and I was no great player."

In the fall of 1968, Youmans arrived at Ashland. Almost instantaneously, Youmans had ambivalent feelings toward Musselman, who at 28 was young himself. Youmans had long harbored a desire to coach and was a willing, enthusiastic student of Musselman. At the same time, however, he sweated out the type of training only Musselman employed.

"Muss was so committed at those times to defense. It was just phenomenal, the amount of work that we put into it," Youmans said. "It was not uncommon to spend two hours a day on defense. Practices were three to four hours. It wasn't fun. I didn't like it. But he was a great teacher, and he really brought out the best in people."

Youmans got a quick education at Camp Musselman.

"It was funny, because he called me up just prior to me going to Ashland for the first time, and he said, 'Gary, what kind of shape you in?' " Youmans said. "I said, 'Great.' I'd been playing in a summer league, typical basketball player. He said, 'Well, we got a little running program when you get to Ashland. It's no big deal. You'll handle it fine.' "

His second day at Ashland is forever embedded in Youman's mind. "We started that running program the day after we got to school," he continued. "He outfitted us in like a 20-pound weighted vest and then we put these ankle weights on which were like five pounds apiece.

"We looked like zombies. Then he takes us upstairs into the gymnasium, and we go through a series of drills he had, a lot of calisthenics and jumping drills and fingertip push-ups. He was a great believer in fingertip push-ups, and he would match each player. If he beat you, you had to run like five sprints. Muss probably did, I don't know, 200 or some 300 push-ups. You had to do 20 or something push-ups. None of us could do it with all that weight on. He would just have a contest with each guy, and if he beat you, you'd have to run. Then you'd get back in line and do it again. He was in phenomenal shape.''

Youmans wasn't. ''We go through these jumping drills and sliding with the weights on,'' Youmans said. ''I thought practice was over. And I was dead. And he says, 'Okay, let's go. We're going to run out to the football stadium.'

''We all looked at each other. What the hell is this guy talking about? It's three miles out to the football stadium and then another three back. And he yells, 'Out.'

''We start running, and we take off, and I'm not kidding you, it was like we were a blur, a little dot in the sky. And we're back there running with these weighted vests which were killing us. And we get about, oh, a half a mile from the stadium. I'm running with this guy by the name of Wayne Sokolowski, who's 6-foot-9, and he's real thin. And Wayne just falls, and I thought he was dead. He can't even talk. This little girl comes up and sees these two giants with these weighted vests on, I'll never forget, she thought we were like space-men or something. She just took off running. She was scared as hell.

''So Musselman comes jogging back. He yells, 'Youmans, where the hell...what are you guys doing?' I said, 'Sokolowski here is passed out.'

''He said, 'Jesus Christ, come on. You guys. I thought you were in better shape than this.' So we finally get to the stadium. He calls everybody together. Sokolowski, we had just left him. Muss says, 'He's done, he's done.'

''And we go out to the stadium. He brings everybody together, and I'm thinking to myself, 'Shit, this guy is nuts,' but I think he sees he kind of over-did it the first day with us. But he brings the guys together and he points to me and another guy and he says, 'Those guys, they're not in shape. They're going to cost us games this year. We're going to have to work harder.'

''I about died. I was thinking about going to the University of Tampa, and I said, 'Holy shit, what the hell am I doing here?' And so he proceeds to make us go through these jumping drills, jumping over the football benches, just going back and forth, back and forth. And we're doing grass drills, running sprints. And then we run up the stadium steps. We're still wearing the weights. I'm just in nowhere land. I'll never forget getting up to the top of the stadium. It was like maybe 100 feet down or something. I thought, 'Well, shit, you know I don't think I would die if I jumped over,' or if I kind of just hurt my ankle a little bit, I wouldn't have to go through this shit anymore.''

He did. "Every day," Youmans said. "And every day I died. Every single day."

Youmans adjusted, though. So did Sokolowski, who became an All-American.

"It was very hard on me, because I was a big guy," Youmans said. "But he pushed us to the limit, and my jumping and everything about me just improved dramatically over the course of two years. That was his intensity. We were in great shape when it was all said and done. That's when Vince Lombardi was around and I read about the Packers and the grass drills they used to do. I'll guarantee you this was every bit as rough, if not rougher. It was intense physical conditioning."

Youmans found the ballhandling routine a pleasant diversion. "I loved that," he said. "At the time it was unique, and it was a big part of what we did. We would get a crowd of 4,000 to watch the JV game. Our game was at 8:00, and at 6:30 the place would be filled. I mean, you couldn't get a seat. The spirit and everything was just phenomenal."

And then there was Musselman's desire to win. "He was just so driven," Youmans said. "He drove you like a madman. But he treated you so well off the floor. I guess that's what kept you going."

Youmans illustrated the point with a holiday story: "At Christmas, everybody else would get to go home, all your friends and stuff. We got like two days or something. We slept on cots in the gymnasium. We had Christmas Eve and Christmas off. I think we had to be back Christmas night or something like that. We practiced twice a day, very hard practices. Then we'd eat downtown at the restaurant, all you could eat. Musselman picked up the tab. Of course, guys liked that. That was kind of good.

"Still, it was really hard. One time around Christmas, four of us went bowling, and we were supposed to be back at 10 o'clock. We got there like at 10:20, and he went absolutely nuts. I had just had a bad game. We lost, and he blamed me for it, just ripped me. That's the closest I had ever come to leaving. As a matter of fact, I was going to tell him the next day that I'd had enough of this shit. I'm leaving."

Youmans and his bowling conspirators shuddered awaiting Musselman's reaction. "He was going to work us out," Youmans said. "Four of us went downstairs terrified of what the hell was going to happen. He made us get dressed, put on the weighted vests, and go upstairs. But he ripped us, and that was it. He didn't take us onto the floor.''

Musselman felt he had made his point. He didn't limit his coaching to merely improving a player's physical attributes. As anyone who has ever played for Musselman will attest, he teaches, preaches, does anything to reach a player's mental condition. His objective is to make each player more focused, more intense, and more committed to winning.

Much of Musselman's dedication centers on playing defense. He breaks every team huddle during a game or at the conclusion of practice with a chant of ''1-2-3...DEFENSE.'' Musselman said, ''I've done that ever since I started coaching. I think I emphasize areas nobody else does. When I coached small college, I put so much emphasis on defense because it was a way to get national recognition for the school. A way to motivate the players, to take pride in something, to be the best in the country. Our fans and cheerleaders yelled, 'Shutout, shutout, we want a shutout.' We went overboard on it. We were so good defensively, it was scary.''

Nobody was more frightened than opposing coaches who feared Musselman's Eagles would obey the chants of their perpetual overflow crowds and actually shut a team out. If not for a game, then for a half.

The closest the Eagles got to pitching a shutout came at Slippery Rock. Ashland blanked the hosts for almost the entire first half and led 29–5 at the break. Musselman eventually had to settle for a 65–19 win.

Undoubtedly, Musselman's patterned slow-down offense, which frequently held the ball for 30 to 40 seconds before shooting, contributed to the amazing defensive numbers. ''You think it was tough coaching against him?'' radio play-by-play man Mike Green said. ''You should have tried announcing the game. I had to take a Valium just to get myself ready for it. I had to slow my heartbeat down.''

Against most opponents, Ashland had a talent and size advantage. However, anybody with the slightest knowledge of basketball appreciated Musselman's defensive genius. He used a match-up zone as a primary defense. Applying man-to-man principles from a 1–2–2, 1–3–1, or 2–3 zone, the match-up zone is intricate and sophisticated. Musselman learned it from a master, Ray Mears, at Wittenberg. Since few other teams used a match-up zone 15–20 years ago, Ashland's opponents seldom had a chance to practice against it.

And Musselman deployed it brilliantly. Ashland led the nation in defense five consecutive years, including a modern-day record average low of 33.9 points a game in 1968–69. The Eagles reached this milestone while at the same time setting another national mark for least fouls per game (10.0). That was testimony of Musselman's ability to teach aggressive defense while maintaining the discipline to avoid fouls. Additionally, the 1968–69 team made only eight turnovers per game, proving the flashy ballhandling drills added more than entertainment. They also improved the players' skills.

Strengthened by Musselman's first crop of recruits, Ashland improved from 10–10 in his first season to 21–3 in 1966–67. The Eagles had two returning Small College All-Americans in 1967–68 and had begun a tradition that would only be heightened by the college's decision to build a new gymnasium and offer grants-in-aid to athletes the following season.

On December 2, 1967, Ashland opened Charles Kates Gymnasium with a 53–17 rout of Walsh College. SRO crowds began packing the gym to watch the increasingly popular warm-up show and Ashland's suddenly powerful basketball team. The Eagles took a 7–0 record into one of several memorable battles between Musselman and Al Van Wie, coach of the College of Wooster. The Presbyterian college not only matched Musselman against his home-town school, but also pitted him against his high school coach, Jim Byrd, Van Wie's assistant.

Wooster, which pounded Ashland 69–57 in Musselman's rookie season, took on Musselman again in the 1968 Wooster Christmas Tournament. Van Wie beat Musselman again, this time 25–24—in overtime.

"We decided beforehand that if we got four points ahead or four down, we were going to stall," Van Wie said. Wooster did, holding the ball for nine minutes in one possession. "People said it was either the finest basketball game they've ever seen, or it was the worst," Van Wie said. "Well, from my standpoint, it was one of the finest. I think what made our rivalry a great one was Bill was from Wooster. His family still lives here, and Bill and I had big egos. So we both wanted to win that game very, very badly."

Musselman had Wooster scouted extremely well for a rematch later that season at Ashland. "We had put in a lot of new things," Van

Wie said. "After we got done practicing in our gym the day of the Christmas tournament, we had left our scouting material up there, and Bill got a hold of it. He really didn't have time to adjust to it that night, but when we played Ashland again later that year, Bill had big signs all over the gym with our special plays on them. As soon as our players came out, they knew he knew what we were going to do."

Mussleman got revenge 41–34. Head games were de rigueur when Musselman and Van Wie squared off. The following year, Ashland beat Wooster again 46–32. Van Wie had to wait nearly two years for another shot at Musselman. It would be the last meeting between the two coaches, who had split the previous four.

The game was for the championship of the Marion Holiday Tournament. Because it had won the tournament the previous year, Van Wie's club was designated the home team.

Musselman and Van Wie got into an argument about which bench they would use because each tournament winner the last three years used the same bench. "When the consolation game was over, I had my manager, who had all our equipment, go right to that bench," Van Wie said. "Bill came out and said, 'Hey, I want that bench.' The officials came out and said, 'Hey, what the hell's going on with you two guys?' I said, 'We're the home team, right? Well, we get the bench. They get the basket they want.' "

Far from being over, the war of wills reached a crescendo during warm-ups. Musselman had a pregame strategy of having his reserves who weren't likely to play that night line up at halfcourt and glare at the opposing team. "They would sort of stare you down," Van Wie said. "So we took some of our kids and we said, 'We want you to go right up to that line. Don't go over it. And look 'em right in the eye.' So there were the starting fives warming up for both teams and 10 kids at halfcourt looking each other in the eye."

This went on for 15 minutes. "We were two guys who had lost our minds," Van Wie said. Chuck Mistovich, at the time Ashland's Sports Information Director and now a columnist for *Basketball Times*, noted: "It was absolutely incredible to see those guys nose-to-nose staring at each other. The crowd was just going nuts. They didn't know about the Ashland–Wooster rivalry."

Oh, yeah, the game. Ashland lost 73–70 in double overtime.

But Musselman had many happy days at Ashland as the victories and acclaim multiplied. He also had more lucky blue shirts than he knew about.

Mardie McGinnis and her husband Ed, the dean of men and intra-murals director at Ashland, were Kris and Bill Musselman's next door neighbors and close friends. How close? "Bill thought he had a lucky shirt, a blue Oxford," Mardie said. "Kris knew she never could have that shirt ready every game. So she had a half dozen. Kris kept them all washed. He never knew it wasn't his lucky shirt."

He does now.

Living next to Bill Musselman was always entertaining for Ed McGinnis. "With Bill, you're out of control to begin with," McGinnis said. Three of his favorite episodes:

1) I saw Richard Speck.

"The night before, the Chicago slayer of student nurses, Richard Speck, was in the news," McGinnis said. "The newspaper the next day had a drawing of this individual and offered a $10,000 reward. Muss and his wife are eating breakfast at the Surrey Inn, and they looked at the paper and saw this fellow there. Bill thought he looked a lot like Richard Speck.

"So Muss comes roaring into my house and says, 'Eddie, Eddie. That killer is at the Surrey Inn. You got to go there with me.'

"I was skeptical all the way, but I went along with him. We crept around outside the Surrey Inn, slinking in and out of the bushes to see who was there. The guy came out, and he went to get in his car. So Muss and I ran back to our car, and we followed him. He went down to the local discount store and he goes in. We follow him clear to the back of the building to the rest rooms. Not being too brave, we decided we weren't going in with him, but we were going to hide. Bill's behind a record counter, and I'm over at another counter slinking down, looking over the edge of the counter. The guy comes out of the rest room, and he walks right in front of us. Bill is motioning to me to get him.

"Then the guy walks behind the jewelry counter and goes to work."

2) There's a prowler.

"Another time, he thought he had a prowler," McGinnis said. "He called me up and I walked over. There's still snow on the ground, and he saw some footprints around his house. I'm walking around, looking all over the place for this prowler while he stands inside, walking back and forth, telling me where to look. The next night, he decides that we have to go looking for the prowler again. We're out in his backyard looking all over the place. Well, he thinks he sees this prowler. He takes off really quick, and I scream at him, 'Hey Bill, watch out.'

"He comes flying across the yard after this guy, and there's a low limb. The limb hits him right square in the forehead. Knocks him flat as a pancake. Knocks him out cold as a mackerel. There weren't any prowlers."

3) Do your ABCs.

"Three o'clock in the morning. I get a call from Kris: 'Eddie, come help. Bill's hurt himself.'

"I go flying into their house, and there he is, lying on the couch in his skivvies. He had let the dog out. They had French doors in the back that were glass. He went to catch the door as it came back, and he put his arm right through the glass. He was a mess.

"He's got a tourniquet on his arm, and the arm's turning blue because she's got the thing so tight. So I loosened the tourniquet. I said, 'Bill, it's okay. But we need to go to the emergency room and get some stitches.' He says, 'Naw, naw, Eddie. I'll gut it out. I'll gut it out.'

'No, no. You got to go to the hospital.'

"We got him up and off we go to the hospital. Bill's got a raincoat on over a T-shirt and his skivvies, and he's wearing a pair of wing tip shoes. I'm wondering what the doctor's going to think with the mess that we have here.

"We go down to the car and it's really cold, and Bill's probably a little in shock and everything. And he starts to shiver. I stall the car about three or four times. He's really nervous. Kris says, 'Why don't you say your ABCs?'

"He's leaning over, almost on the car floor, going, 'A–B–C–D–E–F–G.' "

Fourteen stitches eventually closed the wound. McGinnis never said how far in the alphabet Musselman got.

One of Musselman's sweetest moments in 1967–68 was a payback 41–37 victory at Wittenberg, coached by his college roommate, Eldon Miller. The halftime score was 11–9.

On the way to a 24–6 slate and a defensive average of 38.8 points allowed in 1967–68, Musselman's defense stifled several shooting stars. Bill English of Winston-Salem scored but six points as Ashland defeated the defending NAIA national champion 57–40. In a game two weeks later, English poured in 77.

Kenyon's John Rinka, the leading scorer in the nation (33.9 average), made just four of 22 shots in a 65–51 loss to the Eagles.

Norfolk State, featuring future NBA star Bobby Dandridge, was leading the country in scoring with a 100-plus average before losing to Ashland 61–51 in the second round of the NCAA Small College Tournament. Ashland advanced to the national semifinals with a 45–30 victory against Cheyney State. But then the Eagles stumbled, shooting 25 percent in a 45–32 loss to Kentucky Wesleyan. In the third-place game, Trinity (Texas) beat the Eagles 68–52.

Musselman wanted more entering 1968–69. If there was an omen to the extraordinary season Musselman was embarking upon, it happened at the 1968 football awards banquet. The guest speaker that evening was one of the nation's most revered football coaches, Woody Hayes of Ohio State.

"Afterwards, Woody, Bill and I started talking, and Woody asked Bill what was his philosophy of defense," Martinelli said. "Bill had set a national record for defense the year before, and he said, 'We try to shut people out. Our defense begins with a philosophy that we can shut out an opponent, that we can coach a shutout.'

"Woody looked at me and said, 'Is he crazy?' "

Musselman was confident the winter of '68 despite the graduation of his four top scorers. He had two veterans returning in Kevin Wilson and Jimmy Williams. He also had an outstanding recruiting crop featuring Sokolowski and Youmans.

Wilson, a 6–5 guard, and Williams, a 6–8 center, averaged just 7.6 and 2.2 points, respectively, the previous season. In 1968–69, though, Wilson, Williams, and Sokolowski were named All-American.

The following season, Wilson, Sokolowski, Bubba Jones, and Jay Franson made All-American, but Musselman didn't take the news well. "I think we were the first team to ever have four All-Americans," Mistovich said. "Bill comes into my office and virtually went berserk. He says, 'What am I going to tell the fifth guy? This could crush us.' "

Wilson, dubbed "Defensive Demon," had made a favorable impression on Musselman at Kent State University High School. Musselman liked his willingness to work on defense, his intelligence, and his determination—Wilson played the second half of his 1970 senior season with a broken hand.

Wilson learned how to play with pain in practice. "Bill had these drills," Wilson said. "He would stand below the basket with a guy on either side of him. He'd roll the ball down towards halfcourt, and two guys had to go after the ball.

"My first time, I just thought I was going to go after this ball. Well, the guy I was going against came over like a football blocker, lowered his shoulder, and knocked me on my can. Then he went after the ball. I looked up at Bill like there's a foul or something, right? He didn't say anything. There never was a rule—just go get the ball. The next time we both go to block each other, and we end up wrestling and punching. The ball's going down to the end of the court, and we're still sitting there rolling over each other in a wrestling match. Finally, Bill called it off."

That wasn't the only drill that got physical. "Bill used to put a guy below each basket and the ball at halfcourt," Wilson said. "He'd blow the whistle and the two guys would have to run and dive for the ball. One time, Youmans hit his head with the other guy and was unconscious. They just rolled him over, picked his heels up and just dragged him off the floor.

"We spent all the time on defense with weighted vests. We didn't know any better. We thought everybody played like this and practiced like this."

Nobody else likely did. And probably everybody else ate each day.

"We went to scrimmage Duquesne University in Pittsburgh," Wilson related. "We left like at breakfast time, and a truck overturned on the highway so we got there like 15 minutes before the scrimmage. We didn't have time to stop and eat. We played. We played our butts off against a good club. We played like three halves. I think we won one, lost one by one, and tied the other. We really played well for a small college school.

"But Bill was upset with us because he didn't feel we played well enough or hard enough. Whatever. He said, 'We're not going to eat.'

"We hadn't eaten all day. We were dying. We pull up to this place to go to eat where Bill had already pre-ordered a meal. Steaks. The guy working there said he's already got the steaks on the grill. We had to eat 'em.

"All the players started smiling. Bill reaches in his pocket. He just takes out a big wad of bills. He pays the guy and says, 'We're not going to eat 'em.'

"So now we drive on. We stop at this gas station, and every player gets out. We said we have to go to the bathroom. Bill stays on the bus. He's busy looking at stats or something, and we're all around this candy machine, just pumping in coins as fast as we can. I ate like four or five candy bars. I took my hand and just pushed them in my mouth as fast as I could. I didn't chew 'em. It was so funny. We all came out and got on the bus with these incredible chocolate rings around our mouths.''

Wilson and his teammates survived to pursue championship rings. A key player in the '68-69 season was the 6-7 Franson, from Dixie Junior College in St. George, Utah. Sokolowski (6-9, 210), Williams (6-8, 200), and Youmans (6-8, 225) also were JUCO refugees who provided strength up front. Ohio natives Wilson and John Savage were the starting guards.

Ashland won 21 of its first 22 games. The Eagles finished 26-4 and were voted AP and UPI Small College National Champions. But the team lost its final two games in the NCAA Small College Tournament, 58-48 to Southwest Missouri and 53-51 to American International.

Those two losses ''inflated'' Ashland's defensive average to 33.9 points a game, still a modern record. Three times the Eagles kept an opponent's final score in the teens, beating West Virginia Tech 37-18, Slippery Rock 65-19, and Waynesburg 28-14.

In one game, Ashland committed just three fouls. In another, the team made 77 percent of its shots (23 for 30).

Musselman, whose team won 18 straight in one stretch, was named Ohio coach of the year for collegiate and university divisions. A resolution was passed in the Ohio Senate March 6, 1969, commending Musselman on the award and noting in one of four ''Whereas'' paragraphs that at the age of 28, Musselman ''has established himself as one of the outstanding coaches in the nation, and from all appearances is destined for true greatness in the future annals of American sports.''

The season began with the most revered coach in the history of Ohio State asking Musselman about his defensive philosophy and ended with the Ohio Senate extending ''warmest congratulations.''

Less than three years later, following the Minnesota-Ohio State brawl, Musselman was the most despised coach in Ohio's history. Nine years after that, the citizens of Cleveland were pelting his son with hot dogs. Only in America.

The longer Musselman stayed at Ashland, the more publicity he and his program received. With the aid of Mistovich, Musselman wrote a book entitled *33.9–DEFENSE*. The 105-page book, which thoroughly documented Musselman's precepts and included diagrams of dozens of his offensive and defensive strategies, was printed locally and sold approximately 1,800 copies, according to Mistovich.

Ashland also received exposure on a national level. The December 15, 1969, issue of *Sports Illustrated* presented a four-page story illuminated by eight photographs, one of Assistant Coach Lou Markle's lucky gold shoes, described by writer Peter Carry as "hideous, gold spray-painted crepe-soled."

Carry had kinder words for Musselman: "a bright man in his fifth season whose short muscular frame and light close-cropped hair are archetypal of proper coachly appearance, even if his scenario is not. Musselman blends a pregame ritual of crowd hysteria, raucous music, and Harlem Globetrotter drills with a game plan of sticky defense and tightly controlled offense that results in neither the Eagles nor their rivals scoring many baskets."

Musselman's defense was labeled "a hyperbolic paraboloid transition floating zone" in the *SI* story, which was generally regarded by Ashland's players and fans as the greatest thing to ever hit town. Small college programs aren't usually featured in America's No. 1 sports magazine.

Then again, this was not your ordinary small college program. The publicity helped Musselman's career. "I read a survey once that only eight percent of major college jobs are filled by small college coaches," Musselman said. "Because the odds were slim for a jump from a small liberal arts college to the big time, I knew I would need near-perfection. I had to beat the law of averages."

After the *SI* story appeared, Ashland put the finishing touches on another outstanding season. A 17-game winning streak led to a 23–4 record before the Eagles were again ousted from the NCAA Small College Tournament. Following a 50–43 first-round win against Cheyney State, Ashland was thumped by Philadelphia Textile 45–28.

The following season, Musselman's last at Ashland, was his best. The Eagles took a 24–2 record into the NCAA Small College Tournament and lost in the first round to Evansville. For the second straight season, Ashland had been beaten by the eventual national champion. An 88–65 victory over Augustana (Illinois) in the regional consolation game made Ashland 25–3 and provided a happy ending to a pleasant period of Musselman's coaching career.

6

Crazy George

George Schauer harbored dreams of becoming another Pete Maravich. Schauer had no illusions of becoming a Maravich clone in playing ability; rather, he wanted to emulate Maravich's ballhandling wizardry. "I played on my high school team, but I wasn't a great basketball player," Schauer said. He did, however, know how to handle the ball. "I used to practice about five hours a day on my ballhandling," he said.

Among other gimmicks Schauer mastered was spinning a ball on his nose. With this as his calling card, he went to Musselman's summer basketball camp at Ashland in 1970. Schauer showed Musselman he could spin a ball on his nose. "He told me, 'Go home and practice,'" Schauer said.

He did. Schauer enrolled at Ashland in 1970 and pestered Musselman enough to be placed on the JV team. "I was the 13th man on a team of 12," Schauer said. "He kept kicking me out of practice. But I kept coming back, just like Musselman. Finally, he gave me a chance. His responses went from, 'George, get the hell out of here,' to 'George, what size shoe do you wear?' He gave me an opportunity to play JV and dress with the varsity for the pregame warm-up."

Schauer quickly became the centerpiece of Ashland's pregame routine, which all of Musselman's players practiced diligently. "We got so good at it, the crowd would cheer when someone made a small mistake," Schauer said. "Nobody wanted to make a mistake in the warm-ups, because we'd hear about it when we saw the film."

Who else but Musselman would film warm-ups?

"I'd juggle three basketballs, throw them to our guards, and they'd make a fancy pass to the forwards for a lay-in," Schauer said. "The whole team would do the ballhandling. What was amazing was that the tall guys would do the dribbling, not the guards."

Schauer preferred doing his routines to the music of "Keep the Ball Rollin'." "That's kind of been my song the last 15 years," he said. "I'll be driving along the highway, hear it on the radio, and go crazy."

Schauer got his nickname at an Ashland practice session. "We had a loose ball drill," he said. "Earl Diddle (a teammate) picked me up and threw me into a wall. I was knocked out. When I woke up on the court, a group of players were looking at me and saying, 'Crazy George.'"

George was crazy enough to follow Musselman to the University of Minnesota the following year. "He called me up at 1:00 in the morning and asked me if I wanted to go to Minnesota in the summer of '71," Schauer said. "I had just gotten my draft number, which was 365. I said, 'Sure.' I went to Minnesota and did the drill before 18,000 people. We came running through a 17-foot high wooden gopher. I dribbled the ball to start our warm-ups. The crowd would go nuts. One night we were playing Marquette, and Al McGuire didn't bring his team out. He didn't want his kids to watch the warm-ups."

Opposing coaches didn't have to worry about watching Schauer in a game. He played rarely for the Golden Gophers, scoring all of two points in three seasons. "George is the only guy to get into a metropolitan newspaper for scoring two points," Musselman said. Indeed, the banner headline of the *Minneapolis Tribune*, February 12, 1974, blared on the front page of the sports section, "Schauer scores as 'U' defeats Illini."

Schauer has a unique perspective of Musselman because he's the only person to play for him at Ashland and Minnesota. "Practices at Ashland were a lot tougher than at Minnesota," Schauer said. "He made us run 19 suicides once. You would never be late for practice. You'd be better off to stand in front of a bus. One guy was late for practice, and he made him run laps for 40 minutes.

"The guy's not a madman. He's just a man with a purpose. He's the hardest-working man I ever met. The guy's got a big heart, and not a lot of people know about it. Every day a guy gives me a paycheck for a routine, I think of him.''

Schauer estimates he has performed 5,000 shows in 49 states and 15 foreign countries. He's frequently featured at NBA games and performed at the 1987 NBA All-Star Game. His repertoire includes juggling four basketballs in the air, writing a letter while spinning a basketball on top of the pen, and spinning a basketball on a spoon while feeding ice cream to a volunteer from the crowd. ''The ice cream trick, boy, it gets them every time,'' he said.

One of his career highlights was touring Europe with the Munich Eagles team. ''Bill got me the job,'' Schauer said. ''I was a player on the team. I didn't play that much, but I did a lot of promotion. I used to go to cities ahead of the team and dribble in the streets as a promotion. In the streets of Paris, I juggled two basketballs and a loaf of bread. In Copenhagen, there was this old crippled guy selling flowers. Nobody was buying them. I bought one and spun the ball on his fingers. He was so happy. He looked like he was going to cry. I started dribbling the ball, and about 10 people gathered around. I kept it up, and there were about 100 people watching. I went into my whole act for them. I bought another flower, and then everyone started buying them. The old man sold all his flowers in 10 minutes. That's the best I ever felt in my whole life.''

Schauer elicited a cooler response one day in Berlin: ''I was dribbling a red, white, and blue ball near Checkpoint Charlie on the painted line on the street which separates East and West Berlin. I was dribbling on both sides of the line: Communist, Free, Communist, Free. Then I started bouncing the ball off the side of the Berlin Wall. I looked up and saw a guy pointing a machine gun at me. I kind of walked away. I didn't want to cause an international incident.''

He prefers inducing children to laugh. ''There's no greater satisfaction than making a little kid smile,'' he said.

Crazy George is one of Musselman's favorite disciples: ''George wasn't that good a player, but he worked at ballhandling eight hours a day. He still does. He's an amazing story himself. His goal was to make one million kids laugh. The guy makes six figures. He's a 37-year-old guy still dribbling a basketball around the world. He'll do that till he's 65.''

More than any other quality, Musselman loves Schauer's dedication, his relentless pursuit of a goal. ''This kid transferred 'cause Ashland didn't need him,'' Musselman said. ''He couldn't make the ball club at Minnesota. He came there because I had the pregame warm-up. He came up on his own, transferred and paid his own way the first year. Then I put him on scholarship. The guy slept on a concrete floor." Musselman freezes the image in his mind, when Schauer worked at a plastic bag factory and had nowhere else to sleep but the cold floor of a basement apartment. "He slept on a concrete floor."

7

Minnesota the First Time

The University of Minnesota's undefeated basketball team of 1918–19 won the Big Ten championship. The 1936–37 team went 10–2 to tie for first.

The highlight film stopped there for fans of the Golden Gophers, who managed to avoid an undisputed Big Ten title through five decades. Fifty-three years.

Then Bill Musselman became head coach.

When he was hired for a salary of $18,500, the Gophers' average attendance was less than 8,000. In the ensuing decade, attendance nearly doubled. Musselman was the impetus, compiling a 69–32 record, the best of any Minnesota coach. However, the bookends of Musselman's four-year tenure will forever be The Fight in his first season and the 128 NCAA violations that shadowed Musselman's sudden departure in his last.

The team Musselman inherited in 1971 was coming off an 11–13 season and a 5–9 conference record. He was the fifth coach in five years, and the second choice of University officials for the 1971–72 season. Murray State (Ky.) Coach Cal Luther had the position for two days before changing his mind April 2, 1971. Musselman was hired two days later. "I didn't mind being their second choice," he said. "It still was a great opportunity, a great challenge."

Days of unicycles and a Big Ten title; of players named Dave Winfield, Ron Behagen, and Crazy George Schauer; of coaching wars with a boyhood rival; and chunks of shrapnel from 95 seconds of mass insanity dotted Musselman's comet-like career at Minnesota.

Bill Musselman did survive his bloodied success.

"There's two real tragedies from the fight," said Bill Klucas, a Musselman assistant at Minnesota who previously was an assistant at Ohio State. "The first tragedy is, one, it happened. The second tragedy is that Bill Musselman took the whole rap for it. I don't understand it, either."

The biggest riddle is how such a key element to the melee, an act of aggression by an Ohio State player against a Minnesota player as the teams ran off the court at halftime, was blatantly ignored.

Dave Winfield played only one season of high school basketball. However, his natural ability—Musselman calls him the best rebounder he's ever coached—was enough to enable him to earn All-City honors in St. Paul. And though he would eventually roam the outfield of the San Diego Padres and the New York Yankees during his outstanding baseball career, Winfield grew increasingly curious about the sport of basketball, the way it was played under Musselman.

Winfield played intramurals as a sophomore, leading the Soulful Strutters to the campus championship. The following year, the Soulful Strutters were asked to scrimmage the freshman team.

When freshman coach Jimmy Williams watched Winfield, he had trouble believing what he saw: "I had no idea who he was or where he was from. He'd soar above the rim and land like a deer. I told him I was going to mention his name to Bill Musselman, but our season was already going on.

"Bill said he didn't believe a kid playing intramurals could help our basketball team. I let it slide. We scrimmaged them again, and he impressed me even more. That's when I got real tough with Bill, telling him, 'Let's give him a look.' Bill agreed."

In Winfield's first day at practice, he was treated rather coldly. "There were a half dozen NBA prospects—Jim Brewer, Ron Behagen, Clyde Turner, Keith Young, Bob Murphy, and Corky Taylor," Winfield said. "When I showed up, they didn't exactly put out the welcome mat. Each of these guys had serious hopes of playing pro ball, and they needed to shine under the new coach to attract pro scouts. There I was, not even officially on the team, an interloper from the baseball team of all places, practicing with them, often outhustling them in scrimmages, threatening to take away someone's job.''

Not the first day, anyway. "He was very raw," Williams said. "The thing I remember the most is that David attempted about 10 shots and got nine of them blocked. I remember Bill came over to me and laughed. He said, 'This guy can't play a lick.' I encouraged Bill to have a little patience. You could still see some of his athletic ability.

"We invited him back the next day. David wasn't really excited about coming back. But he got better and better. He became a starter after the fight. He was one of those players who rebounded with reckless abandon. It was unreal how high he could jump and the power he demonstrated."

The more Musselman watched Winfield, the more impressed he became. "I couldn't believe he was floating around," Musselman said. "Extraordinary athlete. I couldn't believe it."

Winfield, who joined the varsity six games into the season, liked many things about Musselman—especially his brashness in predicting immediate success for a team with an entrenched losing history. He wrote about it in his book, *Winfield: A Player's Life*: "Bill said when they hired him that he intended for his team to win the Big Ten title his first year. Gutsy talk, but I liked it. I wanted to play for a guy who knew he was going all the way."

Winfield recalled the good vibrations he experienced from a Musselman locker room, which the coach set up to exemplify the class and attention to detail he saw Ray Mears always provide his players: "You make your way into the maroon-and-gold-painted locker room where you find clean socks draped over your locker, your uniform all laid out. You get taped, walk the halls bathed in the clean smell of adhesive and talcum powder. You're wearing a brand-new jock, a 'Bike' right out of the box. Band music and crowd noise filter down, keep the adrenaline flowing, the anxiety high. 'It's going to be a big crowd tonight,' the coach says. He's nervous. He's pacing. He goes through his scouting report, his strategy, tells you how important the game is.

"Upstairs, on the court, you warm up like you're a Harlem Globetrotter, to the strains of 'Sweet Georgia Brown.' The fans eat it up.

"After your warm-up's over, you disappear back downstairs for a few minutes. A quick pep talk, then hands together one more time.

"Back up on the court, it's suddenly lights out! The arena goes completely black. A split second later a single spotlight picks out an enormous cutout of a gopher dribbling a giant basketball. The critter's sitting at the edge of the court, and there's an open circle in the basketball big enough for a man to run through. Which is precisely what you do, poised, ready, waiting until they call your name, until 17,000 Minnesota fans cheer for you and then each of your teammates, a cheer that builds to a crescendo when you're finally all standing there together on the court.''

To please the SRO crowds and to have any chance to contend for a Big Ten title, Musselman knew he needed to surround Brewer, the best returning player from the previous regime, with talented new players. He found three of them at junior colleges. Musselman needed an immediate fix because, as one of the three, Behagen, pointed out, ''You can't win the Kentucky Derby with Francis the Mule. We had the talent.''

Behagen's route to Minnesota began in the South Bronx in New York City, then passed through Twin Falls, Idaho, where he was a Junior College All-American at the College of Southern Idaho. ''I was all set to go to either Washington or Hawaii,'' said Behagen, now an insurance broker and part-time referee in Marietta, Georgia. ''Then I met Musselman at the Pan American Games in Colorado Springs.''

Behagen visited Minnesota and found enough reasons to play there instead of Hawaii. ''I met Brew (Jim Brewer) and Clyde (Turner) and Corky (Taylor) and those guys,'' Behagen said. ''They pretty much convinced me. I was serious about ball, and I was the piece that Bill was looking for, I guess, to round things out. Then, the other thing was, my wife, who I was dating then, was from Minnesota. That helped.''

By recruiting Behagen, Turner, and a third transfer, guard Bob Nix, Musselman had fleshed out significant strength to complement Brewer, Taylor, Keith Young, Bob Murphy, and Winfield. Behagen and Taylor were 6-9, Brewer and Turner 6-8, Winfield 6-6, and Young 6-5. In the rugged Big Ten, Musselman had the size and the talent to win. And he said so publicly.

''I believed we were going to win,'' Musselman said. ''So why shouldn't I tell how I felt? We needed something; we didn't exactly have what you would call a winning tradition.''

Fans of rival Big Ten teams couldn't do anything but dislike Musselman's prediction at a school that had proven, year after year, it was not a championship team.

Worse yet, he was right.

"He was very brash about saying things of that nature," Nix said. "I guess it's just his personality. It really turned people the wrong way."

Musselman's debut at Minnesota was a 68–49 defeat of North Dakota. The Gophers were 6–3 when they played their first Big Ten game against Indiana. Musselman vs. Knight, first Big Ten game for each.

Minnesota won 52–51 on two last-second foul shots by Nix. "It was the most intense game I've ever seen," Schauer said.

Three more victories put Minnesota at 4-0 in conference play. Ohio State was 3-0. The teams' January 25 meeting at Minnesota's Williams Arena would be their only match-up of the season.

Perhaps the best summary of the fight that night comes from former Ohio State guard Dave Merchant: "Maybe there isn't one answer. You have a lot of opinions. The answer is somewhere in the middle of all of them. I have nothing against Bill Musselman. We saw it from two different sides."

The Ohio State coach was Fred Taylor, a living legend who was two-time Coach of the Year. He took the Buckeyes to the national championship game three consecutive seasons, winning the title in 1960 and then losing the next two to Cincinnati, the first one in overtime.

On the other side was Bill Musselman, a rookie Division I coach. When Taylor coached his first Ohio State team in 1959, Musselman was a 19-year-old student at Wittenberg.

Taylor's legacy in the Big Ten was deep-rooted success in a national spotlight. Musselman came from a small college program, yet beat out Taylor to win Coach of the Year honors in Ohio in 1969.

Taylor gobbled up many of the best high school players in the Midwest annually. Mussleman shipped in junior college transfers from places such as Southern Idaho.

Taylor's team was predominantly white; Musselman started four blacks.

"The Vietnam War was still winding down and the civil rights movement was going on," Behagen said. "Racial relations were not exactly the best. Everything pointed to certain fears people had."

Merchant said, "You wonder if it wasn't Ohio State was more white and Minnesota was black. You wonder if it was a subconscious thing. Who knows? We were different kinds of kids."

The kids Musselman had were talented. "At the time he came to

Minnesota, he built a team instantly with junior college guys,'' Merchant continued. ''That was frowned upon. It wasn't a classy way to build a program. I think there was a stigma attached to junior college guys. It hadn't been done. You were supposed to bring in high school seniors and develop them. I think there was a lot of envy that he could build so quickly. Plus, that image. A good guy to hate. His expressions, his demeanor didn't let people who weren't on his side like him. People resented his success.''

Fred Taylor was one of collegiate sports' greatest coaches. ''While I was in high school, he was my idol,'' Musselman said. ''The fight bothered me more than he'll ever know. I always respected Fred Taylor and his program. There's no way I wanted something like that to happen. And if it had to happen, I certainly didn't want it to happen against Ohio State.''

Asked to comment about Musselman in April 1989, Taylor said, ''I don't want to talk about him. I'm sorry, but I just don't ever want to talk about him. I just made it a practice not to. I don't think he was a very good part of the Big Ten.''

Nor does Witte. ''I no longer have a severe hate,'' said the former Buckeye center. ''I feel sorry for him, as opposed to at the time, when I hated him because he ruined a game that I really loved. It's taken a long time to fight through it, a lot of years. It's not only physical damage, which cleared up relatively quickly, though I've still got a real bad eye.

''Here was a situation where there's a coach and he is teaching young men—and this is quote unquote from one of his players at that time—a 'Get Witte' campaign: To stop Ohio State, we have to stop Witte at all costs. And that's very unfortunate, because you have 18- to 22-year-old men that are under the impression winning is the only thing. I disagree with that 100 percent.''

Witte's father, Dr. Wayne Witte, a philosophy professor at Ashland College, was quoted in *Sports Illustrated* after the fight: ''I'm not surprised. Musselman's intent seems to be to win at any cost. His players are brutalized and animalized to achieve that goal.''

Musselman said: ''I don't think that's true. If I animalized and brutalized players, obviously at my size, coaching 6–7, 6–8 guys, they could throw me across the gym floor.''

Musselman said he's puzzled that the fight still elicits such strong feelings after more than 17 years. ''I can't believe it. I'm amazed by the lingering reaction to it,'' he said.

"People criticized our pregame warm-up for over-exciting fans and players. But that had nothing to do with the fight. Our fans and players were excited because we were 4–0, playing the perennial Big Ten powerhouse, and hadn't won anything since the eighth grade picnic."

Musselman made sure they were excited. He had two of his assistant coaches, Williams and Kevin Wilson, telephone Minnesota students in the dorms that fall. "We told them we were from Ohio State, that we were up here to buy football tickets and we could hardly wait for basketball," Wilson related. "We said, 'We're going to kick your butt!' Those kinds of things.

"We had a pep rally the day before the game. Bill had us go around with all the cheerleaders. We got all the students we could on campus, beating a drum. We opened all the doors to the arena, and the students came in and totally surrounded the gym floor and clapped in unison. The last thing we did was the pregame warm-up, because it was kind of fancy like the one at Ashland. We got the players just sky-high the day before the big game."

After the game, two of Musselman's players, Behagen and Taylor, were suspended for the remainder of the season. The fight would leave scars to last a lifetime.

Musselman likely will never outlive the fight. Nor will anybody involved.

"You'd think we were Ted Bundys," Behagen said. "It is totally, totally ridiculous. I meet people to this day (March 1989), because of the bad publicity we got from the fight, they'll say: 'You know, you don't seem like that person that was in that fight.' Hey, I'm the same person, a little older, a little wiser, but the same person that got into that fight.

"That either tells you that I'm a latent crazy or they painted a bad picture," Behagen said. "Fans came out of the stands. We did not do that. We weren't fighting by ourselves. We didn't jump anybody. It wasn't like we were lurking behind the bushes or sprang out on this unsuspecting team. It was a sports fight. I was 19. And they painted it like I was a Gestapo. Corky was the same age as me, and we were monsters. We did this terrible thing, and we hurt this sweet kid Witte. The kid was a rough player, man."

The damage done to Luther E. "Luke" Witte, Ohio State's 7-foot center, has been clearly identified, labeled, and stored for 17 years.

With Ohio State leading 50–44 and less than a minute left in the game, Witte busted loose on a fast break.

"I had gotten a rebound and thrown it out," Witte said. "Minnesota was trying to press, and I took off downcourt. I'm down there all by myself. I'm yelling, 'Hey, there's nobody guarding me.' Finally, somebody (Allan Hornyak) sees me and throws the ball to me. I had to go back for it. Somebody coming from the other end with a full head of steam could catch me, and that's why I was caught. Clyde Turner was the first person that came to me."

Witte was fouled hard by Turner and Taylor, almost simultaneously, with 36 seconds left in the game. Turner was called for a flagrant foul and ejected. Taylor reached out to help Witte to his feet, but instead kneed him in the groin. It was a singular moment of unconscionable brutality, forever frozen in the mind of anyone who saw it.

Merchant went to the aid of his teammate, pushing Taylor out of the way. Brewer and Taylor chased Merchant down the sideline, and then Behagen, who had fouled out with nearly 14 minutes left, came off the bench and stomped on Witte's face and neck.

"I saw Taylor knee Luke right in the groin," Merchant said. "They keep saying Luke was spitting at them. He was down on the court. I don't see how he could have. I pushed Taylor away to keep him from hitting Luke again. I think Jim Brewer was kind of walking to the lane. All he saw was me pushing Taylor. So he starts coming after me. Then all hell broke loose."

For 95 seconds, a crowd of 17,775, which earlier in the game had been threatened with a technical foul for throwing objects on the court, went berserk.

"I was scared," Merchant said. "You were out there. The fans were pouring out of the stands. It was a raised floor, an old arena. There were little tiny exits to go down to the locker room.

"It seemed like it lasted hours, truly a scary situation. The fans made it crazy by going out on the floor.

"Brewer was coming at me. He's 6–8 (Merchant is 6–1), and I was in the corner of the floor. I got out of the corner, thank God, or I'd still be down there. The longer it went, the more people came down."

Witte, Wagar, and teammate Mark Minor were taken to University Hospital. Minor was treated and released that night. Witte spent an hour in the emergency room and was released the next day. So was Wagar, who suffered a concussion.

Witte suffered a nasty gash on his chin, damage to his right eye that forces him to wear contact lenses to this day, and, one teammate suggests, permanent damage to his enthusiasm for basketball. "It had an effect on people who were involved in it, especially Luke," Hornyak said. "To experience anything like that, to be ganged up on and trampled on. . . .I think it affected him and his playing. Up to that point, I think he was one of the best centers in the country. But after that, I don't think his mind was into the game as well as it should have been."

Different players retain different memories from the fight: Hornyak, now a highway worker in Belmont County, Ohio: "There was nobody out there to control anything. There was a pretty bad snowstorm and all the policemen left to control traffic outside. There were 18,000 fans inside and another 7,000 on the ice rink watching on closed-circuit TV. The policemen went out with about a minute and 20 seconds to go, and there was nobody inside to help."

Ohio State's Bob Siekmann, an insurance man in Columbus: "Brewer had Merchant by the shirt, and (Ohio State's) Gregg Testerman knocked him off. From that point, Brewer picked up Testerman and threw him in the stands. Then he came after me. Fans were coming out on the floor. I got back out of the way. Somebody was chasing Merchant about the time I was coming the other way. At about that time, it was over. At least it slowed down. Everybody stopped."

Minnesota's Bob Nix, a purchasing agent for United States Shoe Corporation in Cincinnati: "I never saw the initial foul. On all foul shots I'd head to Coach Musselman, who was at the other end of the floor, to get any information on what he's doing next. So I'm going in the opposite direction. By the time I turned around, all hell had broken loose. Pandemonium. It was almost a case of getting the hell out of there."

Ohio State's Wagar, a corporate vice president of a Fortune 500 company in Agoura Hills, California: "I can give you my personal account of what I remember, and then I can give you my account of what I saw from the films. It's mixed; part of the time I was aware of my surroundings and part I wasn't.

"I got the crap knocked out of me. At the time the incident started, I remember in fairly rapid fashion there were several events. It was apparent that people were hitting or pushing or shoving, and I was sitting on the bench. I ran out on the floor, and all I recall was grabbing hold of somebody. I didn't take a swing or anything. It was one of those things where you grab on to somebody and try to get everybody to sit still.

"I remember my roommate, Dave Merchant, was playing. He was being chased down the floor. Then somebody jumped me from behind. According to the films, that was Dave Winfield. I took several pretty good shots to the head and face. I was down. I started to get up, and I remember being hit once or twice more by a fan and, I think, by the Gopher, as I was trying to get off the floor. If there'd been a drunk with a knife, somebody would have been dead. I was kind of down for the count for a period. Then I recall coming to my senses on the bench on the sidelines. I was talking to another friend, Gregg Testerman. He had given me a towel because I had a cut over my eyebrow and stuff. That's when they were trying to get Luke off the floor. So I got up and walked back out there and helped carry him off the floor.

"I remember going down (to the locker room) below the stands. They had tunnels you go through before the stairs. People were throwing things and spitting and swearing. Saying they hoped we die. It was pretty spooky. During it, I'm sure it was all adrenaline as to what you did, but as you started to realize what happened, you realize how close you may have come to real serious injury. And we did have some serious injuries. Later on, in the locker room, I guess there was a period of time when we were in there and they were trying to determine how badly Luke was hurt.

"I was kind of going in and out of reality. I guess I'd had a pretty good concussion because at one point, I was having difficulty remembering exactly what happened. Some of the other players said, 'Maybe we ought to take a look at Wagar and take him to the hospital, too, because he's not with us.' So I think Mark Minor and I were taken in a police car. I remember vividly there was still a crowd outside, and it was almost a riot. They were throwing rocks at the police car as they were taking us away to the hospital. We went to the ER, got treated. I called my folks and spent the night in the hospital. I guess, as it turned out, I did have a pretty substantial concussion. I didn't play the next couple games."

Behagen: "The game was just rough. Witte got knocked down. Corky went to help him up. As he was pulling him up, he kneed him because the guy spit at him. Somebody saw Corky do that and hit Corky. Clyde saw them hit Corky. Clyde hit somebody. Somebody hit Clyde. Their bench emptied. Our bench emptied. The fans came out of the stands." (Behagen didn't mention his actions after he left the bench.)

Brewer, an assistant coach at Northwestern, declined to comment on the fight specifically. He said he was in the process of writing a book about it.

Winfield: "I saw Brewer getting grabbed from behind while another guy wound up to hit him. I turned a player around who was about to haul off on one of our men and, boom, knocked him down. Fans got into the act, climbing from the stands onto the elevated court. At the same time, Ohio State guys and our guys are running the perimeter of the court just to get out of there, all of us by now scared of what happens when 17,000 screaming fans are added to the mix. I was never so happy to be inside a locker room. That night, the videotape of the fight is played on virtually every newscast in the country. The next week, it's a *Sports Illustrated* cover story. A hell of a way to make national news. Deserved or not, Mussleman takes virtually all the heat for the incident."

Ohio State's Minor: "The bottom line, to put it in very simple terms, they were a little bit upset. Once it was obvious they were going to lose the game, they just decided to go ahead and cause a little bit of damage, which they did. That's what it amounts to. I think those players were very, very aggressive, and I think Musselman gave them a green light to go ahead and do just about anything they wanted out there. He was that type of coach.

"When you're out there playing ball for all those years, you're always in a little scrap here and there. I didn't think much of it at the time. It happens to everybody throughout their career. You win some, you lose some."

Minnesota's Taylor, working in community development in the Twin Cities: "Luke was gong up to take the shot, and Clyde Turner and myself fouled him. It was really how hard I fouled him that precipitated my helping him up. Basically, it was a situation where he had an easy two points, and we were trying to make sure he didn't score. I think Clyde was ejected from the game for a flagrant foul. When I went to help Luke up, he spit at me and I got pissed. It was a very tough game, and I kicked him. And then I walked away.

"What happened as I walked away, one of their players came up. At that point, Jim Brewer turned around and saw this other player swinging at me, so he pushed me aside to swing at him. I think two players then knocked him down, and I went over to pull one of the players off of him. When I turned around, the entire floor had erupted. It was scary. It was a scary situation.''

Minnesota's Turner, a consultant for Big Brothers/Big Sisters in Minneapolis: ''I find it very difficult to talk about. To be very frank, I think you're dealing with economics, you're dealing with a major institution. There's going to be racism. I don't care who it is or where it's at. When you're dealing with the white community, there's going to be racism. There's going to be prejudice. For someone to deny that . . . I don't think they're really looking at the whole picture.

''I think Fred Taylor and Ohio State were really out of line. As I look at it, they were perpetrators as well. There's two sides to every story. There's a cause and effect. In a sense, Ohio State was basically an all-white team. We were an all-black team. It's like they're saying, 'Hey, they're guilty without due process.' I didn't appreciate it at all. I didn't appreciate it then. I don't appreciate it now.''

Musselman's assistant coaches on the fight:

Williams: ''Taylor fouled Witte. He had knocked him down on the play. Witte was knocked to the floor. And Corky, who is one of the nicest people you'd want to meet, he went to give him a hand. He gave him a hand, and helped him up, and that's when the knee in the groin thing happened. Knowing Corky, I think it was a case of frustration more than anything else.

''As soon as this happens, as you can imagine, both benches came out on the floor. My immediate reaction was to run onto the court and try to get players back to the bench. Fans had gotten onto the court. Fights were breaking out on different parts of the court. We were trying to get our players off the floor. Bill was on the floor, too, trying to get our people off the court.''

Wilson: ''This was a very wild moment. A lot of guys were running around for cover and scrambling around. The major guys were Witte, Hornyak, and Mark Wagar. Wagar got leveled by Winfield. He murdered him. It was a Mike Tyson punch. And Winfield never got in trouble, because you couldn't tell who he was on the film. But he was awesome. I mean he came running from about 50 feet away and just leveled him. I turned away. I couldn't even look.

''I really didn't know this during the fight, but looking at the film, Bill got up. He had to stand up on the bench to get up on the raised floor. He came out and wrapped his arms around Clyde and pulled him out of the melee that was going on. His basic focus was on Clyde, trying to break it up by getting Clyde out of there. When the fight was over, Bill said, 'Hey, don't worry. This will blow over.' That's what he told Jimmy and I. Because about a week before there was a fight between Marquette and South Carolina, and not much happened with that.''

Klucas: ''I saw Corky Taylor go over, and I'm sure if he had to do all that over, he wouldn't have done what he did. It got ugly because some people came on the floor. I think if people wouldn't have come on the floor, and wouldn't have gotten all excited. . . . It got to be a semi-mob scene. The things I remember that were really ugly were security guys hitting fans; fans wouldn't get off the floor, and some fans were after Ohio State players. I still contend the fans did more damage than the players. I'm not making light of the incident. It was very ugly and something that all of us wish never happened. But I also think, largely due to the *Sports Illustrated* story, public opinion was formed that we were a bunch of barbarians just beating up people.

''Bill was stunned. I mean, he was really lower than a snake's belly.''

Said Musselman: ''It caught me off guard. Then I reacted and tried to do what I could to help break it up.''

Musselman criticized the officials: ''Someone from the Big Ten came into the dressing room immediately after the game and told me not to say a word about the officiating. Well, in fact, a lot needed to be said about the officials. They allowed the game to get out of hand, allowed things to be done by both teams. One of the officials never worked a game after that season.''

Musselman tried to understand the fight and the personal ramifications for him: ''A lot of things were said in print that were wrong. I was blamed for the fight or for not stopping the fight, yet the fight was the last thing I wanted. My insides were torn up. My hopes and dreams were shattered that night. I couldn't believe life was like that. I believed if you were dedicated and outworked everyone, you'd be successful. That night it seemed like everything I believed in was wrong. I went home and got down on my knees and prayed. And I thought then, 'Well, you asked for this; you wanted to coach in the big time.' Since then, my beliefs have been reaffirmed. But it was my background that got me through that situation. If I hadn't been mentally tough, I wouldn't have survived that incident.''

The officials, Orlando Palesse, Tony Tortorello, and George ''Red'' Strauthers, called 30 fouls in the game, 16 on Minnesota and

14 on Ohio State. Ohio State was 12 of 19 at the foul line; Minnesota 12 of 17. Thirty-six free throws is not an unusually high number.

Opinions vary as to whether the game, before the fight, was inordinately physical:

Nix: "It was a very physical game from beginning to end. It was like the officiating got out of control early. Every time the ball went on the boards, it was just banging and people getting knocked around. Very few fouls were being called. It was a physical game outside as well as inside. You could get away with almost hacking people as long as you weren't just outright slapping somebody."

Hornyak: "It was very physical that night, and the score indicated it, 50-44. There was hardly any fast-breaking. It was just get the shot and pound the boards. Whoever got the rebound, they walked the ball down and set up. When you get a type of game like that, there's a lot of shoving and pushing underneath. You can crash everybody (to the boards). There's a lot of lumber underneath."

Wagar: "It was typical Big Ten. I wouldn't say the main part of the game was any more or less physical. Anybody who plays organized sports at that level, you can kind of tell the difference between a game that's being played hard and fast and one that's kind of played with deliberate monkey business. I wouldn't say that the bulk of the game was being played that way."

Witte: "It was a physical game, but you watch the Big Ten today or 20 years ago or three years ago . . . the Big Ten is physical. I recall it as being a very normal game. No worse or no better. I mean, there was nothing abusive about it. It would be easy for me to say yeah, they were trying from the very beginning (to get me), but no, they weren't."

Witte returned to the Ohio State lineup after missing one game. He later played 118 games during three seasons, 1973–76, in the NBA in Cleveland, where one of his teammates was Jim Brewer.

Witte said a severe ankle sprain sustained in a Cavaliers–Bucks game curtailed his professional career. After running a sporting goods store in Alliance, Ohio, he became an insurance broker for John Hancock. He and his wife, Donita, have two children, Erin, 9, and Lyle, 7.

Basketball fans will always link Witte to Musselman through the fight. Yet while Musselman's responsibility for the incident has been dissected ad nauseam, Witte's role hasn't.

"What normally causes a sports fight?" Behagen asked. "Combination of things. Sometimes it's rivalries. Sometimes a game gets out of control because of the officials. I officiate high school games in Georgia, and you can feel when games need to be called tight. Normally, if it's not done, things happen. And that's probably one of the main reasons (the fight happened). It was a volatile situation."

Especially at halftime. The first half ended with the score tied 23–23. As the players ran off the court toward the locker rooms, Nix signaled to the pumped-up crowd by raising his fists. "Luke Witte crossed in front of me," Nix said. "There's no question in my mind or anybody's that saw it. It was a deliberate elbow to my face.

"He just threw it, and he damn near decked me. It was all I could do to stand on the floor when he hit me. It stunned me so bad I didn't know what happened. I turned and almost, before I realized what I was doing, took off after him. Then I realized who it was and figured, 'Whew! I'm 6–3 and he's 7-foot. Back off here. See what's going on.' But it was seen by a lot of people. Except the officials."

Witte himself said the "only (physical) thing that had occurred was right at halftime. What the hell was his name? Nix. A little kid, a little white kid. Well, he came up in front of me right at halftime and raised both fists right in front of me. He stuck a fist right in my face. I shoved it off and there was a little shouting. I didn't even say anything. I mean, somebody jumps into your face with both fists raised like a boxer. . . .Just a little kid. Why, I just put my hand up to get his fist out of my face. I kind of shoved it over to the side, and he said something to me, and I didn't respond."

Musselman, Nix, an Associated Press story, a Big Ten investigation by Commissioner Wayne Duke, and a bevy of Minnesota players and the three Minnesota assistant coaches gave starkly different versions of the incident.

Ohio State's Hornyak, who said he didn't see the incident, nonetheless spoke of its importance in what happened that night: "Today, you get a fight here and there, but nothing with this magnitude. It was all built up. Both teams undefeated. Big crowd. A lot of emotion, and it just stemmed from there. I still say that we had the best of them. I thought they were beat and there was some tension during the game at halftime. I just believed it was caused by that. They blamed Luke for taking a cheap shot at one of their guys. If they'd have won, it wouldn't have been anything. But they were down. I think they were frustrated, and they took it out on us. I recall coming down (to the locker room at halftime) behind Luke, and one of their players telling him that they were going to get him. And it was because of an altercation. I guess an elbow was thrown. I didn't see that, but they did and they just stood there pointing at him. They said they were going to get him. But you never knew what they're going to mean by that."

Nix: "I threw my hands up when they missed the shot. I'm going off the floor with my hands raised. I don't even know where he came from. He came across in front of me and elbowed me as he went past. Hard enough that my head yanked. I'm moving in a forward motion, going forward, and my head snapped backward. He hit me upside the head. It just stunned me."

Kevin Wilson: "Bobby Nix was a little white guard. When the two teams filtered through each other to get to go down to the locker room, Luke Witte gave Nix a punch in the mouth. No question. He saw Bob coming. Witte punched him hard.

"I bet you I saw it a thousand times with the 16-millimeter film on the analyzer. Clicked it back, forth, back, forth, back, forth. Bobby's head clearly snapped back. When the half ended, Nix did put his fist up in the air like John Carlos and Tommy Smith (black power salute in the Mexico City Olympics in 1968), but it was pointing to the scoreboard. Luke Witte clearly looked downward. He looked at Nix, took about three steps, looked up at the scoreboard, took his left hand from right to left, and gave Bobby an uppercut. Nix immediately ran over to the referee and started complaining, and Luke Witte just kept his stride and took off. Luke Witte was bad news in high school. The guy was bad news, a Bill Laimbeer-type player. That was the rap on him."

Winfield saw it, too: "Witte crossed in front of Nix and punched him right in the face. Bop! Our guy was hot when he went downstairs. Behagen and a couple of others including Musselman saw the whole thing; and as we went into the locker rooms, Behagen screamed down the hall at Witte, 'Hey, you motherfucker. I'm going to get you.' He was mad. A bunch of us had to hold him back."

According to Kevin Wilson, Behagen's belligerent feelings toward Witte went back to the previous summer. The pair had been involved in a couple of altercations at the Pan American Games.

Winfield, Nix, and Wilson all said that Musselman tried to calm his players at halftime, not incite them as is popularly believed. Musselman wasn't doing this for altruistic concerns which suddenly sprouted in his personality. The answer is simple. Musselman's one concern, one that he's had in every single game he's coached, is his own: to win. On this night, it meant preventing the halftime incident from affecting his players' concentration for the second half.

"In the locker room, he was saying, 'Calm down. Calm down,' " Winfield said.

Wilson said Mussleman's message didn't come through: "The players really weren't paying attention. Behagen was talking about this and that, low tones, but they're talking to each other about, 'Hey, we're not going to let this crap happen.' So the thing was building. I don't think Bill incited that part."

Musselman's alleged incitement of his players was important enough to be investigated by Duke.

The results of the Big Ten's investigation of the fight and the league's subsequent disciplinary action were unveiled three days after the fight at a press conference in Chicago. Associated Press told of the Big Ten's decision to join Minnesota in suspending Behagen and Taylor for the remainder of the season:

"Wayne Duke, Big Ten Commissioner, told a news conference that a lengthy investigation by his office showed that the disruption of the game 'was precipitated by an unsportsmanlike act by a Minnesota player.'

"Duke said that extensive interviews with coaches and players indicated that several factors contributed to the brawl which broke out in the final 36 seconds of the game. He refused to elaborate on the exact cause of the incident. He said, 'We could find no evidence of racial overtones involved.'

"Duke added, 'In only one instance were charges of excessive physical contact against Ohio State's players at all justified. At the end of the half, the films revealed Ohio State center Luke Witte, in what appears to be unpremeditated action, making contact with Minnesota's Bob Nix as the two crossed paths on the way to their locker rooms.' "

The Big Ten documented Witte's action against Nix and singled out the incident at the press conference, demonstrating its significance.

The American audience, however, had been shown only the game-ending fight. The highlights demonstrated the brutality of Taylor and Behagen against Witte and the ensuing mob violence against the Ohio State players. The public never saw film of Witte's elbow to Nix's head.

Behagen said, "Everything pointed to problems. You have to remember, we were 19, 20 years old. I've been labeled a militant since then, and that's the furthest thing from the truth. I'm an insurance broker. I'm just an everyday person. I work in the morning. I have a family. I raise my kids. I have a wife. I grew up. I mean, I have a certain background, but I'm no worse or better than the average person out there. Fights happen in sports, and all of a sudden it turned out like we were the worst people in the world. There was a fight. Now it's over with. It got out of hand.

"The public reacted the way they did because the press, I felt, painted it into a black-white thing, and it wasn't that. That's the sad part about the whole situation. Yes, it was black athletes, predominantly a black team and a predominantly white team, but it was not a racial situation. (Players) got into a confrontation—that's all it was. But once you add ingredients that are explosive and emotional, you have problems. If it had been kept in context, it would have been just a fight."

Behagen said Minnesota's pregame ballhandling routine wasn't a contributing factor to the fight: "But as far as Bill being responsible for the things that happened, he had a great deal to do with it because he did set the atmosphere in other respects. He came in and said we were going to win the Big Ten right away. That alienated a lot of people. Also, you've got to remember, this was the early '70s. You know the joke about what do you call five black guys and a white guy? A basketball team and a coach. That joke was (generally) not true back then, but it was true for our team. He had eight or nine ballplayers that were black, and that was a first. But the fight happened because of the game. That was basically it."

Behagen said he should have gotten more support from Musselman: "I'm sure Bill has learned a lot since that happened. I'm saying he was a young man (31) at the time, probably didn't know how to handle it himself. I know Paul Giel, the athletic director, and I had plenty of talks. The fight happened about a month after Paul got the job. He was like in limbo. Everything pointed to timing, and the timing was bad."

"It turned out we were the pawns. Unfortunately, we didn't get much backing from the people that should have backed us. Every indication to me was that Bill did the suspensions on his own."

Sports Illustrated told its millions of readers about the brawl with a February 7, 1972, cover story by William F. Reed that pointed a national finger of guilt at Musselman.

"The fight had a tremendous effect on his career," Jimmy Williams said. *"Sports Illustrated* painted him as a man who would win at all costs. That was the image a lot of people got. They thought that was the way he is... until this day. There have been other fights, but they haven't gotten the exposure this did. From this fight, that's how most of the nation was introduced to Bill Mussleman."

Reed wrote: "Fights always have been a deplorable part of college basketball, a game that thrives on emotion and contact. Lately, though, the brawls have developed in number and intensity to the point where thoughtful basketball people are concerned about the sport's direction. Millions saw the recent donnybrook between South Carolina and Marquette on TV. That was sobering enough, but Ohio State-Minnesota was different—and far worse. Instead of a fight erupting from the heat of competition, this was a cold, brutal attack, governed by the law of the jungle. It could be considered the inevitable result of the malaise that affects the sport these days, a stunning example of responsibility abdicated by a coach, the players he recruited and taught and the fans who followed them."

Reed told of Musselman's sign in the Minnesota locker room: "Defeat is worse than death; you have to live with defeat."

There were plenty of other signs in Musselman's locker room, too, such as "Quitters never win, winners never quit," and "It's easy to be ordinary, but it takes courage to excel."

Reed wrote, "As a whole, the game was tough and nerve-wracking, but also cleanly played and well-officiated. The only incident of any sort before the slaughter came when the teams were going to the dressing rooms at halftime. As Nix passed in front of Witte, his left arm raised in a clenched-fist salute, the Buckeye center tried to shove the fist out of his way with an elbow and in the attempt clipped Nix lightly on the jaw."

Reed portrayed one team, Minnesota, as brutal and savage while dismissing Witte's action because he "lightly clipped" Nix.

Yet Reed disclosed later in the story that Duke "was satisfied that only in the Witte-Nix incident 'were charges of excessive physical contact against Ohio State's players at all justified.' "

Any notion that the fight was premeditated by Musselman is just plain dumb. Does a coach wait until there's 36 seconds left to precipitate a brawl which will cause him to lose two of his best players for the rest of the season and damage his career for years?

The first physical transgression that night was Witte's against Nix at the end of the first half.

In no way does it justify what followed. To ignore it, however, is foolish. Musselman said Witte's ''light clip'' of Nix before halftime was strong enough to ''snap Nix's head back.''

Reed wrote, ''Musselman made no attempt to stop the fight and showed no remorse afterwards.''

Musselman said he did: ''I was at the hospital after the game to see the Ohio State players. There was no way that I didn't have feelings for what happened.''

Ohio State's Merchant offered his personal conclusion about Musselman: ''It's easy for a guy from Ohio State to say he's a jerk, but I don't know what was said in the locker room. The thing blew up. It just happened. I can't imagine a guy saying I'm going to get this guy and wait until there was 36 seconds left. I can't imagine it was anything more than frustration. The important things were how the institutions handled the situation afterwards, and how there was no crowd control.''

There's one other important item. The fight will never go away for those who were involved.

''I can go somewhere and if I run into a person who's very sports-minded, I say who I am and his head goes spinning,'' Clyde Turner said. ''People come up with Ohio State. They'll say, 'Oh, you were the guy.' ''

Nix said, ''Being from Kentucky and coming back and working in Cincinnati, it's hung with me. I still get jokes from people because there's a lot of Ohio State graduates that are employed at the same place I am. I get comments every now and then. I threw the *Sports Illustrated* article away after about five years. I had it a long time. I said to hell with it.''

8

After the Fight

Lost in the outgrowth of the fight was this question for Musselman to ponder: If Minnesota couldn't beat Ohio State at home at full strength, how could it contend for the Big Ten title without Behagen and Taylor? Behagen had averaged 16.3 points and 10.4 rebounds, Taylor 4.3 points and 6.3 rebounds. There was another concern, too. How would hostile crowds react when Minnesota played on the road? "The situation was that we didn't have a choice except to go out and play," Brewer said.

How would they play? "We don't have Behagen," Assistant Coach Klucas said at the time. "We don't have Taylor. We have no depth. We don't know what's going to happen."

For openers, Musselman inserted Winfield into the starting lineup—less than five weeks after he was playing intramurals. Musselman had been using a seven or eight-man rotation before the fight. Afterward, he went almost exclusively with a five-man lineup: Turner, Brewer, Winfield, Nix, and Keith Young. Bob Murphy served as sixth man but was seldom used. The remaining five members of the squad took a total of five shots—for the entire season.

"We were called the Iron Five," Turner said. "We played defense all over the court. Plus we played the match-up zone, and we had to press. We did that as well. We were just in excellent condition, not only physically but mentally and emotionally as well, because we felt some injustice had been done. Politics had entered into the suspensions of Behagen and Taylor. We just felt like we had to salvage the season. The best thing we could have done is win the Big Ten and devote it to Behagen and Taylor. They were part of our family."

The family, however, was unwanted at rival Big Ten universities. "They really didn't want to know the truth of the story, so we were made the villains," Turner said. "We had to play through all of that. We had to just dig down and achieve what we wanted. And that was to win the Big Ten championship."

They started with successive games against Iowa. Iowa officials reportedly loaded up on plainclothes officers for the first meeting in Iowa City. Security measures, however, didn't extend to the court, where a scramble for a loose ball produced a collision. "One of their players got hit in the head," Musselman said. "The guy fell, hit his head on the floor, and it was bloody. I was thinking, 'Oh my God. We're going to get lynched here.' "

Winfield said, "They went crazy, I'm telling you. They're carting this guy away, dragging him off the court, blood on the towel, and somebody threw a chunk of ice onto the court. It hit their own guy right in the head. And the place, don't you know, went wild because you could see it. Whap! More blood. You had to worry about your safety.

"The fans were vicious. One of them grabbed me. One of them threw beer on me. It was tense. That's the way it was every game, every week—tense, always with the sense that a fight might break out. Maybe it prepared me for what I go through now. But it was tough, everywhere you went."

Minnesota won the game 61–50. "We thought, 'Boy, if we're going to have a chance for the Big Ten, we've already won short-handed at Iowa,' " Klucas said. "I think it really turned the season around and gave us a chance to win the Big Ten."

The chance materialized when Ohio State dropped three of its next six Big Ten games, beginning with an 88–78 loss at Michigan as both Witte and Wagar sat out. "It just seemed to go downhill from then on," Hornyak said. "I don't think we were quite as emotional. I think what happened was still in the back of our minds."

One observer who had breakfast with the team the morning of the Michigan game said the players "looked like war casualties." Wagar said the game at Minnesota "basically was the end of our team's chance of fulfilling its potential."

Musselman was determined to push his Iron Five toward the Big Ten title he had predicted. Never mind that two of his starters were gone. "Bill always had some kind of speech or presentation that every game was bigger than the last," Winfield said. "Every game. Never rest on your laurels, and always prepare yourself. Never take anything for granted."

Opponents couldn't. While shooting only 43 percent from the floor, the Gophers limited opponents to 39.6 percent. They outrebounded opponents by 8.9 per game, yet, despite their aggressive defense, committed 69 fewer fouls in 25 games. And, naturally, they led the nation in defense.

The Big Ten crown was theirs for taking. Ohio State lost at Indiana and beat Michigan State to finish 10–4 in the conference. Minnesota took a 10–3 record to Purdue for its final league game. A win would give the Gophers their first outright Big Ten title in 53 years (Minnesota and Illinois had tied for the championship in 1937).

Purdue had possession when Musselman, trying to nurse home a 49–48 lead, called time out with 15 seconds left. "We're supposed to be the best defensive team in the league," he said in the huddle. "Now's the time to prove it." With time running out, the Boilermakers missed an inside shot and then one from the outside. Winfield grabbed the rebound just before the buzzer sounded. "What else could I do but jump up and snatch it," Winfield said. "No one, but no one was going to take that rebound away from me."

In its first NCAA Tournament appearance ever, Minnesota lost to Florida State 70–56, then beat Marquette 77–72 in the Mideast Regional consolation game. Minnesota finished 18–7. Behagen and Brewer were named All-Americans. Brewer was also voted the Big Ten MVP, averaging 11.0 rebounds and 9.8 points. Turner led the Gophers in scoring (18.6).

In Musselman's second season, Minnesota started 9–0 and took a gaudy 14–2 record to Ohio State February 10, 1973, for a long-awaited, nationally televised rematch with the Buckeyes.

The Gophers stayed in Springfield, about 45 miles from Columbus, and timed it so they would arrive at St. John's Arena an hour and a half before the game. "Bill must have asked me five times, 'How long will it take us?' " Klucas related. " 'We want the bus there right on time. We don't want to be early or late.' "

Musselman low-keyed the game, with the exception of telling Behagen he didn't have to play if he didn't want to. He did—and scored 33 points as Minnesota prevailed 80–78.

Of Musselman's many anxious moments in the game, the most frightening instant was when an Ohio State player went up for a rebound and came down bleeding. "He fell and cut his chin," Klucas said. "There's blood on the floor. And I thought, 'Oh Jesus Criminy, here goes the media again.' "

Instead, Minnesota kept going for a second consecutive title. The Gophers were 20–2 overall and 10–2 in conference play before they lost to Iowa and Northwestern. Indiana went on to win the Big Ten title, while Minnesota settled for an NIT bid, beating Rutgers 68–59 and losing to Alabama 69–65.

The next season, Minnesota struggled through a 12–12 year which included a 102–68 loss to New Mexico, the first time in nine years a Musselman-coached team had allowed more than 85 points.

Other numbers were even more unsettling for Musselman the following season: the number of players transferring away from his disciplined regime and an ensuing NCAA investigation that would uncover 128 violations.

Assistant coach Wilson saw the trouble coming. "Probably my first two years here were okay," Wilson said. "My third year, there was a guy, Dennis Shaffer, who was a first-team All-American junior college player. We brought him up here. I liked him a lot, and I felt Bill was mistreating him. Bill started yelling at players, and our philosophy started changing. Bill was always...if we lost a game, he'd say, 'You guys lost. You're no good. We got to get out and get new players.' If we won, Bill said, 'Great. We won.' It was either 'they lost' or 'we won.' Bill was getting a reputation. Whenever we'd recruit, we'd have to keep Bill away from the player, guys like Adrian Dantley (who went to Notre Dame), because Bill turned some guys off. And the way some of the guys were getting treated; I just didn't think it was right."

Wilson and Musselman went back a long way, before Minnesota and before Wilson's All-American career at Ashland. Wilson was on the first team Musselman coached, Kent State University High School. When Wilson got sick after one game, Musselman insisted he spend the night in Musselman's house. "His wife fixed me a steak," Wilson said. "Bill used to let me use his car. He got me a job at a printing company. I used to baby-sit Eric."

Wilson followed Musselman to Minnesota in 1971. "Bill did a lot of wonderful things for me,'' Wilson said. ''For that, I'll always be grateful. But I also saw Bill hurt a lot of people. I mean, he wrecked a lot of people's lives.

''I've always felt Bill's dealing with people is a major shortcoming. And the fact that Bill never could not be intense and get away. You tell me how many times Bill sat down and read a book. I mean the guy is on the phone, the guy is hyper, he's intense, and it was very, very hard to work for him. I busted my tail. I was his right-hand man. I did all kinds of things there, but I just didn't enjoy it. My stomach was always upset.

''He was very intense, and the No. 1 thing in Bill's life was success in basketball, not his family. When he got up to Minnesota, I think he forgot what got him there: the teaching, the motivation, and being close to the players. The year after the fight, the players just took over. The guys didn't even listen to Bill anymore. They all wanted pro contracts, and they just fired the ball when they felt like it. He'd tell them to pass it around. They'd just shoot it anyhow. We lost control of the team, which was never Bill's style.

''He got caught up with the boosters and the alumni and wearing leather jackets and going to country clubs and doing that kind of thing. I think that's what got him in trouble. The guy got caught up in a whirlwind and didn't know how to get out.''

Others, including Wilson, did. At Musselman's summer camp in 1974, Wilson told him he was leaving: ''I said, 'Bill, this will be my last year. I'm done. I just can't take it.' ''

Nor could 11 players who transferred during Musselman's final three seasons at Minnesota. Young departed for University of the Pacific. Tommy Barker, a highly touted 7-foot recruit from Texas, left after his freshman year. Chad Nelson headed to Drake. Rich McCutcheon, a starting guard in 1973, transferred to Arizona State in '74. A year later Mark Lansberger, a 6–8 forward who would play seven seasons in the NBA, joined McCutcheon.

Musselman's world was crumbling around him. In his final season, 1974–75, Minnesota was 18–8 but again played poorly at the end, losing four of its last seven. And in the final collegiate game he coached, Musselman lost to Purdue 100–72.

In the spring and summer of 1975, Musselman was losing everywhere. Word filtered out the NCAA was launching a probe of the Minnesota program, and that the University was conducting its own investigation. More players told the media they might leave.

While he publicly denied thoughts of leaving himself, Musselman was packing. By mid-May, the Twin Cities media reported the ongoing NCAA investigation, and that 10 of Musselman's players had been interviewed by NCAA investigator Bill Hunt. Yet as late as July, Musselman told one local writer, "At this point I'm the University of Minnesota basketball coach, looking forward to what I believe will be my greatest team."

On July 27, Musselman told columnist Sid Hartman of the *Minneapolis Tribune*, "I'm confident that when the investigation is complete, the whole thing was blown way out of proportion."

The next day, Musselman was gone. He was introduced as the head coach of the ABA San Diego Sails at a July 28 press conference. He signed a three-year contract worth more than $135,000. At Minnesota he was making $23,000 a year.

Asked at the press conference about the NCAA investigation, Musselman said, "The investigation is of the University, not a single individual, and I am no longer a member of the University of Minnesota. I have a very clear conscience."

He also had three years left on his five-year contract with the school. In 1973, Musselman had been courted by Charles Finley's ABA Memphis team and by the University of Florida. To entice him to remain, Minnesota extended his contract three years to the 1977–78 season.

In an Associated Press story the day Musselman resigned from Minnesota, he said, "Who was there backing me up when I needed it? Nobody. That's probably the big reason I left. I can guarantee you that the NCAA doesn't have 100 violations on the basketball program at Minnesota. Everybody in the country thinks I'm some kind of outlaw because of the stories saying we had 100 violations. And that's simply not true."

The very next day in an interview with the *Minneapolis Star*, Musselman admitted he violated NCAA rules by giving Behagen rent money and by providing transportation and cash for McCutcheon. Musselman explained, "Behagen had personal problems, and McCutcheon needed money to get home. The money came out of my pocket and my conscience is clear about helping them."

The NCAA was clear, too, disclosing 128 violations of NCAA rules after substantiating 77 of 112 allegations. Fifty-one additional violations were uncovered by the University's own investigation and reported to the NCAA Committee on Infractions. Minnesota was put on probation for three years.

For the first two years, the number of scholarships was halved from six to three annually, and Minnesota was banned from national television appearances and postseason tournaments. Additionally, Assistant Coach Williams was banned from recruiting for two years, and the University was ordered to sever connections with eight volunteer recruiters and boosters.

Following standard procedure, the NCAA did not make any names public in its 13-page report, March 9, 1976. However, the NCAA said all the violations were committed during Musselman's tenure. The NCAA said, "The university's head coach acted contrary to the principles of ethical conduct inasmuch as he did not on all occasions deport himself in accordance with the generally recognized high standards of honesty normally associated with the conduct and administration of intercollegiate athletics. Furthermore, his involvement in the violations set forth in this report demonstrates a knowing and willing effort on his part to operate the university's intercollegiate basketball program contrary to NCAA legislation."

A university faculty-student committee report about the violations was disclosed two months earlier in the *Minnesota Daily*, the University student newspaper. Musselman was cited for: 1) providing cash, airplane tickets, meals, lodging, employment, car usage, and eyeglasses for players; 2) arranging for other people to deliver such goods and make donations; 3) a visit to Barker's home near Houston, where he tried to persuade him to return to the University; a few minutes after Musselman left the home, an unnamed associate gave $500 to Barker's mother; 4) observing preseason conditioning drills and practices prior to the official starting date, and 5) using a credit card from booster Harry Cox for personal use. The report listed eight boosters connected to the violations including Harvey Mackay, president of the Mackay Envelope Co., and Jack Berklich, operator of Mr. Joe's Restaurant in St. Paul.

The report said Musselman was involved with nearly half of the 128 violations; Jimmy Williams in more than 20, and Mackay in 22. Violations ranged from furnishing personalized envelopes to an athlete's mother to free trips and lodging for athletes; free dental work, meals, and a refrigerator; direct handouts of cash to players, and players scalping tickets.

Even before the NCAA announced its sanctions, Musselman had

weakened the program he left behind. In a Buffalo, N.Y., motel room August 20, 1975, he signed Mark Olberding, who had led the Gophers in scoring and rebounding his freshman season, to a multi-year contract with San Diego. Olberding was 19.

Minnesota center Mychal Thompson, currently with the Los Angeles Lakers, said Musselman tried to sign him out of college, too. "Bill offered me $500,000 for seven years, but I declined," Thompson said. "It wasn't the money so much, but the length of the contract. Seven years is just too long."

Minnesota signed Jim Dutcher, an assistant coach at Michigan, to a five-year contract August 20, 1975.

When news of the NCAA sanctions broke, Musselman maintained the NCAA ruling concerns "a lot of things where I don't even know what they're talking about. They say a lot of things were arranged through the head coach. A lot of those things were never arranged through me."

Musselman told the media he would maintain silence: "If I say anything, I'm going to incriminate others. That's why I haven't said anything."

Having hot-footed it from Minneapolis one step ahead of the NCAA posse, he didn't have to say more.

Sailing into Oblivion

9

Musselman's first coaching offer from the ABA wasn't from either of the two teams he coached during the 1975–76 season. Charles Finley offered him a package worth $250,000 to be vice president, general manager, and coach in Memphis in 1973. "He personally guaranteed it. I turned it down three, four times," Musselman said. I was at Minnesota. I just thought I'd stay where I was. He was honest with me and up front, and I'll always respect him."

Respect was something painfully lacking for the ABA franchise in San Diego in 1975. The Conquistadors entered the league as an expansion team in 1972. The Q's were neither successful (101–173 in four seasons) nor popular. San Diego businessmen Frank Goldberg and Bud Fischer sought to change that when they sold their interest in the Denver Nuggets to assume command of the born-again San Diego franchise they renamed the Sails. One of their first moves was signing Musselman to a three-year contract as head coach.

One of their worst moves was peddling Travis Grant in the preseason to the Kentucky Colonels for cash. Grant had averaged 25.2 points and shot 53 percent the previous year when San Diego finished 31–53. Following their claims to the media that they would spend money freely in the pursuit of players, the San Diego owners created an immediate image of torn credibility.

"If you come into a town with a brand-new franchise, you start at zero," Sails Assistant General Manager Chuck Shriver said. "We're starting at minus 10."

Welcome, Bill Musselman.

Camp Musselman was based at the Naval Training Center. San Diego *Evening Tribune* columnist Steve Bisheff wrote, "The military setting fits Musselman better than his snug sweatsuit. He seems in complete command. Even Gerald Oliver, the new assistant coach from Tennessee, can be heard barking out orders in his best Jim Nabors voice."

Oliver and Musselman traveled many miles together. They first met when Musselman spoke at a weekend clinic at Tennessee, where Oliver was an assistant to Ray Mears. After Musselman gave a lecture on the match-up zone, he, Mears, and Oliver stayed up to 3:30 in the morning in the hallway of the Stokely Athletic Center. They discussed the subtleties of the match-up zone, using wastebaskets to simulate players. "We stayed an awful long time moving trash cans and wastebaskets," Oliver said.

Musselman ran into Oliver again in 1973 when his Minnesota team stopped overnight in Knoxville en route to a game at Furman. That night, Musselman and his assistant coaches decided to see a movie. The taxi ride to the theater cost $3.35. On the trip back to the hotel, a different cab driver asked for four times as much. Musselman refused to pay. Oliver got a late-night call from a policeman he knew. "He said, 'Coach, we got trouble with Coach Musselman over at the hotel. He won't pay the taxicab driver,'" Oliver related.

Oliver rushed to the hotel, called the owner of the cab company, and settled the problem. The owner instructed his cabbie to desist. Musselman and Oliver celebrated by indulging one of their common vices, ice cream. Then they talked hoops well into the night. "Bill was going to go to jail before he was going to pay," Oliver said. "He just would not be robbed by someone. Bill will stand up for things that he thinks is right."

In the infant stages of his first professional basketball training camp, Musselman felt things would be right. He wouldn't have to do much to improve on San Diego's 31–53 record in 1974–75. He had a strong, young club that included Mark Olberding, centers Caldwell Jones and Dave Robisch, and guards Bo Lamar, Bobby Warren, and Kevin Joyce.

Musselman and Oliver would drive from their hotel to practice in the morning, then return to the hotel for a Jacuzzi. "Bill loved Jacuzzis," Oliver said. They'd get out, settle in near the pool and go over plans for that afternoon's practice. "It was great weather," Oliver said. "Everything was perfect."

Paradise didn't last long, despite Musselman's zeal. "In practice, he'd clap his hands and get things going," Oliver said. "It was a very enthusiastic practice. He had a lot of college in it. You have to realize at that time, which was '75, the world was different then. There was still a lot of this rah-rah enthusiasm. Bill had all that. And the players picked up on it."

Musselman hoped his players would also pick up on his work habits. "I saw him work in pro ball 16 hours a day some days," Oliver said. "I don't mean sit around. I mean work 16 hours."

Neither knew how few hours the Sails had left. Jack Murphy, the legendary sports editor of the *San Diego Union* (who was the first sports writer to have a stadium named in his memory), wrote in his column October 14, 1975, that Goldberg claimed the rights to 39-year-old Wilt Chamberlain. Musselman told Murphy, "If he reports, he can run up and down the baseline along with the rest of 'em."

Chamberlain never made it to San Diego, but another center of considerable fame did. Bill Walton, a graduate of Helix High in nearby La Mesa, brought the Portland Trail Blazers of the NBA to the San Diego Sports Arena for the Sails' lone exhibition game that season. Walton reported in full beard and played despite bruised knees he suffered in a minor automobile accident three days earlier. A gathering of 2,871 watched Walton get 11 rebounds and 10 assists while being outscored by Jones 27–6. Portland won the game, though, 98–85.

Injuries to Joyce and Lamar weakened Musselman's backcourt as the season got underway. The attendance at home games was even weaker. Following a 3–8 start, the Sails sailed into oblivion.

Musselman sued for the substantial money still due from his three-year contract. He was awarded $177,800 in personal and punitive damages following a three-week trial.

Musselman was unemployed in the ABA for less than three weeks, taking over as head coach of the 1–12 Virginia Squires. He didn't do much better, going 4–22 while getting into a feud with the Squires' leading scorer, Luther "Ticky" Burden. The rookie guard, from Albany, N.Y., an All-American at Utah, had burned San Diego twice earlier in the season for 40 and 45 points. He was averaging 22.6 for the Squires.

Before Virginia's road game against Julius Erving and the New York Nets at the Nassau Coliseum, November 29, a cameraman went into the Squires' locker room. Then during warm-ups, a photographer from the Associated Press went onto the court to get a picture of Burden for Burden's hometown newspaper in Albany.

Burden subsequently had a poor game, six points in 22 minutes, as the Squires let an 82–78 fourth quarter lead dissolve into a 116–97 loss. Dr. J. scored 31. Musselman fumed afterwards: "I know what Ticky's problem was tonight. I don't blame the kid. It's not his fault. People were doing stories and taking pictures right before the game. A cameraman came into the locker room. Would they do that in football? What do they think basketball is, Mickey Mouse? It's my fault. I shouldn't have let them in. I feel sorry for the kid. Snapping shots. It's a shame. He's played good."

Soon he wasn't playing at all. Burden and fellow starters Johnny Neumann and Jan van Breda Kolff were benched by Musselman, who played a new starting five the entire 48 minutes of one game.

The situation quickly deteriorated from there. Neumann and van Breda Kolff were traded to Kentucky for Marv Roberts. After Burden was left home for two road trips and kept out of practice for a week, two of Virginia's veteran players, Willie Wise and Mack Calvin, spoke to management on Burden's behalf. An ensuing meeting between Musselman and General Manager Jack Ankerson resolved the situation. Musselman, 7–30 in his ABA coaching career, resigned.

"When I first went there, I thought the financial problems had been straightened out," Musselman said. "Then I found the players were talking more about the financial troubles than basketball. They worried more about the next payroll than they did about the next practice. It was difficult for them to concentrate on basketball."

It was difficult for Musselman to accept losing. In 10 seasons at Ashland and Minnesota, he had never coached a losing team. He hadn't experienced a losing season in 20 years, not since his sophomore year at Wooster High School. "It was very frustrating for me," Musselman said. "I couldn't sleep nights. It was killing me."

Soon after Musselman's resignation, the Squires became the third ABA team to fold during the '75–76 season, the league's last before four of its teams, the Nets, Denver, San Antonio, and Indiana, were absorbed by the NBA.

In six months, Musselman's coaching career had taken him from the University of Minnesota to the San Diego Sails to the Virginia

Squires to nowhere. Kris Musselman recalled the afternoon her husband came back from Virginia to their home in La Jolla, California: "I can remember that he sank into a chair, reached into his wallet, and pulled out a small card he always carried with him. He had given it to his mother when he was only in about the fifth or sixth grade. On the card was the inscription that his goal was to become the best basketball coach in the country.

"He looked up to me and said, 'Kris, what am I going to do now?' "

Musselman surfaced at Sport Court of America, Inc., which installs basketball, tennis, handball, racquetball, and other types of courts in the backyards of homeowners. "I sold tennis courts," he said. "If the backyard wasn't big enough, I'd try to sell a 'foo-foo' court."

Musselman worked for Sport Court for nearly two years during his exile from coaching. "I enjoyed it," he said. "I love warm weather. And I was my own boss with my own hours. It was nice to have that freedom."

On idle nights Musselman frequently went to San Diego Padres games, where he could watch his former basketball study, Winfield, crunch home runs and sign autographs after the game. Musselman had tried getting Winfield's autograph on a basketball contract with the Sails, and Winfield gave the offer serious consideration.

"I was playing with the Padres, and they weren't paying big money at the time," he said. "I was making around $45,000, and anything would augment my salary. I was up for the challenge. I know I could have done well, and I wouldn't have been the first person in history to do it. Look at Bo Jackson. I could have done both sports for a while." The collapse of the Sails made the matter academic.

Meanwhile, Musselman adjusted to life without coaching. "My dad was a lot more relaxed," Eric Musselman said. "He played racquetball and ran with the dog every day and went to games at night."

After one Padre game, Musselman walked up to Padres President Ballard Smith, then the team counsel, in the parking lot and began a conversation that evolved into a close friendship.

"Bill is so intense, I was a little taken back at first," Smith said. "This guy came up to me introducing himself for some reason. He knew I was connected to the ball club. I didn't understand what he was trying to do.

"By the time the conversation was over, he had arranged for my wife and I to come over and to have dinner at his house. He just wasn't going to take no for an answer. I mean, I really didn't want to go. I didn't know him, this guy in the parking lot. Well, we end up having a really good dinner, and the four of us struck up a friendship from then on."

Ironically, Smith had graduated from Minnesota Law School in 1971, missing Musselman's arrival by two months. No matter. Musselman and Smith had plenty in common, including an affinity for Winfield. "I've talked to Dave many times about Bill," Smith said. "Dave is very, very fond of Bill."

Musselman and Smith frequently went running and played basketball. "We spent a lot of time together until he got the job with the Cavaliers," Smith said.

And Smith did what he could to help him get that job: "When Bill was going after it he called me and said this guy, Ted Stepien, who owns the Cavaliers, knows me. I said, 'Where the hell does he know me from?'"

Smith had practiced law in a small town in northwestern Pennsylvania. "Ted Stepien apparently had been a client of my small law firm, and I knew the man. Bill wanted me to call the guy," Smith said. "So I called Ted Stepien, my long-lost friend. This guy was obviously acting like we're bosom buddies. I didn't really remember the face, but I recognized the name. So we talked for a while. I may have had some impact on Bill getting the job, but I don't know.

"After Bill got the job, Ted Stepien was in San Diego, and Bill called me and said Ted wants to get together. I said, 'That's fine.' So I invited them to a ball game. Bill walks in with this guy and I mean, I swear to God, I'd never seen him in my life. I didn't have the foggiest idea who this guy was, but I went along with the story anyway. As it turns out, I think it was really unfortunate that Bill got that job, because he never had a chance to be successful there. He was dealing with somebody that was just not going to allow him to do the job that he could do."

Smith's involvement in Musselman's fortunes didn't end when the Stepien/Musselman era concluded in Cleveland. As Smith said, "Bill always had some scheme going." One of them was a coast-to-coast effort to make Musselman, and anyone who dared to assist him, big bucks. The time: 1984. The idea: sell buttons before the Los Angeles Olympics proclaiming, "Kick the Big Reds' Asses."

Smith first heard of Musselman's venture when they were flying back to San Diego in a helicopter from Yuma, Arizona, site of the Pa-dres' spring training camp. ''There's three or four of us, and he's got this crazy scheme about these buttons,'' Smith said. ''He's going to have guys standing on the corner selling them. He finally talked all of us into putting like a thousand bucks into this thing. We made an initial run of 10,000, 20,000 buttons.''

That took care of the West Coast. In Florida, Musselman shared his brainstorm with one of his former players at Ashland, Gary Youmans. ''He sold these people on doing these buttons, and he had this big scheme,'' Youmans said. ''Christ, he was going to make a for-tune selling these gall-darn buttons. He came over to St. Pete, and he and I went to talk to this guy about distributing them on the beach. Oh Christ, he was into this thing. He was all set to make a killing.''

That was before the idea was killed when the Soviet Union de-cided to boycott the Olympics. Five years later, Smith said, ''I've still got a set of them around.''

10

Reno and Bighorns

Bill Musselman returned to coaching November 10, 1978, leading the Reno Bighorns in the first game of the Western Basketball Association's only season. Of course, it wouldn't have been authentic Musselman without controversy.

Billy Martin supplied that. As a favor to his long-time friend, Martin appeared at the Bighorns' opener against the visiting Las Vegas Dealers. In his book *Number 1*, Martin explained why: "Bill thought my appearance would bring customers to the gate. Bill was an old friend, so I didn't even ask for a fee. I made just one request: no press interviews. I would show up at halftime, wave to the crowd, and after the game I'd stay and sign autographs for the kids."

After the game Ray Hagar, a Reno sportswriter, pursued an interview with Martin that Martin had no intention of allowing. Martin asked for Hagar's notes; Hagar refused. According to Martin, Hagar "took his glasses off, and he made a move like he was about to go after me. At that point I pulled the trigger and I hit him with my left hand, gave him two good pops. I gave him a black eye and a cut lip...I found myself in another fight I didn't want to be in."

Nor did Martin want to be in the ensuing stories detailing his latest brouhaha. And he wasn't too keen when he learned of a lawsuit by

Hagar against Martin, the Reno Bighorns, the Centennial Coliseum, and the WBA. Hagar also filed criminal charges against Martin.

Musselman set up a meeting in New Orleans with himself, Martin, and Judge Eddie Sapir, Martin's long-time adviser. Then Musselman got the Bighorns' owner, William H. Myers, and Myers' attorney to talk to Hagar's attorney. A deal with Hagar was worked out with the Bighorns paying Hagar $5,000 to cover doctors' bills in return for Hagar dropping his criminal charges and lawsuit against Martin.

Musselman as peacemaker. Truth stranger than fiction.

By helping Martin out of a jam, Musselman became even closer with the off-and-on Yankees manager. When Martin was roasted at a March 1989 banquet in Las Vegas, Musselman was asked to join select company on the dais. ''I'm sitting there and I'm thinking, 'What the hell am I doing here?' '' Musselman said. ''Whitey Ford was my idol. Ernie Banks. Harmon Killebrew. And Jimmy Piersall. I saw the movie *Fear Strikes Out* four times.''

Musselman had always wanted to be a major league catcher. He didn't make it past college ball, but in Vegas that evening he was pitching zingers to the most famous manager in baseball. When it was his time to roast, Musselman fired away: ''Billy decided to go to college for two terms, Truman's and Eisenhower's. Billy called me before the roast tonight and asked what I thought he should wear. And I said, he should go down to Cox's and get a seersucker suit. Instead, he went to Sears.''

Opening night distractions aside, Musselman quickly built a successful franchise in Reno, one of six which lasted the season (the Las Vegas Dealers eventually ran out of cards and folded).

The WBA seemed to be stepping into an ideal situation. The Eastern Basketball Association was just beginning to expand from a weekends-only semipro league into the Continental Basektball Association, now the principle minor league for NBA teams with a multi-million dollar player and referee development contract with the NBA.

The Reno franchise was operated by a conglomerate of businessmen who wasted little time in selecting a coach. ''There was only one coach I was after, Bill Musselman,'' said Allen Dunn, the team's Executive Vice President. ''He was the best coach available anywhere.''

Musselman hadn't coached a game in more than two and a half years, and he wasn't certain he wanted to leave a pleasant life in San Diego to return. ''I really had to think over whether I wanted to get back into the game," he said. "But they made it attractive enough. Plus, it was the challenge of putting something together from the ground floor. They told me I had complete freedom selecting the players. I think that's where I'm at my best. Evaluating talent, being on the floor, teaching players. I don't think there's anybody who's any better at that."

Musselman's first team included Ira Terrell, the first of 26 players sent to the NBA by Musselman. The team also included two future college head coaches: John Kuester, currently at George Washington University, and Randy Ayers, recently hired by Ohio State.

The idea was to make it to the NBA—players and coaches. Coaching in the WBA gave Musselman vital visibility when he scouted NBA exhibition games and the L.A. Summer League. Most important at Reno was his success, which wiped away the frustrations of two brief, losing terms with failing ABA franchises in San Diego and Virginia.

Musselman convened his first WBA practice at a Reno high school. He pointed to a court he'd never seen before and said, "This is my home, right there. I've spent hours of my life out there. I was choked up when I got off the plane today. I'm not kidding you."

Reno raced to a 24–14 start despite 21 roster changes by Musselman, who received much of the credit in Curry Kirkpatrick's story in *Sports Illustrated*. Kirkpatrick called Reno's success "testimony to Coach Bill Musselman's stable leadership, defensive teachings and passing-game offense, which has tended at times to dominate a league overpopulated by perimeter gunners." Kirkpatrick said Musselman had "matured both in his on-court and off-court attitudes, seems less uptight, more cordial and resigned to the frustrations of coaching. Because of Musselman's newfound tranquility, the Reno club had escaped the problems present on other squads, where NBA egos have clashed with WBA realities."

Musselman didn't seem tranquil to Ballard Smith. Their friendship had been forged in San Diego when Musselman wasn't coaching. Smith saw Musselman in action for the first time during a WBA playoff game in Tucson, Arizona. "I got a seat right behind the bench," Smith said. "In the first 45 seconds of the game, I heard every four-letter word I've ever heard come out of his mouth. I never had seen him swear before. It was almost like he had a split personality. It struck me as very funny. I didn't realize he had that emotion in him. I can still see it."

Reno finished third in the regular season, 28–20, then swept second-place Washington 3–0 to advance to the finals against Tucson. The best-of-seven series matched Musselman against Tucson's Herb Brown, the former head coach of the Detroit Pistons.

The Bighorns split the first two games in Tucson, then won two of three at home for a 3–2 series lead. Tucson's Bill Paterno threw in a desperation three-pointer at the buzzer to give the hosts a one-point win. Tucson then blew out Reno in the final game.

Brown called Musselman ''probably the best coach that I've ever coached against on the minor league level. The one thing about Muss is that he'll do anything that's humanly possible to win. I've heard all the stories about him calling players up the night before a playoff game to disrupt them.

''The only thing I can remember is when we were in Reno and it was right before a playoff game. We had to change hotels at three o'clock in the afternoon. He's never taken full responsibility for that, so I can't really say that it was his fault. But it's the only time it's ever happened to any team that I've coached.''

11

Suddenly One Summer

Bill Musselman couldn't find a locale where he'd want to succeed more than Ohio. It's where he was born and raised, where he went to college, where he made his debut as a successful high school coach, and where he became an even more successful college coach at Ashland. It's where his mother, his sister, and his brother lived.

In the minds of Ohio basketball fans, though, the above wasn't worth squat. Musselman had long before been painted the enemy, the man fans held responsible for The Fight against Ohio State. If you loved college basketball in the state of Ohio, you rooted for Ohio State. If you loved pro ball, you suffered with the Cleveland Cavaliers.

And there was a history of suffering long before Ted Stepien and Musselman surfaced in Cleveland. The Cavaliers entered the NBA in 1970 along with the Buffalo Braves and Portland Trail Blazers. Cleveland lost its first 15 before defeating Portland 105–103. Then the Cavaliers dropped their next 12. After a two point defeat of Buffalo, seven more losses followed. Cleveland was 2–34 and on its way to a 15–67 maiden season. The Cavs were 23–59, 32–50, 29–53, 40–42, 49–33, 43–39 twice, and 30–52 the following years.

Cleveland eventually reached a clear pinnacle under Bill Fitch, who coached the University of Minnesota from 1968 to '70. The Cavs won the Central Division in 1975–76 and beat the Washington Bullets in the first round of the playoffs before losing the Eastern Conference finals to eventual champion Boston, four games to two.

On May 21, 1979, Fitch announced his resignation. Two days later, he was named head coach of the Celtics. Just 11 days later, a banner headline streamed across the Cleveland *Plain Dealer*'s Sunday sports section: "Musselman stumps for Cav job."

Musselman was interviewed by phone from his San Diego home. He told reporter Bill Nichols, "I want that job more than any other in the world. I know I would work at it 24 hours a day. If I get it, I say right now I can sell at least 2,000 season tickets myself. I would devote my life to it. I feel I'm at the right age (38). I can make the team a winner again. I really feel that strongly about it."

President and owner Nick Mileti wasn't impressed. On July 23, 1979, he hired Stan Albeck, an assistant with the Lakers, as the second head coach in Cavaliers history. Jimmy Rodgers, now coach of the Boston Celtics, was named director of player personnel and Ron Hrovat was hired as general manager. Musselman, meanwhile, kept installing tennis courts in San Diego.

The new management failed to produce. Despite winning 11 of its final 14 games, Cleveland finished 37–45 and failed to make the playoffs for the second straight season.

Along with the losing record was a third straight season of declining attendance. The Cavs averaged 13,913 in 1976–77, then 11,097, 7,942, and 7,873 the next three seasons.

And already, the pre-Musselman Cavaliers had traded away their first-round picks in 1980, '82, and '83, and their second-round choices in '80 and '81.

Subsequent trades retrieved some picks. The Cavs got an All-Star guard in Randy Smith by sending their 1980 first-round pick to the Clippers. The Cavs then sold their 1982 first-round pick to the Lakers, who used it to select forward James Worthy, a key member of their three championship teams the last five seasons. In return, the Cavs got the Lakers' 1980 first-round choice. However, it was the last pick of the first round because the Lakers had just won the NBA championship.

Thus, Cleveland had just one pick, No. 22, of the first 46 players taken in the '80 draft. Among the first-round choices were several players still making an impression in the NBA nine years later: Kevin McHale, All-Star forward of the Boston Celtics; Kiki Vandeweghe of the Knicks; Joe Barry Carroll of the Nets; Mike Gminski of Philadelphia; and Utah Jazz guard Darrell Griffith.

Cleveland drafted Chad Kinch, a 6–4 guard from North Carolina-Charlotte. He scored a total of 80 points in 29 games before being traded to Dallas. In effect, the Cavaliers traded James Worthy for Chad Kinch.

Enter Ted Stepien.

"We were really criticized by the media unfairly, even before we got started," Stepien said. "It was terrible from Day One."

Stepien considered himself a hero for purchasing the Cavs and keeping them in Cleveland. To this day, he has trouble understanding exactly how he became Darth Vader to Cleveland fans.

He had been such a success in everything else. In 1947, at the age of 22, Stepien founded his own advertising agency, Nationwide Advertising Service, specializing in recruitment advertising. "I started with $500 and built up a $94 million ad agency," he said. It was enough to indulge a fantasy; Stepien bought a 5 percent interest in the Cleveland Indians. But he was one of 57 partners, "so I really had nothing to say about the Indians."

He wanted control.

By 1980, the parameters of Stepien's life seemed permanently in place. His wife of 26 years, Ann, had died in 1979. But the six daughters they raised provide Stepien unending pleasure.

His business had become the No. 1 recruitment advertising agency in the world and ranked among the top 30 of all advertising agencies internationally. When he stepped into professional basketball, Stepien expected the same success he had achieved in the business world.

He created his own first problem by telling anyone who would listen just how well his Cavaliers were going to do: "We're going to be a winner in the NBA," he told readers of the Cavaliers' game program. "And we're going to give the fans of Northeastern Ohio the best in basketball and the best in entertainment."

Stepien purchased 37 percent of the Cavaliers' stock for $2 million in April 1980, finally solidifying control of the franchise after three previous front office reorganizations that year. The NBA Board of Governors unanimously approved Stepien as new owner, but, apparently concerned with the franchise's instability, decided to move the 1981 NBA All-Star Game from Cleveland to L.A.

Stepien hadn't started, and already he was linked to a decidedly negative development. "I'm elated that I was approved, but disappointed that we lost the All-Star Game," Stepien said.

Strike one.

Cleveland fans seeking ammunition against Stepien had already been given quick assistance by the man himself. A series of damaging statements by Stepien made their way into print. The lu-lus included a remark that he'd like Cleveland to have at least five white players. He also made a reference to the NBA's "Jewish clique." Stepien said his statements were "misunderstood."

Amazingly, before Stepien's ill-conceived comments reached the general public, they had first been printed in *Rave*, the in-house magazine of the Richfield Coliseum, home of the Cavs. Stepien was quoted in an interview saying, "This is not to sound prejudiced, but half the squad should be white. I think people are afraid to speak out on that subject. White people have to have white heroes. I, myself, can't equate to black heroes. I'll be truthful. I respect them, but I need white people. It's in me. And I think the Cavs have too many blacks, 10 of 11. You need a blend of white and black. I think that draws, and I think that's a better team."

Stepien later said that he was speaking strictly in a marketing sense. "I'm not a racist," he said.

Strike two.

Rodgers, the team's director of player personnel, informed Stepien he had been offered an assistant coach's position with the Boston Celtics. "I didn't have controlling interest yet, and I recommended he take the Boston job," Stepien said. "That left open the personnel job, and then Bill Musselman contacted me."

So did Billy Martin and Dr. Glenn Clayton, the President of Ashland College. Each called Stepien on Musselman's behalf. The calls helped, because Musselman hadn't even met Stepien until mid-April of 1980.

But there wouldn't have been an opening for Musselman to pursue if Mileti hadn't sold the team. Or if Rodgers hadn't been offered the Celtics job and left a vacancy in the front office. Or if Albeck hadn't jumped ship despite a three-year contract he had signed just a month before Stepien's takeover.

"My immediate concern is to solidify the coaching situation," Stepien told Cleveland reporters following a board of directors meeting that passed the club presidency from Mileti to himself.

Albeck had already set his sights on San Antonio, which couldn't publicly acknowledge interest since he was under contract to Cleveland. Stepien said of Albeck, "First of all, I would like to have him coach here three years. Secondly, he can stay one year. Thirdly, if he goes, we must be compensated. I tried to call Stan, but he never got back to me. But if he leaves, without reservation, Bill Musselman can do the job."

Stepien hired Musselman as his director of player personnel June 7, 1980. "How bad did I want to get back into basketball?" Musselman asked at the time. "You should have seen my monthly telephone bill. You could've made the monthly mortgage payment on a new house. You can't believe what a feeling it was for me. And to be back in basketball in Ohio, where we have so many friends and where we got our start."

Musselman's "we" were wife Kris and children Eric and Nicole, then 15 and nine. During his exile from basketball, Musselman had interviewed for NBA jobs in Houston, San Diego, and Detroit, as well as waging his one-man campaign for the Cleveland job a year earlier when Albeck was hired. Before Stepien hired him, Musselman had been offered the head job at Tennessee-Martin, where his college coach, Ray Mears, was the athletic director. "It was a gamble to turn down that job," Musselman said. "The biggest gamble I could make."

He'd take a lot of gambles in the ensuing months as he and Stepien tried to glue together the remnants of a moribund franchise. The problems were just beginning. For openers, Stepien had to coordinate the Cavaliers' selections in the NBA draft just one day after he became team president. This meant eliciting common goals from Albeck, assistant coach Mo McHone, and Musselman.

Two stories the week before the college draft documented the tense situation. One story said "Albeck reportedly wants out" and that he reportedly had been unhappy about: 1) remarks Stepien made about Albeck's three-year contract; 2) Stepien's decision to hire Musselman as director of player personnel; and 3) Stepien's decision to hire Don Delaney, coach at Dyke College, to be general manager, replacing Hrovat. "I think my position is that Albeck wants out," Stepien said in the story.

Another story in the *Plain Dealer* June 6, four days before the draft, featured the headline "Albeck 'is gone,' headed for San Antonio job." In the story, Dick Miller, the Cavs' second-leading stockholder after Stepien, raged at Albeck: "Stan is gone. He was the only coach at the (NBA) Board of Governors meeting, and he was very visible. He's obviously trying to leave. How come he wasn't in Cleveland doing his homework for the college draft?''

Stepien said of Albeck, ''I think we could get along. We're better off if he is the coach, but I think he is unsure of himself.''

It was a hell of a way to start a new regime.

Half an hour before the draft began and just 15 minutes prior to their first selection, Cleveland signed 6–10 free-agent center Dave Robisch to a four-year contract. Albeck told the press that now the Cavs were free to draft Kinch instead of a center.

''I think Kinch can be an influence right away,'' Albeck said. He forecast Kinch as a replacement for Austin Carr, who was taken by the Dallas Mavericks in the expansion draft: ''With Randy Smith and Foots Walker, Kinch is ideal. He is very quick, strong, and can play defense.''

He couldn't play a piano. ''I didn't have anything to do with Chad Kinch,'' Musselman said. ''I didn't have much to do with that first pick.''

Stepien felt signing Robisch was the most important move the Cavs made on draft day: ''We had to go higher than we probably wanted, but I wanted to start right out and show we mean business.''

In the previous season, Robisch played in all 82 games and averaged 15.3 points and 8.0 rebounds. He would play just 11 for Musselman, averaging 9.4 points, before being shipped to Denver.

Musselman was appointed coach June 11, the day after Albeck left town to become the head coach of the San Antonio Spurs.

Strike three. Enter Bill Musselman.

Perhaps it was sheer coincidence that Stepien introduced his new coach to the Cleveland media at a press conference on Friday the 13th. Stepien didn't wait long to stick his foot squarely in his mouth: ''Welcome to the new Cavaliers organization. What's happened in the past is all over with.''

Then Stepien discussed the Minnesota–Ohio State brawl with reporters: ''I realize he had a past reputation. I don't believe in hiding anything. He wasn't on the floor fighting. He was sorry for it. I don't think a person should be punished all his life for something that happened a long time ago. Bill will take care of things on the court. I can handle things off the court. I can control Bill.''

Stepien announced the resignation of McHone, who joined Albeck with the Spurs, and declared ''the Mileti–Albeck thing is over.

They are gentlemen. We are still friends with those people. We have too many other things to do now. We've been set back six weeks by this thing.''

Stepien signed Musselman to a one-year contract, telling the press, ''In this organization, we're all under one-year contracts. I get quality personnel, pay them well, and then whip the hell out of them. All I ask is that you give us a chance. We want to be judged when the season is over. With our front office and players, we'll be in the play-offs next season. Not the championship—give us three years for that one.''

By not giving Musselman more than one year, however, Stepien fostered a win-now environment, one that Musselman didn't particularly enjoy. ''You get a one-year contract, what are you doing?'' he asked. ''You can't put the guy where he makes a decision based on whether or not he's going to win the next ball game. It's not fair to you, the ball club, the organization, or the coach. I learned that in Cleveland.

''That's one thing about pro ball. Anybody gives a guy a one-year contract, he's hurting himself and the coach. The coach knows he's got one year; he's got to do something quick. Almost every college coach gets a four-year contract. One-year contract? Who are you kidding? That's the first thing you should look for in an organization. They give a guy a one-year contract? That's the first sign that they don't know what the hell they're doing.''

The one vital plea Stepien made to the media was something he wouldn't concede to Musselman: wait to make judgment until after the season was over. Worse yet, Stepien had predicted unconditional success to the media and, thereby, Cavs fans, who had to be skeptical. How could they not be with the organization's in-fighting and the flight of owner and coach?

In 1989, Stepien questioned the wisdom of his win-now philosophy: ''I should have given myself a three- or four-year program. I should have kept the team low-budget instead of going out for free agents the next year. We had Bill Laimbeer, who was just a rookie, starting at center. We had Kenny Carr and Mike Mitchell. We had a pretty good team. I think if we had just held in there and built from that, we would have been all right.

''Going back, I think the reason I was successful in my ad agency was that I hired good people. I was loyal to them and they were loyal to me. With Bill, I didn't realize how good a coach I had. I think if I would've held and stuck with him, it would've been a lot better for me. My mistake was firing Bill.''

He didn't say which time.

Musselman, only the third coach in Cav's history, said at his initial press conference that he would ''stress defense, shot selection, and the transition game. We'll also use a lot of ball movement. It's important to play with intensity. Ted is a workaholic, and expects that out of his people. My job is to help him toward that goal.''

Cavalier forward Campy Russell was at the press conference, and offered his assessment: ''I'm kind of glad they got the situation together. It's important for the guys to know who is going to be here. I have to reserve judgment on (Musselman). You can't worry about what he did in college, high school, or the past year. My main concern is to be on a winner. And Musselman proved he was a winner in the past.''

Russell was traded before the season started.

At the press conference, Stepien labeled Musselman a ''super coach'' before adding, ''I would never fire a coach in the middle of the season.'' He didn't mention at the end of a season.

Would he fire Musselman? Twice.

But on that day of optimism in June, Stepien envisioned a much happier scenario, telling reporters, ''We're all in this together.''

The media began taking shots immediately. Stepien hadn't helped matters by discussing the Minnesota–Ohio State fight, whether he could control Musselman, and whether he'd fire him—just two days after he named him coach.

In the June 16 *Journal Herald*, columnist Ritter Collett wrote, ''ALL LOVERS of sportsmanship and lofty ethics will have to applaud the return of Bill Musselman to the Ohio sports scene.

''Musselman's questionable coaching philosophy led to one of the most disgusting episodes in memory in college sports.

''That was the infamous brawl at Minnesota in 1971 [*sic*] during which Musselman's Gophers knocked Ohio State's Luke Witte down and sent him to the hospital after he was kicked in the groin and the head.

''Musselman, who once coached at Ashland College, has emerged as coach of the Cleveland Cavaliers, having been hired by new owner Ted Stepien. Stepien has said he wants to run his NBA franchise in the manner George Steinbrenner runs the baseball Yankees. Translate that as ruthlessly.

"Stepien is also on record as saying that he wants to balance the racial makeup of his team. Translate that as more white players.

"Musselman and Stepien. Translate that as a pair who deserve each other."

On the positive side, in an analysis in the *Plain Dealer* by Nichols, with the headline, "Stepien, Musselman deserve their 'honeymoon,'" Nichols stated in his opening paragraph: "Cavaliers owner Ted Stepien and his coach, Bill Musselman, probably are the two most pre-judged personalities in Cleveland sports today.

"Stepien took over the Cavaliers with the reputation of a man with an enormous ego who consistently says the wrong things at the wrong time. Musselman is still trying to erase the memory of that awful night when Ohio State center Luke Witte was beaten up in a game at Minnesota in the early 1970s.

"Normally, owners and coaches come to town and enjoy a honeymoon period. Then the critics come out of the woodwork and begin chopping at them. But not so with Stepien and Musselman. The woodwork is crawling already.

"But they deserve the same courtesy that those who have preceded them received."

Less than a week later, *Plain Dealer* columnist Dan Coughlin's piece about Musselman appeared under a headline "A huge obstacle."

Coughlin's first sentence was accurate enough: "Bill Musselman faces a tremendous obstacle in achieving a smooth transition as head coach of the Cleveland Cavaliers."

Coughlin then continued: "That obstacle is himself. He never has coached in the NBA before, but his reputation as a little Napoleon driven by a 'win at all costs' philosophy has made him a marked man in the world's top professional basketball league."

Coughlin said the previous year, Musselman was one of five candidates for the Cav's vacant head coaching job, and that then-owner Mileti submitted the list to his players: "They said four of the names, including Albeck, were 'fine,' but Musselman's was 'flatly rejected.' "

Coughlin said Jim Brewer of the Portland Trail Blazers was "almost antiseptically non-committal" about his former college coach: "I can't pass judgment. I don't know whether I would like to play for him again or not," Brewer told Coughlin. "I didn't like his style of coaching in college. I thought we should have been more of a running team. I don't know how he'll do with the Cavaliers."

"Judge him by what he does. This is now. Bygones are bygones."

Coughlin next cited Luke Witte, a former Cav and the unwitting Ohio State victim in the infamous brawl. "When you pump up 19- and 20-year-olds with a 'win at all costs' philosophy and then put a gun in their hands, what are they going to do?" Witte asked.

Coughlin concluded: "Personally, I prefer to give the guy a chance, especially someone I barely know. Musselman's NBA debut is going to be rocky, as it is. This is truly a remarkable setting. Perhaps no manager in Cleveland history has been greeted with more antagonism."

Good thing Coughlin was giving Musselman a chance. Musselman had been head coach for half a week.

Between recounts of the brawl and the Cavs' inordinate amount of front office and coaching changes, the mood in Cleveland was rapidly turning gloomy. Musselman headed west for the summer.

The Southern California Summer Pro League has been operating since 1970. As many as 70 NBA players and dozens of prospects gather each summer for three to four weeks of intense competition.

They play games from 1 p.m. until midnight, offering the scouts and coaches in attendance new barometers to gauge talent. Rookies mix with veterans; high draft choices play with longshot free agents as NBA teams test new players.

"It's quite a training and learning session for a lot of NBA players and even referees," said Larry Creger, who has owned and operated the league since 1980.

It's the first place that new Cavaliers Coach Musselman went hunting for players. Creger knew Musselman when both were in the WBA. Creger was also familiar with his work ethic.

"When he goes to the Summer League, I believe that he just outworks people," Creger said. "Other coaches will go and watch a game or two. Bill will camp out and watch every game. That's what all NBA teams should do, and they should have a whole staff of people doing that.

"Bill would not waste time. He would talk a lot about the players, but when the games were going on, he was up there paying a lot of attention. I was there from one in the afternoon to midnight with him every day."

When the WBA closed shop in 1979, Creger was hired as an assistant coach with the Detroit Pistons. One year later, Musselman wasted little time in approaching Creger and proposing he come to Cleveland to serve as director of player personnel and assistant coach.

Creger said he didn't want to be considered for the post, but Musselman wanted him and continued the assault. Sooner or later most people give into Musselman, if for nothing more than to end the incessant phone calls in the middle of the night. After about a month, Creger gave in.

Creger would divorce himself of the Cavaliers organization after one season, but he has remained friends with Musselman and speaks well of his personal association with Stepien.

Asked the amount of pressure Stepien exerted on Musselman, Creger responded: "Tremendous. On all of us. Ted was always concerned when we weren't winning. He just didn't understand the patience it takes to build a basketball team that's not really on top. Bill would've been all right without the push he was constantly getting from Ted. If Ted would've said, 'Bill, you're going to be here for five years if we never win another game,' that would've have made so much difference in Bill's approach."

Musselman would never find out. "When a guy comes to you and says you've got to win tonight or you're fired, the perspiration drips off your face pretty damn heavily," Musselman said. "Under Ted, it happened a couple times...three times: 'If you don't win tonight, you're fired.'"

Musselman inherited a team that had missed the playoffs; changed ownership four times in the off-season; sacrificed key draft picks; been fashioned to another coach's (Albeck) liking, and been ordered by its new owner to make the playoffs. Behind him, Musselman had the dubious backing of an entire state that hated his guts from an unrelated fight eight years earlier and all the security a one-year contract entails.

Musselman left the L.A. Summer League impressed with Bill Laimbeer and unimpressed with Chad Kinch.

As preseason camp approached, Musselman became increasingly wary of the presence of Delaney, the team's general manager. Musselman saw Delaney as his potential successor. "Ted offered me a three-year contract for a different position. He didn't want me to coach at first," Musselman said. "After two weeks he wanted to fire me, not fire me in his eyes, but he wanted to make me vice president 'cause he originally wanted Don Delaney to coach. The guy who coached his slow-pitch softball team. I mean, to go from there to the head job of an NBA team? I'm not saying that he couldn't have come in as an assistant and been there and made it. But you don't jump from slow-pitch softball to the NBA."

A revealing first paragraph in a Cleveland newspaper reported, "Don Delaney will continue as the Cleveland Competitors' (softball team) manager despite being appointed Cleveland Cavaliers general manager earlier this week."

Phew!

Musselman's first day in preseason camp didn't go well. Eighteen candidates showed up at the Cavs' initial practice for rookies and free agents. The workout was scheduled for Richfield Coliseum, but auxiliary baskets hadn't been put up as planned and the regular practice court wasn't ready. Musselman salvaged his first day in charge by moving the practice to a local junior college.

An interesting note appeared in the *Plain Dealer* the following morning: guard Foots Walker and forward Mike Mitchell, both represented by Jack Manton, were trying to get their contracts renegotiated.

One day of practice, one major headache for Musselman. "Ted told me we're only going to keep one of them because he didn't like the idea that they were represented by the same agent," Musselman said. "And they wanted to renegotiate their contracts, and they were doing it together.

"So we got rid of Footsy Walker. I should've never gotten rid of Footsy, because he was a good point guard. But it was him or Mitchell. So we end up with no point guard. So now I'm running around with no point guard. Now what do I do?"

The answer arrived September 16, when the Cavs made the first of their infamous trades. They sent a 1984 first-round pick to the Dallas Mavericks for Mike Bratz. Dallas eventually used that selection to acquire forward Sam Perkins, who averaged 13.8 points and 5.5 rebounds in his first four NBA seasons. Bratz played in 80 games in 1980–81 for the Cavs and played well, averaging 10.0 points and 5.7 assists. The following season, he played for San Antonio.

Eight days after Bratz arrived, Stepien followed through on his directive to Musselman: Walker was sent to the Nets in exchange for Roger Phegley. "The attitude of the community was negative toward the team," Phegley said. "I could sense that from day one."

Cleveland's first preseason under Stepien and Musselman wasn't going well. The desperation in Musselman's voice is quite apparent as he relives the process of acquiring Bratz: "Ted said, 'Okay, we don't sign Footsy, now what are we going to do? Don't worry. You don't have a point guard. We don't win, don't worry about it.'

"We don't have a point guard, but we want to win. Where are we going to get a point guard? Dallas takes a first-round pick for Bratz. You think I thought Mike Bratz was (worth) a first-round draft pick? No. It was a dumb move. I had nowhere to go for a point guard.

"When you've got a one-year contract, you've got to find somebody. I didn't know...I had Jimmy Price, who was 30-something-years-old. I played Randy Smith at 32; I liked his scoring, but I still had no point guard.

"After Ted got rid of Footsy, he should have never asked me what to do. And I like Ted. Anybody I work for, I'm loyal to. I think the world of him now, and I don't care what anybody says. I like Ted Stepien, because if his worst enemy had a problem and went to him, he'd help him. I judge people by that. It hurt my coaching career working for Ted Stepien. It hurt a lot. But yet, I still like him and respect him."

Musselman thought Laimbeer, a 6–11, 250-pound hulk, could help the Cavs after playing his first pro season in Europe. "Well, this was the first thing that happened to the Cleveland Cavaliers, and it was a positive thing," Creger said. "Bill Laimbeer is a story of Bill Musselman's tenaciousness. A lot of guys would have not even known he existed and would not have gone after him so hard. He wasn't that good in those days. He didn't look that good in the Summer League. You have to give Bill Musselman credit for Bill Laimbeer being in the NBA."

Laimbeer would be the center of an unhealthy difference of opinion between Musselman and Stepien, leading directly to the Cavs trading Robisch. Laimbeer would eventually get traded, too, to the Pistons on February 16, 1982. Didn't everybody in Cleveland get traded?

"Everybody said Laimbeer couldn't play," Musselman said. "Not one NBA guy said he could make my club, let alone start."

Musselman saw potential in Laimbeer, even though his numbers in college, 6.4 points and 5.5 rebounds per game as a senior at Notre Dame, were downright ordinary.

Veteran guard Randy Smith was one of many people unimpressed with a first look at Laimbeer: "I would have never guessed at the time that he was going to achieve all the things that he has. But he was extremely competitive. And the reason Bill Laimbeer is where he is today is because he worked extremely hard to get there. So Bill Musselman must have seen something in him.''

Musselman didn't like what he saw in Campy Russell.

12

Sinking Rapidly

Campy Russell wasn't the greatest player at the University of Michigan. He wasn't even the best C. Russell. That distinction belongs to Cazzie Russell. Campy Russell, however, strung together several impressive seasons in Cleveland after he went hardship and was taken by the Cavs as the eighth pick in the first round of the 1974 draft.

At 6–8 and 215 pounds, Russell was strong enough to score inside and smooth enough from the perimeter to create match-up problems. He improved his scoring average four consecutive seasons with the Cavs, from 6.2 as a rookie to 15.0, 16.5, 19.4, and a gaudy 21.9 in '78–79, when he also posted personal NBA highs in rebounding (6.8) and assists (4.7) and was selected to play in the All-Star Game.

Injuries sliced the following season in half, but he still averaged 18.2 points in 41 games. Nine years later, Russell's name could be found throughout the Cavs' record book: third all-time scorer, fifth in rebounding, fifth in minutes played, sixth in games played, second in free throws made and attempted, third in field goals made, and eighth in career scoring average.

Creger remembers Russell as "the one Bill first got mad at."

How mad?

Just a week after trading for Bratz, the Cavaliers played an exhibition game in Youngstown, Ohio, against the Indiana Pacers. "We had about four or five of our better players that were injured and did not play," Creger said. Accordingly, the Cavs were creamed.

The team headed back to the Sheraton in Cleveland where several of the players were living during training camp. Players got off the team bus and dispersed.

Musselman, Creger, and the Cavs' other assistant coach, Gerald Oliver, sat down at a table in the lobby. "This coffee table was solid, from about 3 1/2 feet down to the floor. It was really a heavy thing," Creger related. "Bill looked around, and finally when nobody was there except myself and Gerald Oliver, he hit that table with his fist. I swear, it's probably still bruised. That coffee table literally jumped, and it must have weighed 400 pounds. I was embarrassed. Fortunately it was really late and there weren't many people around. And Bill said: 'We have to trade Campy Russell.'

"Bill had in his mind that Campy, with his attitude and maybe even with his clubhouse lawyer talk, was dragging the other players down. Bill said, 'I know you've been trying to tell me since we've been together with the Cavaliers to never talk about trades and to take your time and all, but I think he's going to ruin this ball club if we keep him. I want him traded tomorrow.'

"That's when my veto power went out the window.

"Bill insisted, and he was the head coach. I would have quit the team on something like that, but my personality is kind of cool and easy going, and so I didn't get too excited about it. I said, 'This isn't what we agreed, but you are the head coach and if you insist on this move, we'll have to make it. But don't say anything to anybody.' He was so excited that he did."

Russell was traded the next day, just one day after Phegley had arrived as Foots Walker's replacement.

"I got a call from Cotton Fitzsimmons (coach of the Kansas City, now Sacramento Kings)," Creger said. "Bill had already talked to Cotton. Cotton told me, 'I know how badly that Bill wants to get rid of Campy. I'll give you Bill Robinzine.'

"I knew Bill Robinzine quite well as a player. I knew that he was maybe 60 percent as good as Campy. But we checked around the league, and that was the best we could get for him. They were all trying to steal Campy. So we took the deal."

In the meantime, Fitzsimmons had traded Russell to New York for the Knick's first-round pick. Russell average 16.4 points, 4.7 rebounds, and 3.3 assists in the '80–81 season. Robinzine, a 6–7 for-

The Minnesota Timberwolves' first college draft choice, UCLA's Pooh Richardson. Musselman hopes Richardson, the tenth pick overall, puts the Timberwolves' running game in high gear.

(Photo courtesy of UCLA Sports Information Department)

Known for intensity, Musselman leaves no doubt what he wants his players to do.

Minnesota Timberwolves President and Chief Executive Officer Bob Stein introduces Bill Musselman as the new head coach of the Timberwolves.

The Albany Patroons' Sidney Lowe drives against Steve Burtt of the Savannah Spirits. An integral part of the Patroons' CBA championship team, Lowe has signed a two year contract with the Timberwolves.

Tod Murphy, shown here as an Albany Patroon, is one of several free agents signed by Minnesota this summer who Musselman is depending on to make the Timberwolves' first season a success.

The Minnesota Brain Trust: Director of Player Personnel Billy McKinney and Coach Musselman discuss the Timberwolves during a preseason practice.

Starting with the Timberwolves' open tryouts, Musselman instructs his players in the finer points of the game.

ward, appeared in eight of Cleveland's first 11 games, accumulating 33 points and 13 rebounds before Musselman traded him.

In the span of two games, Russell matched Robinzine's scoring output for the season.

"One thing I learned out of Cleveland about pro ball is everybody waits for somebody to panic," Musselman said nine years later. "Then you get players for wholesale price. Ownership can cause panic and a coach to panic. I did learn things in Cleveland."

Not soon enough.

If one player had been affected the most by the exit of Mileti and Albeck, it was Robisch. The 6-10, 240-pound center had posted solid numbers in 1979-80. He would turn 31 on December 22, 1980, but the Cavs were sure enough of Robisch's future to sign him to a four-year contract on draft day. Instead of four years, he barely lasted 14 days under Cleveland's new regime.

Now a coach in the World Basketball League, Robisch explained his deep-rooted ties to Albeck: "I had played for Stan the year before in Cleveland. I had a good relationship with him because he was my coach in Denver when I first started playing professionally, and also in Los Angeles with the Lakers when I was there. I felt we were coming back on the right track in Cleveland, so it was disappointing that Stan left. All that was happening was out of my control."

Was anybody in control?

"I met Ted (Stepien) personally, and he was a nice guy and very successful in his business. But he didn't have any idea what the National Basketball Association was like and how things happened in the league," Robisch said. "You lose Stan Albeck and you lose Jimmy Rodgers, you lose some pretty quality people. You bring in a whole new staff and it's disruptive. They have certain ideas and certain ways that they want things done."

One thing Musselman has always wanted is players in shape. How did veterans react to Camp Musselman? "I think as far as conditioning, he did a good job there," Smith said. "I got in shape much earlier than I had previously. And that's because of the college type of mentality where you do suicide drills (a series of sprints in which a player goes from one baseline to the near foul line and back, to halfcourt and back, to the far foul line and back, and then to the other baseline and back). In the NBA, most players like to play themselves into shape or skate through the training camp without going extremely all out."

Not in Camp Musselman. In fact, the coach was criticized for using Smith too much in exhibition games. "I respected his condition," Musselman said. "Randy Smith to me was the most marvelous athlete in shape. And I'm big on that. People said why didn't you save this guy because of his age. I thought, shit, this guy is in better shape than 25-year-old guys. And I thought he was the best player we had. I said, 'Hey, we're going to the guy. We don't have much.' "

While Smith played on—he still holds the NBA record for most consecutive games (906)—Robisch grew increasingly unhappy. "Training camp was hard," he said. "Bill had to come in as the new coach and change from a system that the players were used to. He had, of course, his own way of doing things, which was a little different. It's hard to come in and change everything."

While Stepien applied the pressure of trying to win immediately, Creger continued to preach patience to Musselman. "Bill had a great desire to win," Creger said. "He didn't understand when you play all these games that you're going to lose some, and you're going to really blow some out the window. Your players can't get ready every night. But he started getting panicky really early during the exhibition games because we had some injuries on our team. We were blown out some games, and it really bothered him.

"And Ted was on him constantly. Ted and Bill were kind of neophytes on the pro level; Ted especially, but even Bill somewhat. Remember, he'd only had been at the ABA level, and he only had a few months there."

There were moments in the preseason that offered hope. A win against the Chicago Bulls stands out in Musselman's memory: "They started (David) Greenwood, (Reggie) Theus, and (Artis) Gilmore. We started Walter Jordan, Jimmy Price. We had Laimbeer, Kenny Carr. Mitchell wasn't even there. My backcourt was pick-ups. Phegley just arrived. He played. And we beat 'em something like 20 points."

Still, it was in an exhibition game. The real season began October 10. Even the schedule seemed unkind to Musselman. The Cavs would open at Boston (which would win the NBA championship), and 11 of their first 17 games were on the road.

Musselman's NBA debut was a 130–103 pounding administered by the Celtics. The Cavs returned home the next night and lost to the New Jersey Nets 99–96 before an embarrassingly small turnout of 5,731. Only 4,071 and 4,046 watched the Cavs reach 2–2 with consecutive home victories against Detroit and Washington.

Any hope Musselman had of building momentum was quickly

shattered by a 98–79 defeat at Chicago, followed by successive losses to Milwaukee.

The Cavs' next game was in Washington against the Bullets.

"I'm talking to the team before the ball game, and then somebody said I had an urgent phone call," Musselman said. "I go, 'Oh, my God, something happened to my kids.' I go out and answer the phone. It was Ted. I'm on a pay phone in the lobby outside the locker room of the Bullets. I said, 'Ted, I'm talking to the team.'

"He said, 'I just wanted to let you know, I hope we start Laimbeer.'

"I told Ted, 'I can't do it. I like Laimbeer, too, but Laimbeer's young. We'll bring him off the bench.' "

"No, no, no. I like him, too," Stepien said. "You like him. We both like him. He should start. He's our discovery.' "

"People never ever understood why we got rid of Robisch," Musselman said. "It was because he was going to start if he stayed, although I love Laimbeer. And Ted insisted Laimbeer start."

Robisch played 48 minutes, Laimbeer didn't play at all. Washington won the game 109–96.

Stepien's response to his coach's insurgence? "Nothing," Musselman said. "He got the message. I can't go around getting a phone call before a game and a guy telling me who to start. He didn't call me again on who to start. Robisch, he was mad as hell. I didn't ever explain to the players why I did what I did. They were upset. They held a team meeting, discussed how I wasn't going to substitute."

News of the team meeting reached the press. The *Plain Dealer* ran a story in its October 24 editions, and United Press International picked it up and sent it across the country.

"Low morale hits Cavaliers" was a fitting headline for a floundering team (2–6) under a controversial coach and owner. The UPI story detailed the players' concern after meeting with Oliver prior to that night's road game with the Nets. According to UPI, all 11 players met with Oliver to "air grievances over Musselman's coaching methods. The main issue was over the number of playing minutes being logged by starters and the lack of playing time for the reserves. Some questions were also raised about Musselman's practice schedule and coaching philosophy."

The story noted that Smith had played nearly every minute of the preseason games and had averaged 44 minutes a game to date. Said

Smith: "Eventually we're going to wear down. We're exhausting our-selves at the end of games."

The story added, "The players are unhappy about Musselman's concept of practice. A major beef simmered last Friday when the rookie coach called a practice in Chicago as soon as the team bus ar-rived at the hotel. The Cavs were to meet the Bulls that night, and had played at the Coliseum the night before."

Worth noting is that the Cavs won at New Jersey 126–112, then whipped Indiana 118–100 at home. The team was 4–6 despite playing eight games in 12 nights. A 119–101 loss to Philadelphia ended Robis-ch's career in Cleveland.

"I just didn't feel comfortable, and I thought it was definitely the best thing for me to go somewhere else," Robisch said. "That's nothing against Bill. I don't think I ever really sat down and told Bill that I was unhappy, but he could see it."

In two days at the end of October, as the Cavs began a six-game West Coast road trip, Musselman's world began to fall apart. Robin-zine, who averaged 4.1 points and 1.6 rebounds in eight games, was sent to Dallas along with Cleveland's first-round picks in 1983 and '86. The Mavericks used the selections to get guard Derek Harper and forward Roy Tarpley, each a vibrant member of the current team.

In return, Cleveland received forward-centers Jerome Whitehead and Richard Washington. Washington wasn't thrilled about leaving Dallas, where he'd been a starter for the expansion team. "Cleveland had always been an NBA horror story," he said. "The joke around the league was that if you played for them, you have two seasons left in your career—if you're lucky."

Washington wasn't. He played in 69 games for the Cavs and aver-aged 9.9 points and 5.4 rebounds, then suffered a knee injury that lim-ited him to 18 games the following two seasons. Meanwhile, Whitehead was waived after amassing two points and three rebounds in eight minutes of action in three games.

The next day, the Cavs made an even worse trade. Robisch went to Denver for Kim Hughes, a 1981 third-round pick, an '82 second-round choice, and unannounced future considerations. With Denver, Robisch played 73 games and averaged 10.4 points and 5.7 rebounds.

Hughes played in 45 games for the Cavs. He scored 32 points and somehow managed to play 331 minutes without attempting a single free throw, which may have been a positive development. The preceding season with Denver, he pursued NBA history for worst free-throw percentage by a regular player, shooting .366 (15 for 41) in 70 games.

The Cavs used the '81 third-round pick to get Mickey Dillard, a 6–3 guard from Florida State. He scored 73 points in 33 games in 1981–82. Cleveland traded away its '82 second-round pick acquired from the Nuggets.

Hughes, Dillard, an unused draft pick, and future considerations for Robisch, a player who only 4 1/2 months earlier had signed a four-year contract with Cleveland, was a lopsided trade that only added to Musselman's growing problems.

The Cavs began their Western road swing with starters Bratz, Phegley, Washington, Whitehead, and Hughes. None of the five had been with the team for more than six weeks.

The road trip began with a 107–98 loss to the Lakers. The Cavs fell 102–96 at Portland two nights later.

They played the following night at Seattle and were annihilated 118–83, but that wasn't the worst news of the day for Musselman. Stepien called.

"Ted wanted to fire me," Musselman said. "He said we didn't play any defense. I asked him:

" 'How do you know we didn't play defense?'

'I heard it on the radio.'

'You heard it on the radio? I'll tell you why we lost. We shot a terrible percentage. We didn't shoot well because we had no legs. We lost because of our offense. We always play hard defense.'

'No, no, no. You're not playing any defense.'

'You got to be kidding me. You weren't even here.' "

A lot of people were wishing they could say that about being with the Cavaliers.

Fans. Media. Players. Even Creger, who was being advised by long-time friends in the NBA to get out.

"Ted wanted to win, wanted to make the playoffs," Creger said. "You see, Ted's situation was that he'd been laughed at a little bit in Cleveland in sports. When he bought the Cavaliers, he made some statements about what he was going to do, and they were a little bit, shall we say, optimistic. And when he realized that we were beginning not to live up to those promises he made to the press, he thought it would reflect personally on him.

"He wanted to make the playoffs so bad, he almost cried watching when we would lose. When we would win, he'd go too much overboard the other way. Ted didn't have the background of knowledge about the NBA, the patience it takes, the fact that a change in coaches, a change in player personnel, a change in anything is not necessarily going to help. He did a lot of things that were very positive, but his impatience tore him down.''

Musselman and Creger's concern was to stop losing games. ''I would tell Bill, 'We've got to get these players used to each other. We've got to stay stable and stay with players,' '' Creger said. ''I had 12 years of pro experience with good people. I was around Bill Sharman and Pete Newell. All that experience taught me patience.

''Bill would start out with severe criticism of some of our talent, that some of the players weren't playing hard or they weren't very good. He kept thinking moves would be the answer because it had worked in the WBA. At that level it will work, especially if those moves get you an equal player or maybe even a little better player who'll play hard for a while.

''In the NBA, that's not the point. Other teams aren't going to let go of somebody who's going to help them win. They're only going to let go of the guy who has a problem cooperating, or is going down in his talent level, or maybe to get a real great player back. And we didn't have any real great ones to trade anyway.''

Creger felt he was having increasingly less input on Cleveland's personnel decisions while his name—after all, he was director of player personnel—was diminishing in stature among his NBA peers because of the Cavs' poor decisions. ''(Then-Atlanta Coach) Hubie Brown was on an airplane with an assistant coach, Brendan Suhr,'' Creger said. ''Hubie likes to read the sports pages when he's flying. Well, he read how we gave all these draft choices to get Richard Washington. And he looked up at Brendan and said very seriously, 'Is Larry on drugs?' He was serious. He said, 'He could not have done that unless he's on cocaine or something.'

''And Brendan said, 'No, Larry and I've been talking, and he's having difficulties stopping Bill from making those moves. Bill's panicking a little bit along with Ted Stepien about losing. He wants to turn it around overnight with trades. I'm sure that's probably Bill Musselman's trade, and he's going over Larry's head.'

''Brendan was exactly right, and we talked later about it. But Hubie thought I was out of my mind. He thought I'd gone insane.''

Creger began getting advice from friends in the NBA to abandon ship. ''They wanted me to get out of Cleveland because they thought the thing was going to go down the tubes," he said. Regardless, Creger stayed aboard the NBA's version of the Titanic for the whole season.

Musselman also endured a slow torture, one worsened by the paradox of values by which he lived. He couldn't win with Stepien's direction, yet he felt extremely loyal to the man who had resurrected his coaching career and put him where he always wanted to be—the NBA.

"The guy paid my paycheck," Musselman said. "I respected him for it. I don't care what his decisions were. If I didn't want it, I should've walked away from my contract. You work for a guy . . . you may not agree with him, but he's the boss."

Norm Sonju, general manager of Dallas, offered his perspective of his deals with Musselman: "He was on a short leash. He didn't have an opportunity to build long-term through the draft and take his time. The players that we traded him, we took a lot of heat in the newspapers when we made those trades. I want people to know that. One guy blasted me personally, saying that we were messing with our fans by only thinking of the future.

"I think those cynical, sardonic people who are on Bill Musselman because of those trades are being unfair to him. Richard Washington was just one classic example of a guy who just had everything going for him, and unfortunately, through circumstances totally out of Bill's control, wasn't able to deliver his end of it. Now if he's scoring 20 points a game for four years, I'm not so sure people would be talking about it."

They were sure talking about it in Cleveland. In an extensive interview in the *Plain Dealer*, Musselman responded publicly to the increasing criticism. The Cavs were 8–18 at the time.

"Why did you make all the trades?" was the first question. He gave a blow-by-blow account of the Cavs' deals, saying absolutely nothing about Stepien's involvement. That was a public stance Eric Musselman understood but disliked: "Some of the things that were done were not Bill Musselman's decisions. I remember reading stuff in the paper and him getting blasted for things that Mr. Stepien decided on."

Musselman mounted the most secure public posture and rationalization he could muster. He justified the Walker trade for Phegley by citing Walker's long holdout (but not Stepien's ultimatum to Musselman that either Walker or Mitchell would have to go), that Phegley was five years younger, and that ''Roger is one of the better shooters in the NBA. Keep in mind, we got Mike Bratz without giving up a player (the Mavs eventually drafted Perkins). Mike doesn't have Walker's speed, quickness, and ability to pass out assists, but he plays hard and is intelligent.''

Nine years later, Musselman said, ''I had better guards in the CBA.''

Musselman next discussed the Campy Russell trade, explaining that Russell had approached the Cavs during the summer and asked to be traded. ''He didn't think we could win,'' Musselman said. ''From our point of view, the Cavs won 10 of their last 12 games last season and did it without Campy Russell, who was injured. He wanted to be traded, and we felt it would be in the best interest of Campy and our club to move him.

''However, after the Walker and Russell trades we saw that we needed more height, and then came the trades for 6–11 Richard Washington and 6–11 Kim Hughes.'' (Musselman called Whitehead, who'd already been waived, a throw-in in the Washington deal.)

Citing his research of each NBA championship club since the 1973 Knicks, Musselman declared, ''To improve in the NBA, you do it with size and obtain the players who can control the boards. If we had the chance to make these trades again, we would do it.

''For someone to say the trades are not good without seeing the people play or the role the coach wants them in is not being objective.

''When it's time to knock us, it's time to knock us.''

There had already been a major knock, not from the press, but the NBA. Following the back-to-back major deals, the league placed a moratorium on Cleveland trades pending an investigation by NBA Director of Operations Joseph Axelson. The moratorium eventually was lifted, but the NBA, concerned that plummeting attendance would kill the franchise, reserved a right of approval for Cavs' trades.

In concluding its unprecedented intervention, the NBA ultimately restored the draft picks as part of a deal to sell the Cavs from Stepien to present owners George Gund III and his brother, Gordon. That wouldn't happen for more than two years, enough time for Stepien to fire, re-hire, and re-fire Musselman.

13

Moving On

A funny thing happened to Cleveland on its way to a terrible season. The Cavs started winning.

But first, they ruined Musselman's Christmas.

The Cavs began a five-game December home stand with a 130–122 victory over Denver. They lost the next three to Boston, Kansas City, and Chicago by a total of nine points. Defensively, they played well, allowing an average of 103 points. Their record, however, was 12–27.

In the two-point loss to the Bulls, the Cavs squandered an eight-point lead in the final four minutes. Cleveland had a chance to force overtime, but Laimbeer threw a pass to Mitchell that skittered out of bounds with seven seconds left.

"It wasn't a very good pass," Musselman noted. It also wasn't Musselman's only problem that night.

Yet another controversy had taken root three nights earlier. Smith, upset with playing 24 minutes in the narrow loss to Kansas City, aired gripes to the media, saying he wasn't being "utilized."

Rumors began swirling that Musselman was shopping Smith, a 10-year NBA veteran. Word also leaked out that different members of the Cavs' organization had different opinions about the subject.

The afternoon of the Bulls game, Musselman and Delaney had an argument that found its way into the next morning's *Plain Dealer*. The story called the incident a "gathering storm" and the "first crack in the veneer of solidarity" between Stepien and Musselman.

First, Musselman had a pregame meeting with Smith. Then he took him out of the starting lineup. Coming off the bench for the first time in 121 games, Smith played 28 minutes against Chicago and scored a team-high 23 points.

Smith said after the game, "I'm sure the stories (in the newspapers) were the reason he wanted to talk, but he didn't mention them specifically. We just cleared the air. He told me he wanted me to provide the leadership I did at the start of the season."

Asked if his pride was hurt by not starting, Smith said, "Well, I've started about 50 years in the league. Whatever it takes to win. But I think I am a better player starting. The season's almost half over, and we've got to find a solution."

Phegley expressed surprise that he was part of Musselman's latest solution: "Actually, I think the fact that I started was more a punishment for Randy than anything else. I don't know if I deserve to be starting in place of Randy. I didn't know I was going to start until a minute before the game."

Less than a minute after the game, a spectator rushed down an aisle of seats, shook his fist at Musselman and yelled loud enough for reporters to use in their story, "Musselman...we're going to put you on waivers."

Not quite yet.

Three days after Christmas, an extremely well-written and utterly damning analysis of the Cleveland situation, by Bob Ryan of the *Boston Globe*, was picked up by papers around the country. Ryan painted a bleak montage of the situation, then dissected it. First, Ryan summarized the NBA's intervention: "The Cavaliers have been judged to be incompetent. Both Stepien and Musselman feel highly insulted."

Ryan characterized Musselman as "very charming, invigorating, of good mind, facile with the mother tongue, and consumed by the meaning of his job." While Ryan displayed fairness by quoting Musselman throughout the piece, he also presented the opinion of Musselman's detractors. Ryan wrote, "His critics feel he is both a liar and a conniver—and those are his good points."

Ryan said: "The coach is well-known for his intensity, and the current situation is not geared to improve his mental health. The make-the-playoff edict is absurd and counter-productive.''

Ryan's article then focused on Stepien, beginning with the opinion of Pete Franklin, host of ''Sports Line,'' a talk show on WWWE, a 50,000-watt Cleveland radio station: ''Charles O. Finley was a dirty s.o.b., but he was smart. This guy (Stepien) is a megalomaniac who's dumb. The worst thing about him is that he's dumb. I don't mind you quoting me because he's a schmuck, a dodohead. This team is on support machines. Pull the plug, and they're dead.''

Ryan wrote that Franklin had been ''attacking Stepien on a nightly basis since last June.''

Nearly a decade later, Stepien revealed the impact of Franklin's barrage: ''My wife died at that time, which was hard. I had six daughters to raise. It was rough. I even asked them, 'Should I sell the Cavs?' And they said, 'No, Dad. We can take it.'

''They were taunted at school. Pete Franklin would go on the air and say, 'Ted Stepien is nothing but a pimple on my ass.' He had the No. 1 talk show in sports. How would you feel? He was 50,000 watts. You listen and say, 'Is this America? How can a guy have the right to say personal things?' It was tough. It was tough on my daughters, and it was tough on me, too. I had to look in the mirror and say, 'Who are you? Two people? One, you're running a $100 million ad agency, and two you're like a goofball?' ''

Ryan concluded the latter. After ridiculing the Cavs' cheerleaders, the Teddi-Bears, and Stepien's choice of a polka as a victory song, Ryan wrote, ''The Cavs are not as bad as people think, but Ted Stepien is. By every intelligent account, his is the ultimate Amateur Hour run wild, which does not make him a bad guy. But until he starts listening to Creger (who would like to modify the emotional peaks and valleys of both Stepien and Musselman) and until he is willing to admit that he is not the arbiter of taste for Northeast Ohio, the organization will continue to be viewed as just another Polish–Cleveland joke.''

There were no jokes the afternoon of December 28, when Musselman and Stepien met privately at the latter's home. The two-hour discussion took an interesting turn.

Stepien, who admitted to the *Plain Dealer* that he had entertained thoughts of canning Musselman as recently as the previous night, instead gave him a vote of confidence. ''I'm behind Bill,'' Stepien said. ''The easiest thing to do when things are going bad is to fire the coach.'' Stepien described the meeting with Musselman as ''the first time Bill and I sat down and really talked. He told me what he thought were his strengths and weaknesses as a coach, and I told him my strengths and weaknesses as an owner. I've made mistakes, and there are things I will do differently next year. We like each other, and he is extremely loyal. No one has given him a chance, not even one year. I'm giving Bill the chance.''

Stepien even told the *Plain Dealer* that another home loss that night to Dallas would ''definitely not'' jeopardize Musselman's future.

Musselman didn't find out, because the Cavs ended the '80 part of their schedule with a 112–100 defeat of the Mavericks. Cleveland then won only its third road game in 19 tries, a 111–105 decision over New Jersey. The next night at home, only 3,092 fans, the second smallest crowd of the season, watched Cleveland demolish Washington 132–112.

Six nights later, the Cavs gutted out another road win, 108–107 in overtime against Atlanta. Cleveland was 3–0 in 1981, on a four-game winning streak, and 16–27 overall with home games up next against the Knicks and the Lakers.

The Cavs played well but lost both, 104–99 and 108–104. Attendance was picking up—crowds of 6,321 and 7,316 were poor by NBA standards, yet still a significant increase from earlier Cavs' home games. Those may have drawn as few as 1,000, though announced attendance figures were three to four times higher.

Losses at Boston and Philadelphia preceded another four-game winning streak. The Cavs eventually finished January with a 9–5 record. Until 1989, no Cleveland team ever had a better record in January.

''We had some talent,'' Walter Jordan said. ''It was just a matter of the people in Cleveland being patient. And they weren't. When you have so many distractions, it's going to affect team morale. There was pressure put on Coach Musselman that shouldn't have been, by the media, by the organization. It couldn't do anything but hurt him. He didn't get a chance. We had the nucleus of a good club.''

Briefly, the Cavs were showing it. Add in the final '80 win, and the Cavs had completed a 10–5 string heading into the All-Star break. They held teams under 100 points four consecutive games in a season when Philadelphia would lead the NBA in defensive average at 103.8.

''The trading of the draft choices was not good for the franchise,'' Musselman said. ''I'll be the first to admit it. It was stupid. But the coaching job I did with what players I had that first year . . . we won a lot of games we shouldn't have. Our roster basically was Laimbeer and Washington at center; Mitchell at small forward backed up by Walter Jordan; power forward Kenny Carr backed up by Don Ford; guards were Bratz, Phegley, and Randy Smith. How great a team was that? And Laimbeer was a rookie. Nobody thought he could play.

"We went to Mitchell a lot. Mitchell had his best year. He was an All-Star. Kenny Carr had the best year in his pro career. He was sixth in the NBA in rebounds (10.3 average, Kareem Abdul-Jabbar was seventh) and has never been there since. I utilized those guys, and I went to them all the time. I think I helped their careers because they were focal points on that ball club.

"Next year...they had twice the talent; they win half as many games."

When the bottom fell out, it happened quickly.

"We stopped playing well because of the All-Star break," Musselman said. "Broke our momentum. We were playing so well, then we come back, played Chicago at home, and lost. It just seemed like that loss hurt us."

More would follow. After losing its first three games in February, Cleveland made one more deal, acquiring guard Geoff Huston and Dallas' third-round pick in 1983 for Kinch and Cleveland's '85 first-round choice.

Huston, who works for the law firm Pulvers, Pulvers, Thompson, and Cerbone in Manhattan, said Musselman "did a good job with what he had. He's an excellent coach and a great motivator. Some people question his tactics, but he gets the most out of players. He pushed me to become a better player.

"Bill's always been volatile. That's just part of his personality. I think, when he's winning, he's a great coach. When he loses, everybody has criticism of him."

Huston had averaged 16.1 points and 4.9 assists for the Mavs, who finished 15–67 in their first NBA season. In 25 games with the Cavs, he averaged 7.0 points and 4.7 assists.

From February 7, 1981, when he arrived in Cleveland, until the 1982 preseason, Huston played through five coaching changes by Stepien. "I think not knowing who was playing or coaching contributed to the losing," Huston said. "You never gained continuity. It was hard to establish player relationships in terms of camaraderie."

Still, Cleveland had won 13 of its last 24 and was 25–38 overall entering the season's homestretch.

However, the Cavs would play 13 of their final 18 games on the road. Musselman wouldn't be around for all of them.

As the losses mounted, so did his frustration with players he felt weren't giving 100 percent. "One day in practice, we had lost five or six in a row, Coach Musselman was so pissed at our lack of effort and enthusiasm, he challenged anybody to a fight," Jordan said. "He went through all our names. He said, 'I'll whip anybody's ass.' He said we were all pussies. I looked at Kenny Carr (6-7, 230 pounds) and I thought, 'I wouldn't do that.' "

Jordan felt Musselman was still learning how to deal with NBA players: "I think it took him time to adjust to coaching pro players. College kids are so enthused they'll do anything. They're determined and full of dreams. He couldn't understand that pros, they've already made their dream. They've done this, they've done that, and they're making more money than he is.

"I had no problems with it. I was a young player trying to get established. I look back and appreciate Bill Musselman because he knew my background. He knew I'd work my behind off, and he gave me a hell of a chance to make my dream happen."

Musselman's dream had become a nightmare.

"When you're in a losing situation, individuals have a tendency to take care of themselves first," Phegley said. "Once it's headed in that direction, it's very difficult to turn it around. This got out of hand early and no one was able to get it stopped."

The more Cleveland lost, the more the pressure on Musselman increased—from the media, his owner, and a marriage that was beginning to fall apart.

Musselman, criticized earlier in the season for playing Smith too much, decided to use him less and less. "Bill got upset with his play, and there were times when we had to beg Bill to put him in the game," Creger said. "He had that streak going."

From February 18, 1972, to March 13, 1983, Smith played in an NBA-record 906 consecutive games with four different teams. "When you don't win and you don't have a chance to make the playoffs, it's not enjoyable because it seems like the season was in vain," he said. "The whole franchise had gone through a transition, and the franchise was not stable."

Jordan wondered if Smith's incongruous number of minutes was a decision made by Musselman alone: "Randy Smith was doing everything for us. Then all of a sudden he goes from 48 minutes to hardly playing at all. I don't know how much Bill was in control. To this day, I'm not sure he was able to do what he wanted to do."

On March 11 the Cavs lost their eighth straight game, 101–95 to visiting Seattle. The next day, Stepien moved Musselman into a vice president position and made Delaney head coach.

"A funny thing happened in Delaney's first game," said Creger, who stayed on as director of player personnel until the end of the season. "I would do a lot of the scouting of opponents for Bill, and I would tell our players the best I could how to defend the opponent. So the very first game that Don coached, we were playing at home and I was giving my pregame talk. Guess who came into the room? Bill and Ted Stepien both. They walked into the locker room and sat in the back and listened to the talk from me and later from Don. It was a bit strange for a guy who'd just been removed from the coaching job to be in the locker room."

Breaking up is hard to do, as was winning in Cleveland. The Cavs lost their final seven games. Delaney was 3–8. Musselman had gone 25–46. The Cleveland Cavaliers were going nowhere.

Coaching the Cavs the second time around wasn't any easier for Musselman. "I didn't want the job again," Musselman said. "I didn't want to go through that. For the first time in my life, I said I don't want to coach."

Stepien, however, presented an offer Musselman couldn't refuse. "He took a poll of his staff, and they said to hire me back," Musselman said.

"I like the job I've got, vice president," Musselman told him.

He said, 'You're no longer vice president. You'll take it or you won't have a job.'

"So I took the job."

The volatile environment Musselman walked into in his first season seemed trifling compared to his second tour of duty as head coach.

Delaney went 4–13 to open the 1981–82 season. Stepien dismissed him and made Assistant Coach Bob Kloppenburg an interim head coach for six days and one game. Next up was Chuck Daly, coach of the 1989 NBA champion Detroit Pistons. In Cleveland, Daly did as poorly as everyone else, 9–32.

Hello, Bill Musselman.

"It was an impossible situation from a coaching standpoint," Kloppenburg said. "There was so much pressure on the coach from above. I thought, under those circumstances, Bill did the best job of any coaches that were there."

Musselman wasn't thrilled about being the fourth head coach in a season of disastrous proportions. Cleveland was 13–46 when Musselman returned. "There was nothing I could do at the end of the season," he said. "I wasn't even into it the second time. It was impossible. Who am I to put in a fourth (coaching) system? There was nothing I could do. Things were too far gone."

Regardless, Musselman told his assistants, Kloppenburg and Oliver, things would be different: "I said we've just got to do what it takes to win, and we can't let Ted tell us what to do. And I told Ted, 'Ted, this time around I've got to do it my way, 'cause you're going to fire me if I do it your way. If you're going to fire me, you might as well fire me now.' "

The team Musselman returned to coach March 11, 1982, bore little resemblance to the club he left exactly one year earlier. The top five scorers and the top three rebounders were playing elsewhere.

The lone healthy holdover from the '80–81 season was Huston, who would finish eighth in the NBA in assists (7.6) while averaging 10.3 points. Washington had already injured his knee and would never play again for the Cavs.

Cleveland would go through 23 players in the '81–82 season. No team in NBA history used as many. "It was kind of crazy," said one of them, Paul Mokeski. "You were wondering who was going to be in the locker next to you the next day."

The best of Musselman's new personnel in 1982 was Ron Brewer, a 6–4 guard from Arkansas. He had ambivalent feelings about his trade, which took him from San Antonio, on the way to the second of three consecutive Midwest Division titles, to Cleveland: "The talk around the league was, 'If you don't like what we're doing here, I'll trade you to Cleveland.' But I think I was right at the top of my game. I was happy to get with a team I felt I could help."

Brewer helped all he could, averaging 19.4 points in 47 games. He couldn't prevent the losing. "There was an awful lot of turmoil, and the team was going nowhere," he said. "It was a downfall, seeing all the talent we had, and not mustering up more wins than we did.

"Ted Stepien was free-wheeling. If he wasn't happy, he made a move. A couple of people said some things in his ear: 'You've got to do this and this and this.' Then he made a move. People can see now he really didn't know how to manage a franchise. It started from the top and worked its way down. It was tougher for Bill. He was in a situation where it was a lost cause.''

Brewer came from a winning program in college and a winning team, San Antonio, in the NBA. ''No matter what the situation is, you play until it's over,'' he said. ''I'll never forget the last game of the season. We had lost 18 in a row, and when the last game was over and we got beat again, everybody was...there was champagne. It was almost like we won the championship or something. I just couldn't understand that.

''We were the laughingstock of the whole NBA. I would say out of the 12-man squad on a given night, there were maybe four or five guys who played hard all the time. Most of the people from the outside could see what was going on. They could see we weren't putting 100 percent effort into what we were doing. I think we had one of the best first seven in the league, but we had to maintain intensity for 48 minutes, and that's what we weren't doing. We'd play a team hard 38, 40, even 46 minutes. At some point, we'd lose that intensity, and that's when we'd get beat. We weren't getting blown out every game. We were competing, but there was just another little inch to get over the hump that we were lacking as a team.''

Brewer, now a corrections officer in Portland, Ore., described Musselman as a ''hard-core coach. He was a very, very dominating type of guy. You could sense it in his demeanor. Run it his way or don't run it at all. He meant well. He backed up what he said and he got respect from a lot of players who felt he knew what he was doing. But I knew at that time Musselman wasn't going to be there long because that's who they were going to blame as the reason we were losing.''

Musselman returned to the Cavs' sideline for a four-game home stand. In those four games they displayed marvelous symmetry: lost to Phoenix by six, beat Utah by six, lost to Detroit by six, and beat San Diego in overtime by six.

The Cavs didn't win another game. Nineteen straight losses. An NBA record for worst finish of a season and on the way to two more records extending into the '82–83 season: most consecutive losses overall (24) and at home (15). All three records remain intact. The Cavs finished the season 15–67 and ended Musselman's coaching career in Cleveland with a record of 27–67.

As early as March 14, 1982, just three days after he was rehired as head coach, Musselman revealed the frustration churning inside himself in an interview with Akron *Beacon Journal* columnist Tom

Melody. Musselman and his wife, Kris, had gone to see Eric's basketball game and watched in horror as hot dogs were thrown at their son.

Kris asked her husband on the ride home why their son had to be a recipient of the hatred of Cavs fans. Musselman didn't have an answer. Nor could he explain how the stigma from the Minnesota–Ohio State fight 10 years earlier still thrived in the minds of the fans he cared the most about, the fans of northeast Ohio. "I can't believe it," he told Melody. "I'm still amazed by the lingering reaction to it."

He searched desperately to explain the abuse he and his family were receiving, though he knew the incendiary ingredient was obvious, the pathetic record of the Cavs. He told Melody, "The abuse doesn't happen in other places. Just here. Here, where I was born, where I grew up."

He needed only to turn a radio on to hear the ugliest side of the abuse, of people calling him Musclehead. "Pete Franklin started that," Musselman said. "And when he did, he went too far. Nobody has a right to ridicule my family name. Criticize me and my coaching, fine. Ridicule my family? No, that's wrong."

Then he told Melody and his readers of his feelings about returning as coach of the Cavaliers: "I don't need it any longer. I don't care one way or the other about coaching the Cavaliers next season."

Still, Musselman prepared for '82–83. The Cavs traded Laimbeer and Carr to Detroit for Mokeski, Phil Hubbard, and first- and second-round picks in '82. They drafted Bagley and Magley.

John Bagley, a 5–11 point guard from Boston College, is still in the NBA.

"Like any young guy, I was excited and would go out there and play real hard in training camp," Bagley said. "That excitement just wears down and, all of a sudden, it hits you that this is real work. Training camp was something like boot camp. I never imagined it being that hard."

With Bagley, Huston, and Lowes Moore, the Cavs were overloaded at point guard. There were 14 players in camp with guaranteed contracts, and Moore wasn't one of them. So despite an excellent preseason ("Lowes led us in every statistical category except for rebounding," David Magley said; Musselman said Moore was "phenomenal") Moore was released. He would play for Musselman in Albany six years later. "It seems like everybody comes back and plays for him again," Moore said.

Another Cav who played against and briefly for Musselman in the CBA was Magley, a 6–8 forward from Kansas who would play just 14 games and score 12 points before being cut by the Cavs. "Bill was the one that scouted me and drafted me. And, I guess, took the blame for me," he said.

Magley, a sales manager in Columbus, Ohio, had high hopes of playing a major role with the Cavs his rookie season. He flourished early in Musselman's training camp: "He wanted guys that could run, and I could run," Magley said.

But Magley had trouble understanding the Cavs organization: "Ted Stepien's not a basketball mind. He'd be the first one to tell you. He didn't use good judgment in the people that he chose to help him, and consequently he had all kinds of problems."

Magley developed an interesting relationship with Musselman in the brief time their lives crossed in Cleveland. "It was a thing where Muss could come on the bus and yell and rant and rave at everybody, and I would look at him, and as he'd get ready to sit down, I'd say, 'Excuse me, Coach. Does this mean I don't get to come up to your room and rap tonight?' And he would just laugh. I never minded the guy. He kind of changed toward the end because he was under so much pressure. The last couple of weeks, he wasn't the same person."

On October 21, six days after bringing in Harry Weltman as Executive Vice President of Operations and eight days before the season opener, Stepien fired Musselman and his assistants, Kloppenburg and Oliver. He did keep all three on the Cavs' staff as scouts.

Stepien called Musselman and Oliver to his office for a 10:30 a.m. meeting that day. Musselman walked into Stepien's office alone. "Ted just said, 'Hey, I'm going to make a change,'" Musselman said. "He said, 'You're still getting paid. I still think the world of you. You really work hard, and I really respect you.' He was so sentimental."

Musselman walked out of Stepien's office and waited for an elevator. An anxious Oliver waited alongside. As the elevator doors closed their coaching careers in Cleveland behind them, Musselman told Oliver, "It's over." Oliver said Musselman looked more relieved than angry.

Nobody told Kloppenburg, who boarded the team bus with his players to go downtown for a "Meet The Cavs" luncheon. "I was the only coach on the players' bus," Kloppenburg said. "I didn't think anything of it."

When he entered the Stouffer's Inn, Weltman called him into a room. "I still didn't think anything of it," Kloppenburg said. "We had an exhibition game that night, and I thought he wanted to discuss personnel."

Instead, Kloppenburg learned he was out. "Obviously, Bill already knew," Kloppenburg said. "He handled it very well. Nothing gets him down. Tough, I guess, is the word. He said, 'I'll be back sometime. They won't keep me down.' "

Musselman's replacement, Tom Nissalke, arrived the following day. "It was a shock," Mokeski said. "We just went through a training camp with one coach. All of a sudden, they change in mid-stream. When you go through a whole training camp, you kind of prove yourself to the coach. Then a new coach comes in, and it's like everybody has to prove themselves all over again. It's like a waste of a long, hard training camp."

Nissalke guided the Cavs to a 5–30 start before finishing 23–59. He'd end his association with the Cavs 51–113. From 1979 to '84, before and after Musselman's reign, the Cavs failed to make the playoffs.

On April 7, 1983, George and Gordon Gund, co-owners of the Richfield Coliseum, announced they had secured an option to purchase the Cavs. One month later, Cleveland was awarded bonus first-round draft choices by the NBA owners for 1983, '84, '85, and '86, an arrangement that enticed the Gunds to purchase the franchise. The *Plain Dealer* estimated Stepien's losses at $8 million.

Eric Musselman remembers the day his dad got fired the second time: "The team was playing extremely well in preseason. The city of Cleveland was all of a sudden saying, 'Hey, we're coming around on Bill Musselman. Hey, maybe it's not all his fault. Maybe Stepien and these other guys have something to do with it.'

"I was driving my girlfriend home from school with the radio on, and they said that he was fired. I pulled off the side of the road and just started crying for about an hour and a half. Didn't leave the side of the road. It was so bad."

14

Sarasota: Fired Again

Bill Musselman was running out of leagues: ABA, WBA, NBA.

But he hadn't yet tried the CBA.

A bizarre scenario led Musselman into the Continental Basketball Association, which was in the process of shedding its Eastern League, weekends-only heritage and becoming the primary minor league feeder to the NBA for players, referees, and, ultimately, coaches.

Sam Ketchman, a 75-year-old former football coach and athletic director at Ferris State in Michigan, used to vacation with his wife Hildred, at Siesta Key in Sarasota, Florida.

Musselman's family vacationed there, too.

Ketchman said: "It was like 1966. We used to come down here every Christmas and stay on the beach. We went swimming one afternoon, and I ran into this elderly lady. We got to talking, and she said, 'What do you do?' I told her I'm a coach."

"Well, my son-in-law is a coach," she said. "His name is Bill Musselman."

"Well, I know of him," Ketchman said. So he and Musselman's mother-in-law talked.

Ketchman retired from college athletics in 1970, then took a job in Sarasota with the Kansas City Royals Baseball Academy. That's where Musselman introduced himself to Ketchman. Ketchman remembered Musselman's mother-in-law, and they talked.

About 13 years later, Ketchman's phone rang.

"This is Bill Musselman. Remember me?"

"Right out of the clear blue sky," Ketchman said. But they talked.

Musselman thought the CBA was agreeable to locating a 1983–84 expansion team in Sarasota. He told Ketchman he was back at Siesta Key, then asked him if he thought pro basketball could succeed there.

"I told him I thought it would," Ketchman said. "It's a resort town, and there's a lot of people down here in the wintertime. And there's no great sports activity in Sarasota itself that draws any kind of attention."

First came pursuit of financial backing. Jeff Fisher, a local stockbroker, was interested. He put up the money and hired Musselman, making him the first person to coach in four different pro leagues. (Keep in mind he had coached high school, small college, and major college, too.)

But the success Musselman enjoyed earlier in his career, 129–30 in six seasons at Ashland and 69–32 in four years at Minnesota, was a distant memory. He came to Sarasota with a 62–117 record from his last four jobs at San Diego, Virginia, Reno, and Cleveland.

The Sarasota Stingers did not slow the downward spiral of Musselman's career, though he did learn a fundamental rule of survival in the CBA. "I lost four players early," Musselman said. "We replaced them with guys I cut. I thought this was ridiculous. How many games are you going to win with guys from Marathon Oil? I had the best damn team in the CBA, and then, boom. Broke it up.

"It was the system. When those players go, you better have guys just as good. You work around the clock. The only way to survive is to know where you're going to get players when others are called up."

Musselman learned his lesson. He tracked every potential CBA player, carefully cataloguing more than 1,000 names in a black looseleaf notebook. The phone numbers of each player, his agent, and a family member were constantly updated.

That was later in his career. With Sarasota, he tried to stop the bleeding with Band-Aids. It didn't work.

Clay Johnson, a 6–4 guard from Missouri, was the first to go. The Seattle Supersonics plucked him for the remainder of the season after Sarasota's fourth game.

Nine days later Mike Sanders, the CBA's leading scorer with a 27.7 average, was signed by Phoenix. Ironically, Sanders was a key figure in the dramatic turnaround by the Cavaliers in 1988–89, improving from 42–40 to 57–25, the best record in franchise history. A player that Musselman sent to the NBA wound up part of the NBA's hottest story, one told many times: how the franchise in Cleveland had finally recovered from the Musselman/Stepien debacle.

The departure of Sanders and Johnson was compounded when Dale Wilkinson, a 6–10 center, quit and Bo Ellis was injured. Musselman traded rookie forward Orlando Phillips to Wyoming for center John "Moose" Campbell. He then signed guard Kevin Loder, who was cut by the NBA's Kansas City Kings. Next, Musselman suspended Wilkinson and traded him to Wisconsin for guard Mike Wilson of Marquette.

Wilson, one of the smoothest shooters to grace CBA courts, would average 25.4 points. Loder scored 21.3 per game, but the points came too late to save Musselman's job. Sarasota dropped seven straight, including five road games in six nights. A 3–2 start had become 6–13. Fisher fired Musselman.

Bob Bowman, an assistant coach at Southwest Louisiana, was named Musselman's replacement. He won his first game, then went 9–15 to finish the year. Twenty-four players wore Sarasota uniforms in the 44-game season.

While the Stingers sputtered through the rest of their season, Musselman spent time with Eric in San Diego. Then he retreated to his beachfront condo at Siesta Key. He often played tennis with Ketchman, and they still play spirited matches. Musselman fondly called Ketchman "my idol." Ketchman returned the compliment.

"He's a wonderful person and a strong competitor," Ketchman said. "He's obsessed with winning, and nothing's going to stop him. He wants to be the greatest coach in the world. And he takes good care of himself physically. You look at some coaches and they're slobs, aren't they? They look terrible. Musselman's like a conditioned athlete. He's incredible. He doesn't smoke or drink. And he doesn't drink coffee. Runs that beach like a madman."

Many of Musselman's mornings were spent in a Bradenton health club, where he quickly became friends with the owner, Rich Jordan. And Musselman didn't even know Jordan had a 60-foot-long basketball court in his backyard, complete with glass backboards and lights.

"I don't know how many ballgames we've played there," Jordan said. "Even though he's an NBA coach, he's just another fella with us."

Stroll by Jordan's backyard and you're apt to see an interesting collection of ballplayers. Ohio State product Jay Burson, CBA scoring legend Waite Bellamy, several high school coaches from the area, Eric's buddies from college, and Sidney Lowe and other players from Musselman's CBA teams have all played at Jordan's house.

"It's just a fun deal," Jordan said. "But we play to win, and Bill is the most competitive of everybody. He's got that look in his eye like he does when he's coaching. Bill doesn't like losing anything. None of us do; that's why we get along so well."

Jordan's relationship with area high school coaches occasionally leads to scrimmages, high school varsity teams against Musselman, Jordan and company. "We were going to scrimmage Cardinal Mooney a couple summers back, and I call Bill and I say, 'Come on out. We're going to play the kids,' " Jordan said. "This is the summertime. I mean it's hot in that gym. It might be 100 degrees. Who knows? And we're playing and we're ahead. Now, we've played maybe six or seven quarters, and it's hot in there. These guys have played seven quarters in 100 degrees in the gym. The guys are from 45 to 48 years old. And Bill said:

'Time out.'

'What's wrong?'

'Okay. We'll have to press 'em. Let's pressure 'em all the way up the court.'

'You're nuts. We're not pressing anybody.'

"So, he put the one-man press on them. He was pressing them all over the floor." Battle NFL linebackers for rebounds in a charity game or press 16-year-old kids in a 100-degree gym. Musselman knows only one way of competing.

When Jordan learned Minnesota Timberwolves President Bob Stein, a distant cousin he'd never met, was selecting the team's first head coach, Jordan called Stein and told him: " 'How could you even think about picking anybody but Bill Musselman? You couldn't ask for a better guy in the NBA or anyplace else.'

'Well, Rich, how's Bill going to handle people who are making a million dollars and have no-cut contracts? These guys have a mind of their own. They don't like people pushing them.'

'He's going to work them just like he works players when they're making $50,000 a year. He's out there to win the ball game.' "

Having competed time after time against Musselman and having seen the bond he has with former players who showed up for pick-up games, Jordan said Musselman's ex-players "all had one thing a coach wants them to have. They have a little fear of him. He's got a line drawn between himself and his players. There's great respect, but he's still the coach, and that's the way it's going to be.

"But Bill also understands the difference between the game and life. He's got a soft spot that I don't think people see. I think he really cares about his players."

Musselman frequently spent his Sarasota nights at Blueberry Hill, a nightclub across the street from his condo. "I loved going in that place," Musselman said. "You'd go in there and listen to '50s and '60s music. You'd see a lot of sports stars in there."

The owners of Blueberry Hill, Gil Rosenberg and his 34-year-old son, Jeff, also own a healthy interest in sports. As Musselman got to know them, an idea was born, the pursuit of a CBA franchise to potentially land an NBA team. The Rosenbergs felt Musselman was essential to a new CBA franchise.

"Jeff and I didn't want to go into the CBA with the prospect of having no idea of how we were going to get a winning coach," Gil Rosenberg said. "Bill was a very integral aspect of our decision. We expected we would be competitive because we felt Bill's recruiting abilities were exceptional. He was involved with us right from the planning stage of acquiring a team."

Musselman was convinced his Sarasota team would have been successful with a larger pool of players to compensate for call-ups to the NBA. And his career options were limited. He had interviewed for the head coaching job at St. Cloud State in Minnesota. He considered carving out a career in business. But when Musselman thought about it, an offer of a three-year contract for a CBA team in Tampa Bay was the logical move.

"The Rosenbergs said, 'Hey, we'll be a club based on you being with us. We will not buy a pro club unless you are our coach,' " Musselman said.

"I said, Hell, I got to do it. If I can get back in, though, I'm going to win. That's what they want. They are responsible for me still being in basketball."

15

The Thrillers: A New Start

The Rosenbergs' bid for an expansion franchise was quickly approved by the CBA, which saw the Tampa–St. Petersburg area as a fertile market with a population of 1.75 million at the time. And though the mechanism of using a successful CBA club to get an NBA team didn't happen for the Rosenbergs, the NBA's position on basketball in Florida is as clear as glass. Two of the league's four expansion teams these past two seasons are Orlando and Miami.

The Tampa Bay team was named the Thrillers. The Bay Front Center in St. Petersburg was chosen as their home court. And Gary Youmans, who played for Musselman at Ashland College, was invited aboard by Musselman.

Youmans, who coached St. Petersburg Catholic High School, was set to add on a summer job at the school as Director of Development. "It was going to start in two weeks," Youmans said. "The day I got back from vacation I read in the paper a little blurb that they're going to put a CBA team in St. Pete with Musselman. So I called Muss to see what was going on. He said, 'Yeah, come on. You'll be great with all your business experience (Youmans had owned and operated pizza restaurants). You'd be perfect. You can help me, you know.' "

Youmans was hired immediately as general manager and assistant coach. "I was smart enough to really just sit there and take it all in,"

Youmans said. "Some guys try to look at people and figure out how they're going to use them to get somewhere, but I thought the opportunity was to learn, and that's really what I did. I spent hours upon hours just sitting in Muss's office listening to him talk on the phone, and at practices and at games. I just learned the whole pro game. He had had such a negative experience in Cleveland, and I think he learned.

"The thing about Muss is that he's brilliant. He's got a great mind, and he would talk and talk about the Cleveland experience and the players and putting teams together and all those kind of things. I just engulfed that. I'd just take it in."

The down side for Youmans was taking in all of Musselman's intensity.

The other expansion team for the 1984–85 season was the Evansville Thunder. Evansville selected guard Greg Jones, left unprotected by the Wisconsin Flyers in the expansion draft. Jones was CBA Rookie of the Year. Tampa Bay got 7-foot center Steve Hayes, who was the CBA Most Valuable Player. Musselman, however, wasn't a happy camper afterward.

"We got Steve Hayes, who ended up being the player of the year in the CBA and really the cornerstone for our championship team," Youmans said. "But I remember driving home and Muss was just furious. He felt Evansville had a better draft 'cause Jeff Rosenberg had talked him into taking a particular player. He wanted to take this other guy. And he went nuts in the car. I mean, he pounded the steering wheel yelling, 'They beat our ass today in this draft.'

"I was thinking, I took this job because I listened to Rosenberg, and I shouldn't have done it. Oh my God, I can't believe it. This is terrible. I looked at Muss and had a flashback to Ashland. Holy shit, here we go again."

Where no man has gone before.

Youmans didn't need long to witness Musselman's obsession: "Muss was just driven to get another chance in the NBA. Initially, the Thrillers were going to be a prototype for that area to help bring an NBA team, but Rosenberg wasn't strong enough to do it. Muss's whole thing was to win a championship and get some respect again in pro ball. So after he did it once, then we had to do it a second time. We had to do the impossible. And always he'd relate to Ashland and 33.9. 'Do the impossible. That's the only way you're going to get noticed. That's how I've got to be. That's how I got to be a major college coach, by doing the impossible.'

"Everything was driven. When he won twice, that wasn't enough. He had to do it a third time. Then he had to do it a fourth time. That intensity was just always there. After he won the first championship, he was off and running. People respected him again for winning. He was building his support with the agents, which is how you win in the CBA."

Musselman's obsession had no parameters. Work into the middle of the next day? Sure. Call people at 2:00 in the morning? Of course.

"I didn't travel with the team all the time," Youmans said. "If I was listening to the game on radio, and we didn't play well, I could almost set my watch. About 2:00 a.m. The phone would ring. He'd want to talk and we'd start talking. He'd do most of the talking, of course, and he'd be letting out his frustrations on this, that, and the other. I didn't mind it for one night, and we didn't do it every single night. One or two nights a week. If there were more than two, then I'd take the phone off the hook.

"He'd call the next morning around 8 a.m., about a minute after I put the phone back on. He'd say, 'What's wrong with you? I tried to get a hold of you.'

'Jeez, I don't know. I'm going to call the phone company. I don't know what the hell it is. I was home all night.' "

Right from the start, promotion figured prominently in the Rosenbergs' plans for the Thrillers. "We took a lot of pride in our entertainment," Gil Rosenberg said. "We had promotions all night long. Our program was designed with meticulous care. We took a lot of pride in our uniforms. We took a lot of pride in our cheerleaders. We felt we could take that showmanship and help create more excitement in our team."

There was no better basketball ringmaster than Musselman. And there was no better show in the CBA.

The festivities typically began with the warm-ups. The lights in the Bay Front Center were turned off while music blared over the P.A. system. A spotlight focused on one corner of the building. The Thrillers, clad in silver and black uniforms, awaited their cues. Waiting for their heroes were the young and sexy Thrillseekers, the team's cheerleaders.

The idea was to have each player introduced with a spotlight that followed him from a corner of the court to midcourt, where the

Thrillseekers stood next to a rack of basketballs. A cheerleader handed each player a ball, then the player dribbled between two rows of flashing red runway lights for a fancy dunk. His entire movement was centered by a roving spotlight. Additionally, a smoke machine was belching gray clouds everywhere in the building.

That was the concept. What actually happened was another matter. "It was so crazy, because they'd turn the lights out and all of a sudden you'd hear this music, Duh-duh-duh-duh, duh-duh-duh-duh," forward Brian Martin said. "You're like standing out there waiting for the introduction and the smoke machine is just billowing in your face. You're coughing and hacking, and you can't see. The cheerleader stands out in the middle of the floor then hands you a ball as you run by. Well, the spotlight is right in your eyes, and you're trying to find the ball. We finally figured out that when you grab the ball, just keep it in your hands and run like a running back. Don't dribble. You get up there, take your time, and go up and dunk it."

After each Thriller had been introduced, Musselman emerged from the cloud of smoke invariably wiping his eyes so he could regain sight.

Rival coaches and players took the theatrics about as well as could be expected. "I didn't mind the lights going out and all that," said Herb Brown, coach of the Puerto Rico Coquis. "That's show business, and there was nothing wrong with that, as long as it didn't disrupt the game. Where they got out of hand was the announcer."

Harpoon Howie, a.k.a. Howard Karasick, was an overbearing P.A. announcer who didn't let minor details—such as a game being played—interrupt his schtick. He dubbed each player with a nickname. His best was "The King of Hearts" for Ron Valentine. He had innumerable candidates for worst including Sidney "Sweet and" Lowe and Linton "Toast of the" Townes. The Harpoon Man mixed play-by-play description with advice to the Thrillers, and played a deafening tape of a cannon being fired each time Tampa Bay scored.

Typical Harpoon scenarios were:

The shot clock running out: "Four seconds on the shot clock, shoot it, Linton, shoot it."

Sidney Lowe bringing the ball up: "Look out behind you, Sid, here they come."

Hayes gets a rebound: "Steve, Steve; Yes, shot-blocker Steve."

Hayes, who spent the 1982–83 season with the Cleveland Cavaliers, was a dominant figure in the CBA, averaging 20.5 points and 8.9 rebounds. Musselman built a wall of talent around him.

Freeman Williams, a two-time NCAA scoring champion at Portland State, had five NBA seasons behind him. In consecutive seasons with the San Diego (now L.A.) Clippers, Williams averaged 18.6 and 19.3 points.

Musselman signed him as a free agent. One of the greatest gunners the CBA has ever seen, Williams supplied Musselman with a steady source of outside scoring, averaging 21.9 points, to complement Hayes' inside strength.

A second preseason addition, point guard Lowe, provided a shining example of Musselman's CBA recruiting.

Following an outstanding season in which he helped North Carolina State to the 1983 national championship, Lowe spent his rookie season with Indiana in the NBA. He averaged 4.2 points and 3.4 assists in 78 games while demonstrating his excellent peripheral vision and great court intelligence. But the Pacers weren't convinced the short (he's generously listed at 6 feet) and stocky (197 pounds) Lowe would help them the following season and cut him in training camp.

He had never spoken with Musselman. Yet the morning after he was cut, Lowe got a wake-up call. At 6 a.m.

"You have to respect the homework the guy does," Lowe said.

That wasn't his initial reaction: "First, I wondered what in the world is wrong with this guy, calling me at 6 o'clock in the morning. I'd just been released from a team, so I'm hurt."

Forty-five minutes later, Musselman had a point guard. Lowe would lead three of Musselman's teams, two in Tampa Bay and one in Albany, to CBA championships before being re-united with Musselman this season with the Timberwolves.

"I got Sidney because I researched," Musselman said. "In training camp, I went around and talked to everybody to anticipate who was going to get cut.

"I knew more about Sidney Lowe than anybody before he got cut. I knew who was going to take a look at him next. Detroit was going to pick him up. So I called (Pistons General Manager) Jack McCloskey and asked him if he was going to pick him up.

"He said he was, so I said 'Do me a favor. I've got to sign him before you do because if I don't, I lose the rights to him.' " (CBA teams had the rights to two NBA clubs; Indiana was one of Tampa Bay's NBA affiliates; Detroit wasn't.)

McCloskey told Musselman he'd give him two days to sign Lowe. Musselman faxed Lowe a CBA contract that he signed shortly before the Pistons picked him up. "He was still my property," Musselman said. "I figured he might get cut by Detroit, and he'd be mine."

He was after just six games with Pistons. But Musselman's hard work would have been wasted had he failed to strike a rapport with Lowe. Musselman was beginning to develop an acute ability to deal with traumatized, vulnerable young players who had just seen their NBA dreams evaporate.

"I was very delicate with these guys getting cut," Musselman said. "So delicate that you wouldn't believe it. I called Sidney. I tell him what a great kid he is and everything else. He was as down as anybody I ever talked to after being cut. You have to have the timing. The day he's cut, I'm there."

Lowe would play only 18 regular-season games for the Thrillers before being called back to the NBA by the Atlanta Hawks. But then he returned for the CBA playoffs and quarterbacked the Thrillers to Musselman's first championship.

Musselman won Lowe with one well-timed phone call. At the other end of the Musselman spectrum is 6–11 Lance Burwald, a player he recruited for years without succeeding. Reminiscing through his loose-leaf notebook in mid-March 1989, Musselman said, "He's a guy in Europe I called so many times it's incredible. I tried to convince him to quit Europe. Two, three years I worked on the guy. Worked on his parents. I never got him. I almost got him. I missed him a couple of times.

"Here's his phone number in Spain. There's his parents' number; they're from Minnesota. There's his stepfather's number. I was in touch with those people I don't know how many times. I worked relentlessly to talk to him. One time he came home 'cuz a child of his died. I almost had him talked into staying and playing in the CBA 'cuz of his family situation."

Musselman didn't sound as if he'd given up.

16

A CBA Championship

Musselman cemented the Thrillers' imposing roster with three trades:

• Forward Linton Townes from Lancaster for Don Collins and Kevin Graham in preseason. Townes led the Thrillers in scoring (24.1) and made the most significant shot in Musselman's entire CBA tenure. Collins averaged 24.0 points for the Lightning, while Graham played in just 10 games, averaging 11.0.

• Guard Perry Moss from Bay State for Pete DeBisschop and Kevin Springman, an early December deal so one-sided Musselman is still liable for theft. Moss averaged 16.9 points; DeBisschop 8.7 and Springman 3.3.

• Center-forward Charles Jones from Bay State for Ronnie Williams, two weeks after the trade for Moss. In 24 games before getting called up to the NBA, Jones averaged 8.3 points and 9.5 rebounds.

Additionally, Musselman purchased the rights to forward Ronnie Valentine from Detroit in early January. The CBA's MVP in 1982, Valentine averaged a modest 12.3 points in the regular season and 15.2 in the playoffs.

Brian Martin, a 6–9 rookie forward who averaged a team-high 9.6 rebounds and 7.2 points in the playoffs, came to Musselman on the suggestion of Martin's coach at Kansas, Larry Brown. "I wasn't really well-known," Martin said. "Larry said the best way for me to get exposure if I wanted to play professional basketball was to go to Florida and play in the CBA. He thought Bill Musselman would be the best guy in the league to help me out that way." Martin got called up to the NBA the following season.

The Thrillers began a CBA-record season in attendance (70,705) on November 29, 1984. They beat Sarasota 111–101 before a crowd of 3,776. Tampa Bay bolted to an 11–4 start, lost two in a row, then won 11 straight. Despite their 22–6 record, the Thrillers couldn't shake the defending CBA champion Albany Patroons in the race for the Eastern Division title.

Musselman's major problems during the season centered on NBA call-ups and his own flare-ups with a multitude of people. Two incidents could be labeled as extremely ill-conceived from Musselman's perspective.

In one, he got into it with Dave Cowens, the 6–9, 230-pound former Celtic who was coaching the Bay State Bombardiers. In the other, he nearly began a riot in Puerto Rico (He and Bobby Knight grew up together, remember?).

The confrontation with Cowens happened at Bay State. Thrillers trainer Guy Hill described the action: "Kirk Richards hit Steve Hayes in the back of the head with a basketball. Steve went after Kirk and was chasing him around the arena."

Musselman raced onto the court. So did Cowens. Musselman saw Bay State's DeBisschop heading for one of the Thrillers and pushed him away. Cowens saw his player threatened, and picked Musselman off the ground.

"All of a sudden, they're at halfcourt, him and Dave Cowens," Hayes said. "And Cowens is twice as tall as Muss. Cowens has Muss by his collar, holding him up with his feet off the ground. And Bill, his face is all red and he's so mad. He's punching at him in the chest and screaming, 'Put me down; I'm going to kick your ass.'

"Cowens looks like he's not even struggling. He's just standing there, holding him. He was saying, "You leave my players alone."

"After this, Cowens comes into the locker room and says, 'I apologize. Things like this shouldn't happen. We shouldn't let things like that get out of hand.' Muss is going, 'Oh, yeah, yeah, okay, thanks a lot, thanks a lot.'

"Cowens walks out the door and Muss makes like he's going to kick him in the rear. After Cowens left, we're all talking about it. And Muss says, 'Yeah, he had me. But I would've kicked his ass if he put me down.' "

Musselman didn't reach the same conclusion one night in Puerto Rico. "We had to go across the island to play," Martin said. "We were playing in this gym, and there's not 100, 120 people in the stands. Something happens on the floor, and Muss gets real mad. He just turns around and kicks his chair. The chair flies into the stands about four rows up and it lands about six inches from this little girl. All of a sudden, about eight rows back, this 6-8 Puerto Rican stands up. He's about 300 pounds and he looks like a guy who carries a switchblade and a gun in his back pocket. He just stands up and stares at Muss. Muss forgets his anger. He just goes, 'I'm sorry. I didn't mean to do it. I'm really sorry.' He went up in the stands and was apologizing to the little girl. She was crying and Muss was holding her hand.

"We go, 'Hey Muss, there's a game going on. You want to get back down here?' "

If a single moment epitomized Musselman's brilliance in the CBA, it happened in the 1984 playoffs in Albany, a city whose fans despised him—until he became coach there in 1987.

The Patroons fans' dislike of Musselman stemmed from natural causes as the 1984-85 regular season reached its conclusion. Albany was the defending champion, and Musselman's expansion Thrillers were correctly perceived as Albany's main threat.

The Thrillers and Patroons played six times during the regular season. Each won three. Tampa Bay finished with a better record (35-13) than Albany (34-14), but the Patroons finished first because standings in the CBA are determined by a seven-point system: three points for a win and one point for each winning quarter.

The seven-point system was Commissioner Jim Drucker's masterpiece. He began the system in 1981-82, and CBA fans love it. Separate scoreboards keep track of the points in each quarter, and each quarter has meaning because a point in the standings is at stake. Even in blowouts, CBA fans, unlike NBA fans, see teams playing hard every time a quarter is close regardless of the score of the game. A single standings point can determine whether a team makes the playoffs or wins a championship.

Albany Coach Phil Jackson despised the seven-point system, as did most of his contemporaries, because it placed added pressure on coaches and their players. However, Jackson won more individual quarters during the season than Musselman, and Albany beat the Thrillers for first place by $7^{1/2}$ points. As a result, Albany had home-court advantage in the playoffs.

Both Tampa Bay and Albany won their first round best-of-five series. The Thrillers swept Lancaster 3-0, while Albany had to rally to eliminate Toronto 3-2.

Fans in Tampa and Albany geared for the Eastern Division best-of-five final. They wouldn't be disappointed.

The Thrillers had six more days of rest than the Patroons, an advantage that was dwarfed by the Philadelphia 76ers' decision to bring up Hayes.

Musselman had already lost Charles Jones to the NBA (Jones said Musselman ''helped me by keeping me playing so I could get another chance at the NBA'') and was confronted by the question he'd asked himself after getting fired at Sarasota: where do you go for help?

Coby Dietrick, a 6-11, 225-pound center, had several decent if unspectacular seasons in the ABA and NBA with four different teams, one of them Chicago. That's why he was invited to the Bulls' Old-Timers Game in 1985.

And that's how he became Musselmanized.

''I called Rod Thorn (then GM of Chicago) up, and Rod said, 'God, Coby still looks like he can play a few minutes,' '' Musselman said. ''Half-kidding. I figured if he could play 10 minutes, he can help us. Boom. Called him.''

Musselman didn't let Dietrick's age (36) or retirement (he had last played in the NBA in 1982-83) deter him from finding a badly needed replacement on Tampa Bay's front line.

Dietrick didn't dominate in the playoffs. In fact, his statistics were downright poor, averages of 2.2 points and 2.1 rebounds. However, he played a key role as Tampa Bay ousted Albany and advanced into the CBA finals.

Before that turning point in Musselman's career came the most publicized phone call of his life. He called Patroons guard Frankie J. Sanders in the middle of the night during the middle of the playoffs and allegedly threatened his life.

The bewildering saga just increased already heightened passions.

At his best, Sanders was unstoppable in the CBA. At his worst, he was a pain in the neck, particularly for Coach Jackson. Sanders sulked when substituted out of the game, and chose the first round of the playoffs for his most childish behavior. After Game 2 of the Toronto series, he and Jackson got into a heated argument. Jackson suspended him for Game 3, which Toronto won 117–105 to take a 2–1 series lead. With Albany on the brink of elimination, Patroons President James J. Coyne and General Manager Gary Holle rushed to Toronto to encourage Sanders' immediate reinstatement. Jackson complied, and Sanders scored 27 points in Game 4 and 39 in Game 5 to lead Albany to its victory in the series.

Musselman had mixed results keeping Sanders in check in the opening two games in St. Petersburg. Tampa Bay won the opener 144–129, but Sanders scored 30 in Game 2, which Albany won 113–100 after a bench-clearing brawl. Musselman, Sanders, and seven other players were fined by the CBA for the incident.

What happened between Games 2 and 3 is the stuff of CBA legends.

What's clear is that Musselman and Sanders exchanged unpleasantries during Game 2. The war of words didn't end when the game did. Slightly before dawn, Musselman phoned Sanders in his hotel room in Tampa.

Sanders claimed Musselman threatened his life, alleging Musselman told him. "I have friends who eat nails, and they're going to be in Albany tonight."

Musselman claimed (and still does) he never threatened Sanders: "The whole incident was blown out of proportion. I respect Frankie. Later he apologized. Albany used me to hype up the crowd and get people there."

The story hit the press immediately as the teams flew into Albany that day for Game 3. Sanders said he was scared for the safety of his wife and 3-year-old daughter. What were the Patroons going to do to ensure their and his safety? What was the CBA going to do?

Musselman's players didn't know what had transpired until they saw the local 6 p.m. news on television. "It was just so funny," Martin said. "It was one of the first things they said, something like 'Plane crashes in Lebanon, war declared in Indonesia, and local player threatened by coach.'

"We're like, 'Holy cow; what is this?' And we're sitting there watching the news, and they come on and they say that Frankie J. Sanders reports that Tampa Bay Thrillers Coach Bill Musselman had made death threats on his life with a phone call. Something about if he played well, Musselman was going to get his goons after him. We thought this is ridiculous. Only Bill Musselman could do that."

And follow through. Amid considerable security precautions in the Washington Avenue Armory, up popped three goons. "These three big guys," Martin said. "One guy was called Boot. He tears off beer cans with his teeth." Trainer Guy Hill said he's seen Boot "put a firecracker in his mouth, light it, and hold his mouth shut." Hill also said he heard that Boot used to race German shepherds in pizza-eating contests in Cleveland. Patroons guard Lowes Moore saw Boot in action in Cleveland: "He'd eat light bulbs. I saw him eat light bulbs."

Before the game, CBA Commissioner Drucker, who flew to Albany from league headquarters in Philadelphia, held a closed-door meeting with Musselman, Sanders, Youmans, and Holle. "Drucker's going through the whole ritual about this," Youmans said. "He said, 'Because of this, I'm going to take some serious stands here, and one of them is I'm going to hold back money for the playoffs.'

"And Frankie goes, 'What? I don't have any problems. Hey, I don't have any problems with Musselman.'"

Score one for paycheck diplomacy.

As an extra precaution, a security team was assigned to follow Musselman. "We couldn't go anywhere in the building without a police escort and the German shepherds," Hill said. "So we go downstairs to the community men's room (downstairs in the Armory, players and fans shared the same bathroom). Bill goes to the urinal. The two dogs are standing there, and they're staring at him. Muss turns around and goes, 'You got to turn those dogs around—I can't piss with them looking at me.'"

Musselman was relieved, literally, but returned to the Tampa Bay locker room disconsolate. "We're sitting there, the guard dogs, Muss and Guy and I," Youmans said. "Muss looks at me and says, 'Why does this always happen to me?'"

Youmans' answer: "Could it have anything to do with your intensity?"

There were no incidents in Game 3, which Albany won 93–90. Tampa Bay then won Game 4, 118–113, sending the series to a deciding Game 5.

It was a game of remarkable defensive intensity, every shot challenged, every rebound fought over.

Albany led 89–87. Tampa Bay had the ball out of bounds under its own basket with three seconds left. Musselman called time out and began to diagram a play that would decide the Thrillers' fate. "It was a play that he just invented on the spot," Martin said. "We must have had 90 plays during the year. We ran them every day during practice— it took us an hour just to run through our plays. But he was famous for inventing plays. That year, that team, if Musselman drew something up, we ran it the way he drew it up. And it almost always worked."

"It was peculiar," Townes said. "I looked at Perry Moss and told him, 'We got this game.' It was something I never felt in basketball before. I just felt like we were going to win somehow. I didn't know how."

This was Musselman at his best: "I designed it," he said. "It was perfect execution. I had it all figured out. Townes was on the block. Dietrick's taking the ball out. Back pick. Townes comes out. The first option was to go to Townes for a jump shot on the baseline. We'll make sure we try to force a switch, and Townes would pump fake. If he didn't have the shot, he drops it inside to Brian Martin, who set the pick. Brian was going to drop step and go to the hole. And, as a last resort, if they denied everything, the back pick would go over the top and get the ball. And if that broke down, we call green out. That means everybody just turns and crashes the boards. That means the guard would penetrate and draw the foul because every-body was going to take their man to the baseline."

Dietrick held the ball and watched Martin set a pick on Derrick Rowland, one of the premier defensive players in the CBA. Rowland fought through Martin's pick. "I think I just slowed him up enough for Linton to get the shot off," Martin said. "As soon as he got the ball, I knew the ball was going in the hole."

Townes' 12-footer from the baseline barely cleared Rowland's outreached hands and swished through the net at the buzzer. Tie game. Overtime. Sudden-death overtime. First team to lead by three wins. Dumb rule, especially with the three-point shot (the rule was replaced in '87–88 with a standard five-minute overtime).

Albany won the jump and quickly went for the kill. Moore, who had won three previous sudden-death games, missed a three-pointer. Tampa Bay's Freeman Williams scored a layup in transition. Sanders missed a three-pointer. Les Craft got the rebound and passed long to Williams, who had beaten the defense downcourt. Williams drove in uncontested, pumped a fist to his teammates, and scored the final basket.

The Townes shot was the play of the year, the play drawn spontaneously by Musselman. And the triggerman for the pass to Townes was a refugee from an Old-Timers game.

"It wasn't like it was a lucky thing," Musselman said. "The play was coached and designed. The game was won that way. But it was won because of recruitment. I wanted a veteran who won't fold under pressure and could pass. It was a great pass he made."

Tampa Bay moved on to face the Detroit Spirits for the CBA championship. It would be a tightly contested seven-game series.

Townes poured in 36 points and Martin scored all eight of his points in the fourth quarter to rally the visiting Thrillers from a 70-60 halftime deficit to a 123-119 win in Game 1. Detroit evened the series, getting 41 points by Michael Young and 35 by Tico Brown, the CBA's all-time leading scorer, for a 146-139 win.

The series shifted to Florida for the next three games as the Thrillers changed home courts from St. Petersburg to the University of Tampa. The Thrillers won Games 3 and 4, 127-106 and 134-132. Williams was limited to 30 minutes because of a nagging back problem but still scored 43 in Game 4.

Musselman was a game away from the CBA title, but Brown scored 35 to keep the Spirits alive by winning Game 5 107-103.

Games 6 and 7 were in Detroit, and Musselman was confronted with two major problems. Townes, who was averaging 26.8 points in the series, was called up to the NBA by the San Antonio Spurs. Williams' back spasms limited him to nine minutes and two points in Game 6, taken by Detroit 122-111.

Then Williams went wild. In the first half of Game 7, he scored 34. He finished with 47 points, the second-highest total in CBA Championship Series history.

It almost wasn't enough. Detroit took its only lead of the game, 105-103, with 1:20 left. With 1:02 remaining, Valentine tied the score with a jumper as he completed a 26-point effort against his former team.

After each team wasted one possession, Williams was fouled with 18 seconds to play. He made both free throws, giving the Thrillers a 107-105 advantage. Detroit missed and Tampa Bay scored just before the buzzer, giving the Thrillers a 109-105 win and Musselman his first CBA championship.

"When we actually won it at the very end, we all just screamed and jumped into the air," Gil Rosenberg said. "Jeff jumped into my arms and we jumped the last few rows of the bleachers to get down to the floor. It was absolute bedlam. For the team to have done that in the first year of ownership of the franchise was just a miracle as far as we were concerned."

Nobody appreciated the work Musselman did to achieve that miracle more than Gil Rosenberg: "Bill was absolutely, totally indefatigable. He slept and drank basketball from morning to night."

That night Musselman slept well.

17

Title after Title

Musselman's second and third seasons with the Thrillers encompassed two different owners, a sudden shift of the franchise to a city half a continent away, several more NBA player call-ups, and an unprecedented second and third consecutive championship.

Relocation of the Thrillers' home court from St. Petersburg to the University of Tampa worked well in the playoffs, but proved to be a poor financial decision.

"The thing about it was we led the CBA in attendance that first year," Musselman said. "We drew unbelievably at St. Pete, yet we moved for the playoffs. It was a big mistake. We packed them in for the playoffs over in Tampa, but they were St. Pete people coming over."

Gil Rosenberg explained the decision: "We decided to move for two reasons. One, we had a more favorable lease, and, secondly, we felt that there were more movers and shakers in Tampa. It was just the opposite."

Despite Musselman's continuing success, the Thrillers attracted less than half as many people as the previous season. Average attendance plummeted from 2,946 to 1,340.

"Our most difficult job, one that we were never able to succeed in, was to make basketball important enough to wake up the community," Rosenberg said. "With a championship under our belt and with a strong indication we could be the only team to ever repeat as champion—which we did—what the answers were to the decline in attendance...you can't always come up with a cause and effect relationship. Some have said you have to understand that people come to Florida to be outside. But I can't give you an exact recipe."

Musselman, however, had no trouble cooking up another winner. The more he won, the more confident he grew in his methods of coaching, his recruitment of players, and, ultimately, his steely faith in himself. Typically, players in the CBA feel they have to score big to get a shot at being picked up by an NBA team. Musselman preached a different philosophy: play for me, play to win, and you'll get noticed.

Each season he built a stronger case for his philosophy as he sent player after player to the NBA. "I took pride in guys moving up," he said. "If they paid the price for me, I told them I'd break my back to help them get to the NBA. I had great respect for the veteran players because when they came to play for me in the CBA, they worked as hard as they could. My players worked hard for me because they knew I could move them up to the NBA.

"Every day I explained to my players where they were in their careers, what their weaknesses were, and whether they improved or not. I could do that because I try to find out anything I can about every player I coach. I want to know more about him than anyone else.

"Very few players in pro ball play hard every night. In the CBA, very few people are willing to make a commitment. It's tough to get guys who are great competitors. I can get along with any personality as long as a guy is a great competitor.

"I mean, like Magic Johnson. I'm just amazed. I can't believe his intensity level is so high through all these years. I admire somebody that excels in anything. I don't care whether he's a writer or what he is. You have to respect somebody that can do something well and does it over and over and tries to be the best he possibly can be."

Twelve of the 1985–86 Thrillers were good enough to play in the NBA after playing for Musselman. Several were still playing in the NBA in 1988–89, including Kevin Williams (Nets), a 6–2 guard who averaged 30.7 points for the Thrillers after Musselman traded for him with 15 games left in the regular season.

"Bill was the only coach that believed in me and my talents and was willing to give me an opportunity to show them," Williams said. "Playing in the CBA was fun for me because Bill always wanted to win and always found a way to win. Now, I might not have a good shooting night, but I do other things to win the game. Not just scoring. That's something I learned from Bill: It's not just scoring, it's how you go about playing the game."

Another Musselman veteran in the NBA is Golden State forward Rod Higgins, whose 10.6 scoring average helped the Warriors to a surprisingly strong showing last season. In 1985–86 Higgins was treated like a yo-yo, getting called up to the NBA by four different teams while sandwiching in 11 games with the Thrillers. "Up and down, up and down," Higgins said. "It was frustrating in a sense, but it wasn't that bad because I was enjoying myself down at Tampa. We had the best team in the CBA, and we just wanted to keep on winning."

The Thrillers began the season as if they'd never lose. Their 9–0 start was the best in CBA history and gave Musselman enough of a cushion to weather a midseason slump and a bushel of personnel moves.

The Thrillers' only two losses in their first 15 games were by three points in sudden-death overtime at Toronto, and by one against the Stingers at home. But then the Thrillers dropped three in a row. The third loss was especially galling to Musselman, who once again went wild in Albany in a 131–121 loss.

Thrillers swingman Brook Steppe was fouled hard, injured his leg, and had to be carried off the court. No foul was called, and Musselman went berserk. He threw down his leather jacket on the court, got a technical foul, and only got angrier. After stomping on his coat several times, he kicked it off the court as he got his second technical, an automatic ejection.

"Just being on Coach Musselman's team, you knew that he was all out for you, 100 percent behind you, and vice versa," Steppe said. "It was a relationship where there was a lot of tension at times, but when you went out on the court, you'd do anything to help him win. He was always behind you.

"I saw his coat after the game. He ruined it. It was all torn up. He and I laughed about it in the locker room. It was a nice leather coat. It was the type of thing that he was making a point for his player."

Steppe's Tampa Bay career was brief, 30 games, but never dull. A 6-5 former first-round NBA pick out of Georgia Tech, Steppe mirrored Musselman's intensity on the court. He played at just one speed: hard. "I really enjoyed playing for Coach Musselman," Steppe said. "He was a competitor, which I related to, the type of guy that would do just about anything to win. He would trade his own family: mother, father, whoever. Trade 'em away if he thought he could get a better player to help him win.

"He had a volatile personality that could explode at any moment. You have to understand the whole time with him you're living on the edge, really. You understand that that's him, and you have to let it go. It's not best to confront him, 'cause you'll just make it worse.

"He may get mad and cuss you out, get in your face for one minute, but an hour later you could go out and have a beer with him or something. He's that kind of guy."

Agile, tough, and a good shooter, Steppe could do many things. One of them was not taking care of a dog.

"Brook was rooming with Rick Lamb," Brian Martin began the story. "This dog, a Rottweiler, is as big as a booth, and they're in a little two-room apartment. One day I go over there, and I see all these piles with paper on them. All over the apartment. I bet there's 10 or 12 of them. And it smells. The place smells like a dog kennel with a thousand dogs that someone hadn't cleaned in a month.

"I'm banging on the front door. Finally, Rick comes to the front door. I ask him what's with all this paper. He says, 'It's the dog. Craps in the middle of the floor. Brook just covers it with paper. He won't take the dog out. He barely feeds the dog. He won't bathe it. He won't do anything. I'm stuck back in my room.' "

Martin said, "We went on a 10-day road trip, and Rick said that Brook locked the dog in the apartment with four or five bowls of dog food laid out for him to eat while we were gone. The dog probably ate it the first hour. I mean, this dog was huge, so I'm sure when they got back to the apartment, the place was wall-to-wall crap, and the dog was probably half dead."

When the Thrillers split two games to go 14–6, Musselman started dealing. He shipped guard Michael Holton to the Stingers for forward Ed Nealy. Holton was soon called up by Chicago; Nealy reported 20 pounds overweight, played himself into shape and averaged 15.5 rebounds and 12.9 points in the playoffs before moving up to the NBA himself.

Following a three-game losing streak, Musselman made two major trades. He sent forward Ray Tolbert to Bay State for Kevin Williams, then got Don Collins from the Baltimore Lightning in exchange for Steppe and Valentine. Collins and Williams were the top two scorers in the CBA.

But six days after the trade, Collins injured his back in an automobile accident. "When I was in the hospital, Bill was there every day," Collins said.

To Musselman, Collins' accident was a painful reminder of the one his brother had 30 years earlier. "I think I was motivated a lot by my brother," Musselman said. "Deep down inside, he loved sports. He still does to this day, but he had a head-on automobile collision, broke part of the bone in his face. He was a senior in high school; I was a sophomore. When I came home from school that night, my mother made me go to the hospital to see him. It devastated me. He got tuberculosis because his respiratory system and everything was screwed up. When he got TB, he was 40 miles away in the hospital. I'd go see him before a ball game, and I'd run over anybody in my way."

Collins missed four weeks, returning to action five games before the playoffs. He quickly resumed his high-scoring ways while developing an explosive on-court relationship with Musselman. Musselman would yell at Collins to play defense. Collins would yell back. Obscenities were routinely exchanged. Collins spoke of the fragile line of demarcation in his relationship with Musselman. "Neither one of us crossed that line," he said.

Musselman said his fiery relationship with Collins could work "because Don Collins is a great competitor. He knew me, and I respected him. I told him when he played bad defense. Under one coach, Cazzie Russell, he played defense. Under another coach, he wouldn't."

He sure would for Musselman.

"There were times I knew I couldn't get on Don Collins," Musselman said. "There were times I knew he was vulnerable."

Collins said of Musselman, "If he asked me to jump through a wall, I know I can't do it, but I'd try. Because he'll do anything for Don Collins."

He did. Collins was called up by the Milwaukee Bucks the next season.

Not every player on the Thrillers' 1985–86 roster had NBA scouts on the lookout. Eight of the 22 players were with the Thrillers for five games or less as Musselman worked around NBA call-ups and injuries.

When Musselman needed a player, he'd try anyone. Even Frankie J. Sanders.

"The first year we had the death threats and all this stuff," Martin said. "Every time we played against Frankie Sanders, Muss would talk about how much he couldn't stand Frankie J. Sanders. He said he didn't think he was a very good player, and he said, 'He'll never play for me. I'll never have that guy on my team.' And the next year, two games before the All-Star break, he decided that he was going to bring him in. One day he was talking to me at practice and he said, 'I've got Frankie J. Sanders' rights. He was available, and I didn't want anyone else to get him.' "

A week later, Musselman told his players of their new teammate. Sanders made two appearances in a Thrillers uniform. In a 117–114 overtime loss to Bay State, Sanders had five points in six minutes. Two nights later, when the Thrillers played the CBA All-Stars, he scored 11 points in 22 minutes. The next day he was gone.

Before he left, Sanders tried hitting up Youmans for cash. "We gave him a plane ticket, but he still wanted 75 bucks," Youmans said. "He worked it down to five bucks. I don't think I gave it to him. I can't even remember. He was going to con me for whatever he could get. He's just a piece of work."

Another ex-Patroon who suited up for Tampa that season was Dave Magley, who played with Musselman at Cleveland in the 1982–83 preseason before Musselman was fired. "One of the biggest testimonies to Bill Musselman is, after all the negative things that happened, he went to a league that is very unglamorous and did the best job maybe in the history of the CBA," Magley said. "Not just because of his record. We won the CBA championship in Albany (in '84), but none of us ever got called up to the NBA. So really, what does it mean? To me, the CBA's goal primarily is to get guys into the NBA, and secondly to win."

Musselman was doing both when he phoned Magley in Des Moines, Iowa, where Magley worked as a salesman. "How he tracked me down, I'll never know," Magley said. "I got a call out of the blue: 'This is Coach Musselman. I need you to come down and finish the season for me.' "

"Coach, I can't quit a career job to play in the CBA for three weeks," Magley told him. "I can't do it."

Three days later Musselman called again, at 1 a.m. " 'Mags, I need you. And I need you to come on down with someone, with one other body. I don't care who it is.'

'Well, Coach, my brother lives in South Bend. He's 6–7.'

'I'll fly him down.' "

Magley explained his change of heart: "The main thing I got excited about was he was going to give me a free pair of sneakers, and I was going to get a chance to see my brother for the weekend."

The Magley brothers joined the Thrillers in Evansville for a 130–112 loss to the Thunder. David Magley had 15 points and 10 rebounds. Pat Magley had two fouls and no other stat in a two-minute performance.

"My brother was more interested in winning souls than winning the game," David said. "He was able to kick a lot of bad habits when he turned his life over to the Lord. The funny story was Freeman Williams hurt his elbow and came to the bench, and he's going, 'Ohhhh,' and using a bunch of expletives to describe his luck. My brother looked at him and said, 'Do you mind if I pray for it?'

"There's not many guys in the CBA that are going to come up and pray for your elbow when you're hurt. Freeman really didn't know how to take it. You've got to understand my brother's a big man with a pretty wild beard and a pretty wild hairdo, so Freeman's not going to say anything but 'Yeah, I don't care.' Coach is up yelling at somebody on the court, and my brother is on the bench praying for Freeman's elbow.

"His elbow got better, by the way."

Before 1985–86 ended, Musselman had one more escapade in Albany. Hill described the action:

"We were at the Albany Hilton. In a previous game, Kevin Williams had allegedly spit on an official. Drucker called the Hilton to talk to Muss and tell him Williams had been suspended for the next game (which was that night). Muss got on the phone to fight for this team and fight for Kevin. He got so excited that he ripped the phone literally off the wall. He was holding it in his hands. The wires were just dangling there. And he was still screaming into the phone, 'Drucker, are you there? Are you there?' "

When the season ended, Musselman's Thrillers were in familiar territory. Despite a mediocre midseason stretch of 13–10, Tampa Bay finished first in the Eastern Division with a 34–14 record and 211 points, 16 more than second-place Bay State.

Freeman Williams missed 13 games and the entire playoffs because of his back problem, but Kevin Williams compensated with several monster performances. He scored 40 against Maine, 41 at Wisconsin, 45 versus Kansas City, and 58 in a 135–122 loss at Baltimore in the Thrillers' regular-season finale.

Once again, though, Musselman faced a personnel problem as he prepared for the playoffs. A week earlier, Higgins had been taken one more time by the NBA when the Chicago Bulls called. Once again, Musselman went through his black book and got a replacement. This time it was 6–10 Eric Fernsten, a 33-year-old NBA castoff who mistakenly thought he had retired after the 1983–84 season.

Fernsten was working as a carpenter just outside Boston when he got the call from Musselman. "Bill and I talked pretty straight," Fernsten said. "I wasn't really going to do it for anybody because I got screwed so much in the NBA. He sold me on a special situation where he thought I could help him. I didn't want to get into political and egotistical problems. I was pleased to play for him."

Though he hadn't played for two years, Fernsten averaged 10.1 points and 9.1 rebounds in the playoffs.

Musselman's opening-round opponent in the playoffs was Albany, which had slipped to fourth place with a .500 record.

With Kevin Williams scoring 42, Tampa Bay won Game 1 at home, 128–118. Attendance was 803. Two nights later in Tampa, the Patroons stunned the Thrillers 119–104 to even the best-of-seven series.

Games 3, 4, and 5 were in Albany. With Williams scoring 36 and Nealy providing 24 rebounds (he had 25 in Game 2), Tampa Bay edged the Patroons 104–101 in Game 3. But Albany recovered to win the next two and push Musselman's Thrillers to the brink of elimination.

Kevin Williams exploded for 59 points in a 134–111 win in Game 6. Musselman got even more good news the next day when the Bulls waived Higgins in time for him to play in Game 7. Albany led by 10 at halftime, but the Thrillers won 118–110 behind Williams' 37 points.

The rest of the playoffs was easy for Musselman. Tampa Bay won the Eastern Division title 4–1 against Bay State, the lone loss in sudden-death overtime on the road.

In the finals against the La Crosse (Wisconsin) Catbirds, Tampa Bay made a statement in Game 1 with a 123–94 rout. The Catbirds fell, four games to one.

Higgins averaged 29.2 points and was the playoff MVP. Williams averaged 30.8, while Sidney Lowe averaged 12.3 assists, 6.3 points, and 3.9 steals. Nealy averaged 15.5 rebounds and 12.9 points. Musselman had become the first CBA coach to win consecutive championships. In doing so, he had season records of 45–18 and 46–19.

While Thrillers fans were thinking dynasty as 1986–87 approached, the Rosenbergs sold the franchise to John Tuschman in September. Gil Rosenberg described his two-year ownership in the CBA as a "roller coaster. It was tremendously heady wine. The games here, the games on the road, getting to know the players and the hope for their ultimate success. I don't begrudge a moment of the experience or the kind of effort we got. But it is also a business, and we lost lots and lots of money. I just couldn't afford to do it again."

Musselman did it again, bringing a CBA championship to Tuschman, who owned an investment firm in Houston while living in Vail, Colorado. The Thrillers opened strongly (6–0), had a midseason slump (10–11), and closed like champions, taking 18 of their final 21 games.

Four more of Musselman's players were called up to the NBA: Collins, forward Michael Brooks, guard Eddie Johnson, and guard Ray Williams, who spent just four games with the Thrillers before being signed by the Nets. Collins played six games with the Milwaukee Bucks before returning to Tampa Bay, where he finished as the league's second-leading scorer (27.2).

Lowe took a year off to manage a restaurant in Sarasota, but Musselman quickly found a replacement in Clint Wheeler, whom he got by trading rookie center Greg Grissom to the Patroons. Wheeler, a resourceful and quick guard, was second in the CBA in assists and steals and 17th in scoring. Grissom averaged 6.9 rebounds and 6.0 points.

Persistence worked again for Musselman when he looked for a center. He signed 6–10 John Stroeder, who averaged 10 points and 6.5 rebounds in Tampa Bay's final 17 games, then 10.3 points and 7.1 rebounds in the playoffs. The following year, Stroeder played the entire season in the NBA with Milwaukee. "Two years earlier, I tried getting John Stroeder," Musselman said. "He came back from playing in France and said he was burned out, tired of basketball. I must have called him 10 times in December and January. He just gave in."

So did Lester "The Molester" Conner, a 6–4 guard with four years of NBA experience. Musselman traded for his rights from Toronto two days before the Thrillers faced Albany in the Eastern Division finals. "I tried to get him all year," Musselman said. "But you know what? I worked at it. It's a never-ending process."

For the second consecutive season, Musselman went 34–14. His three-year record in Tampa Bay was 103–41, a win percentage of .711. In the playoffs, the Thrillers beat Pensacola 4–0, Albany 4–1, and Rockford 4–1 to give Musselman his third straight championship and first CBA Coach of the Year award. His three-year playoff record with the Thrillers was 34–12. And in the final 35 games of the '86–87 season including the playoffs, Musselman was 30–5.

So what if the team moved right before the playoffs. Logically, where would a team from Tampa, Florida, move? To Rapid City in the Black Hills of South Dakota, of course.

Musselman didn't find out about the move in the conventional manner. "They didn't tell me," he said. "After a ball game, I came out of the locker room. We'd won. The press comes up, they're surrounding me, and one guy asks 'what are you going to do now?'

'I'm going home,' I said. 'We won the ballgame.'

'No, no, no. The owner held a press conference on the other side of the arena.'

"He told them we were going to move," Musselman said. "I didn't know it."

Musselman said he understood Tuschman's decision: "Basically, he's a good businessman, and he's a bottom-line guy. Hey, we won a regular-season championship, and we didn't draw. Tuschman made a great business deal. He had a championship ball club, and he shopped around. He got the best deal in the country. It was disruptive to winning a championship, but I'm a professional, and I had a commitment to the players."

His players also had commitments. "They were upset," Musselman said. "A lot of them had girlfriends that stayed with them because it was so expensive. They all had leases for the season. They wanted them made up, and I don't blame 'em. They weren't paid anything."

Musselman called a team meeting. "We all go or none go," he told his players. "One guy in here doesn't want to go, I'm not going. Tuschman told me he wouldn't move the first year, no matter what. He told the press he wouldn't move for three years. I says, 'I don't believe you. You're not from around here.' "

Musselman polled his players at the team meeting. They all were going to Rapid City.

"Everybody had responsibilities and obligations in Tampa,'' Wheeler, the MVP of the playoffs, said. "It was heartbreaking to leave. But we had no choice. It turned out to be okay. The people were really nice, and the whole town was excited. It was like a brand-new baby.''

The new baby was a winner. In their first four playoff games in Rapid City, the Thrillers drew more (19,896) than in 24 regular-season home games in Tampa (19,325).

18

The Best Season Ever

"We may lose and we may win, but we'll never be here again..."—
"Take It Easy"—The Eagles

"All right, everybody in. 1-2-3. DEFENSE."

That's how every practice ended, a group of 10 players huddled around Bill Musselman in the frequently chilly Washington Avenue Armory.

The huddle dissolved; the players scattered.

Just a few months before the season began, the players who would comprise the 1987–88 Albany Patroons were in vastly disparate surroundings:

- Forward-center Scott Roth was in Istanbul, Turkey, playing for EFES Pilsen Beer Co.
- Power forward Michael Brooks was in the NBA with the Indiana Pacers.
- Point guard Sidney Lowe was managing a restaurant in Sarasota, Florida.
- Forward Tony Campbell was in Detroit, finishing his third NBA season with the Pistons.

- Guard Micheal Ray Richardson was in Israel briefly before being exiled and winding up in a drug rehab center in Houston.
- Shooting guard Rick Carlisle was in a Boston Celtics uniform.
- Point guard Scott Brooks was at California–Irvine, finishing his senior season as the leading major college scorer on the entire West Coast.
- Guards Lowes Moore and Kenny Natt, forward Derrick Rowland, and center Greg Grissom were in Albany, compiling a mediocre 26–22 season, then losing to Musselman's Thrillers 4–0 in the Eastern Division finals.

The taste of defeat burned inside James J. Coyne, Patroons President and Founder. Not only had Albany been swept by the Thrillers, but the final two losses were agonizing decisions at home, 91–88 in overtime and 113–112 in a game televised nationally by ESPN. It was the third consecutive year Albany's season had been ended by Musselman on his way to three CBA championships.

With Musselman seeking an alternative to relocating in Rapid City, South Dakota, Coyne, who is also the Albany County Executive, reached a perfectly logical conclusion: hire Musselman.

Rowland, Albany's all-time leading scorer, said, "I was psyched, to tell you the truth. He had won the last three championships. It was just good to be on his side for a change."

For a while, anyway.

Rowland, more than any other member of the Patroons, bore the brunt of Musselman's intensity, which frequently raged out of control during games. Michael Brooks was another popular target of Musselman. So was Roth, whose lack of defensive ability tortured Musselman. "Hey, Roth, is there one guy in the CBA you can stop one time?" Musselman screamed at him during a home game. This is the same Scott Roth who was Eric Musselman's best friend in Cleveland. "He's two years older than me, and he used to come over to the house when we were in high school when I didn't have my driver's license," Eric said. "Every time we left the house to go somewhere, Dad would say to Scott, 'Drive carefully. Drive safely.'

"I think a lot of times, the guys that Dad verbally goes after are the guys he cares about the most. Even Scott Roth didn't understand it. Scott had grown up in our household, basically, and then all of a sudden in Albany, here's Bill Musselman, a guy that he kind of looked at as a second father, screaming and hollering at him. There was a point where Scott hardly even played. I flew into Mississippi on one trip. Scott said, 'God, am I glad you're here. Can you talk some sense into him and get me back in the lineup?' ''

Musselman was the magnet who drew the players to Albany to share six months of their lives. The players had written contracts to play for the Patroons for paltry salaries—the CBA's team salary cap of $80,000 during the 1987–88 season mandated weekly salaries of $400–$500. The NBA minimum was $4,000 a week.

There was also an unwritten contract each player had with Musselman. Play your heart out for him, win another CBA title, and help him get back to the NBA, and he'd break his back trying to get you there, too.

"He was pushing us past the limit, but he was pushing himself past the limit, too," Lowes Moore said. "Nobody makes you play. I wanted to prove to Coach Musselman there was nothing he could do— if he sat me on the bench or yelled at me in front of people—to keep me from being successful. When I went home, I felt good about myself. I know who I am. I won the battle."

The Patroon players knew that Musselman, more than any other coach in America, could get them into the NBA immediately. He had done it in Tampa Bay, sending 18 players up in three seasons while winning the CBA championship each time. And he'd do it in Albany, too.

But could he get himself back? He had to.

"A guy can sit back and say I want to coach at UCLA or an ACC school," Musselman said. "That's easy. To me, to coach somewhere just because it's got great prestige doesn't mean a damn thing. Never has. That's why coaching in the CBA never bothered me. I miss Albany. I miss the Tampa Bay Thrillers. I don't care what anybody said, I felt that I did the job in those places. I didn't feel inferior. I felt that I had a great job. I didn't need an NBA job for the prestige. I needed the job to say, 'Hey, I can coach there with those guys.' And I worked hard to get there, and I deserve to be there. It's a higher challenge. I'm not there for the ego thing.

"A lot of coaches, college and NBA coaches, and NBA players and media people . . . you don't know how many people since I've gotten the Timberwolves job have come up to me and made statements like 'God, you earned that job. You really paid your dues.' Some guys who think the CBA is really minor league, say, 'Gee, I can't believe how you went back down there in that league and worked your way up. I mean, you really sucked it up.'

"I think I gained a lot of people's respect. That's what is more important to me than anything—that they know I wasn't handed the Minnesota job. How could they have hired me if I'd flopped in the CBA? I don't care what I did and where I'd been. How can a guy win unless he's willing to pay the price? How can he go back to the CBA and lose players the first year, the second year, and the third, and still win unless he had tremendous drive and purpose? There's no way you can do that.

"My purpose and goal was to say, 'Hey, if this year isn't good enough for somebody and you don't think I've paid my dues, then fine, I'll go back and pay my dues again.' After the second year and the third year, I told Gerald Oliver, I says, 'You know what? I'll just keep winning forever in the CBA. I'll have 10 championship years if that's what it takes.' I mean, it's a league that's supposed to move up players, coaches, refs, trainers, everybody. If that's the case, how can you pass up a guy who's winning consistently?''

Season after season in the CBA, Eric Musselman saw his father's mounting frustration. The obsession. "As a coach I think the longer he was involved in the CBA, the more possessed he became," Eric said. "He said, 'If you're not at the top level, which is the NBA, you have to do something extraordinary to get up.' That's the attitude he took. No matter what, in his own mind he was going to end up back in the NBA.

"In my mind, to be honest, I never thought that he'd get back. After Cleveland, it was just terrible. And then, his first year in the CBA, he only lasted 19 games. I think there was a point where even he was wondering. But due to his competitiveness, nothing was ever going to get in his way."

Right from the first day of training camp, Musselman made that message perfectly clear. When he saw a play executed poorly, he let the world know about it. He harangued his players privately in practice and publicly in games.

Two years earlier, Musselman had unsuccessfully tried to trade for Rowland, who found it easier playing against Musselman than playing for him.

"I was on Derrick Rowland pretty hard," Musselman said after one home game. "Derrick's a great kid, and I know when I took the job he called me and said he wanted me to come to Albany. But I feel that there's certain things that will make the club better. Sometimes it looks like I may be embarrassing a player, but when you teach, you correct a mistake immediately.''

Mistakes never go over well in Camp Musselman.

''The verbal abuse was really frustrating,'' Rowland said. ''Early in the season, it affected my game. I had to make an adjustment and play through whenever he yelled at me. I was one of the guys he stayed on the most, but I'm proud of myself, that I was able to go through it. He's a hard, hard, hard coach because his expectations are high. But it was worth it. It was an incredible season.''

The Patroons' 1987–88 season produced the highest winning percentage (.889) in the modern-day history of professional basketball. Musselman molded a team in his own image, one exuding his personality and radiating his intensity. It was the ultimate CBA/Musselman team, one that crushed weaker opponents and outlasted stronger ones. One that went 48–6.

Simply, Albany became a team that never stopped believing it would win every game it played. ''It was just incredible,'' Sidney Lowe said. ''You could see it, and I've been on a few championship teams. We thought we could not lose.''

Musselman thought they would never lose. Literally.

''When he took the job, once things got going, he talked about 54–0,'' Eric Musselman said. ''I thought the guy was crazy.''

A majority opinion:

- Rowland: ''He said he could take the team to 54–0. And he was serious about it. He thought that he could win 54 of 54 games.''
- Moore: ''He said we're planning on going 54–0. Everybody's saying, ''Oh, this guy's had too much to drink.''
- Lowe: ''He really wanted that 54–0. For a while I thought he was kidding around, but then I realized he wasn't.''

The day after the Patroons won the 1987–88 championship, they flew to Puerto Rico and played three exhibition games against the Puerto Rican National Team. It was a semi-working vacation arranged by Ben Fernandez, a businessman who had purchased the Patroon franchise a month earlier. ''Down in Puerto Rico, Micheal Ray Richardson and all the guys were in the back of our bus laughing,'' Musselman said. ''And they said, 'Come on back here, Coach.' And they were telling stories about the whole year. They said, 'You know when you said we were going to go 54–0, we thought you were crazy. We were laughing. Now we look back and think of the six losses. We think we could've won them.'

"Now there's psychology," Musselman continued. "They didn't think they could go 54-0 because nobody ever heard of it. The season's over; they look back and say, 'We could've won those six games.'

"And they probably could have. It's hard for some people to really cope with perfection. I believe every game, regardless of who you play, regardless of the time of the game, and regardless of the score, you ask your players to execute every time up and down the floor. Not many coaches do that."

Not many have the good sense to repeat one successful play time after time until the opponent stops it. "I make 'em stop it," Musselman said. "If they don't stop a guy, why quit going to him? Why go away from him? I think you go to your strengths to cover up your weaknesses. Until they find a way to stop somebody, keep going to him."

Ram it down their throats. Play to your strengths, exploit your opponent's weaknesses. "He has a very good knack of taking the best offensive skills of a player and designing plays to maximize strengths and minimize weaknesses," said Steve Hayes, Musselman's MVP in Tampa Bay.

It's a successful strategy only if the coach has a thorough knowledge of personnel, both his and his opponent's. This isn't incidental knowledge a coach happens upon. It's the result of hours and hours of hard work. Is there a pro basketball coach who works harder than Musselman? Maybe in the NBA. Maybe not. Certainly not in the CBA.

Musselman's Patroons played the Mississippi Jets in Biloxi, Mississippi, February 5 and 6, 1988. Eric Musselman was there for both games. The Patroons won the first one 117-110 in overtime.

Late that night, Eric made the mistake of trying to sleep. "We were in the hotel room, and the lights were off," he said. "We had been talking, and then we just stopped. I was still awake, but I was on the verge of falling asleep. I figured that he was totally asleep. What happened was he got up, turned the light on, and just started writing down a play on the sports pages. I got up and said: 'What the hell are you doing?'

"And he said, 'Hey, I got this play that I know Tony Campbell, if we put him in and give him the ball five straight times, he will score five times in a row. This thing's going to help us win the ball game tomorrow night.'

"I ended up getting over on his bed and watching him diagram the thing," Eric said. "He went over it two or three times. And the next day at practice, he put it in during the walk-through shoot-around. The thing worked to perfection."

Campbell had scored four points in 25 minutes in the first game. In the second, he scored 33 as Albany again won in OT, 126–124.

"Tony had a quick first step, and he could muscle his way in the lane," Musselman explained. "So I wanted to get him the ball off different picks and within 12 to 14 feet from the basket. I liked Tony setting picks in the lane, making them send his defender past him on a switch. That'd open Tony up inside the lane, where he was so strong. I just wanted to utilize his strength."

Two weeks before, Campbell had an incredible four-game stretch, making 8 of 10, 13 of 15, 14 of 15, and 9 of 12 from the floor. He was 24 of 26 from the line, too, averaging 28.3 points in four home wins.

Musselman's Mississippi maneuver was just another new wrinkle, one he conceived in the middle of the night. "I think best then," Musselman said. "I can put everything aside. My only peace of mind is late at night. That's when I like to make phone calls. I don't care what hour it is."

Musselman's players, friends, and family will attest to that. "I was with him at Topeka one night," Eric said. "It was in the middle of the night, and he puts the lights on."

Eric grabbed his pillow and walked to the door. "Hey, what's the matter with you?" his father asked.

"I'm going to Scott Roth's room to get some sleep. I can't stay with you. You're nocturnal."

Musselman signed with the Patroons June 19, 1987, after turning down a contract from Rockford worth $25,000 more in perks than his $50,000 Patroons salary. "I felt this was the best place to win with the media coverage, knowledgeable fans, and because it's a tough place to play," he explained.

In Albany, he took a small apartment at Woodlake, a yuppie complex three miles from the Armory. Insurance man Jim Laverty, one of 34 members of the unsalaried Patroons Board of Directors, volunteered his services to Musselman and wound up a go-fer, a confidant, and a close friend.

There was little in Musselman's apartment. A bookcase had a single tenant: *The Art of War*. "The premise of the whole book is that the battle is won before it's fought," Laverty said. "I think that's the way he led his whole life. He was so prepared in basketball. He knew how to win the game before the whistle was even blown."

Laverty, as many before him, discovered Musselman's schizophrenic nature: "On the court, he was very serious. Off the court, he was just the opposite. He'd turn the game face off, and he'd be a normal person. He was a funny, very humorous guy. He liked to go out and have a good time as much as anybody, though he never drank. And he was a very caring guy. Despite what you saw on the court, he was concerned about his players. Off the court, he really worried about these kids and how he could get them to the NBA and what he could do to get him there. He knew the players' weaknesses, and he tried to perfect their defense."

When he wasn't on the court for two-a-day practices, Musselman was in the hallway at the Armory, using the building's only pay phone. He called other coaches. He called players. He called agents. And all of them called him, looking for deals or roster spots. Musselman rarely visited the Patroons' office just five blocks away. In fact, he made it the entire season without a key to the office. Musselman either worked at home or put a folding chair next to the pay phone in the Armory and began making his daily quota of dozens of phone calls.

Coyne had the good sense to let Musselman operate on his own. "Jim Coyne treated me with dignity as a coach," Musselman said. "He wouldn't bother me before a game or anytime. He gave me the space to coach. When anybody does that, I can do a good job."

When Musselman broke for lunch, he'd walk half a block from the Armory to Lawren's Deli. He'd ask what the daily special was, and regardless of the response, order meatloaf with at least two glasses of orange or tomato juice.

After a shoot-around one game day during the season, Musselman went to Lawren's with Tim Wilkin, who covered the Patroons for the *Times Union*. "There was some guy in there who looked like he was down on his luck," Wilkin said. "He was dressed really shabbily with a scruffy beard. He recognized Musselman and said:

'Oh yeah, Big Ten.'

'Where'd you go to school?'

'Northwestern.'

'You ever been to a Patroons game?'

'No, I can't afford to go.'

'What's your name?'

'Phil.'

'You come to the game tonight. I'll leave you a ticket.' ''

Musselman did. Phil showed.

Unlike his on-court persona, Musselman is congenial, frequently displaying warmth and self-deprecating humor. He literally created a Patroons fan every time he spoke to a person on the street, and he rarely ignored a comment by a stranger.

He never ignored a good-looking woman, either. If one passed remotely in Musselman's direction, he'd approach her with a question, usually, ''Do you ever go to Patroons games?'' Frequently, their chance encounter ended with Musselman saying, ''I hope you don't mind me saying this, but you're a very attractive lady.''

When he went out, his standards were less stringent. Any female who didn't look like a bulldog and had no male escort was fair game.

His favorite stomping ground in Albany was the Parc V, where he would earn the sobriquet ''Parc Five Willy.'' A five-minute drive from Woodlake, the Parc V had ferns, hanging plants, potato skins, and other trendy appetizers. And a lot of attractive women on a weekend night.

Keith Marder, a sportswriter for the *Times Union*, recounted one of Musselman's frequent visits: ''He was there with Eric and a cousin that came to one of the Patroons games. They're just checking out women on the dance floor. Musselman's going, 'Look at that girl; she's a wild dancer.' And he's just ranting and raving, 'Just look at that guy, he needs intensity.' He's yelling about people on the dance floor. And all of a sudden, he sat down with these women that me and Timmy Wilkin had met earlier. One of the girls was getting married, and we were taking pictures of all of them.

''He sits down at our table. He never really knows who I am. He never knows me. But he sits. He sees me sitting with six women, and he just stops dead in his tracks and goes:

'You know these girls?'

'Nah. I don't.'

'What are you girls doing? Where are you from? You from Albany?'

'Clifton Park. You from Albany?'

'Ahhhh, Pensacola...I'm head coach of the Albany Patroons.'

'I got a friend. She lives and dies for the Albany Patroons.'

'What's her name?'

'Anna.'

'I don't know her.' "

"When the prettiest girl got up to leave, Musselman asked, 'Where's she from?'

'Charleston, West Virginia.'

'I knew I knew her.'

Musselman goes over to this girl. She was talking to a guy. He asks, 'You ever been to a Charleston Gunners' game?'

'No.'

'I used to coach the Gunners.' "

No, Musselman hadn't ever coached the Charleston Gunners. But how could she have known? For one fleeting moment in the Parc V, Musselman switched jobs with Charleston Coach Gerald Oliver; for one second he was coaching the last-place Gunners instead of his first-place Patroons.

There were lots of other women to peruse in the Parc V. Musselman retreated into the noisy background and started looking again.

On the court, he expected each player to learn every one of his 120 plays. Before games, he'd put roughly a third of them on the chalkboard in the tiny locker room in the basement of the Armory. Being in a pregame Musselman locker room is an experience in itself: his intensity grows with each play he puts on the board.

"It's definitely a shock for new players," Lowe said. "He tells us what we're going to run, maybe 35 to 40 plays for a particular game. He'll write 'em all down, and then he'll read 'em off just as fast as he can: 50 Down, 50 Up, 51, 52, 53, 54. Just like that. We're looking and paying attention, and that's it. And we go to play."

And they play just one way. "Winning comes from the top," Michael Brooks said. "Coach Musselman doesn't like to lose. He only knows how to coach one way, and that's hard. When he's not coaching, he's a hell of a guy."

When he is coaching, Musselman himself says, "It's just like I'm in another world."

The players who sought entry to that world convened at Patroons training camp headquarters, a meeting room at the Howard Johnson's Motor Lodge on November 5, 1987.

Musselman seemed surprisingly serene as he gazed at the prospective Patroons. Next morning was the first practice, and several key players hadn't yet arrived. Lowe came the next day, Michael

Brooks the day after that. Grissom made it to the meeting, but was late. Campbell and Tod Murphy would join the team in midseason.

Musselman's captive audience at the first meeting was an interesting mix of players: Patroons veterans Moore, Rowland, and Natt; rookie Scott Brooks; newcomer Scott Roth; and a bevy of young hopefuls.

Musselman coddled the veteran Patroons and spoke glowingly of how well they had played against his teams in the past, and how they could make it to the NBA with the right amount of work: "Derrick Rowland...I tried trading for you two years ago. I thought you were the second-best player in the league. I almost traded three players for you. But last year, you were soft on defense. We're going to get you back to the level you were at two years ago. Kenny Natt...we're going to improve you defense. Lowes Moore...you're not too old to get back to the NBA (he was 30). Greg Grissom...you've got pro potential. Hey, we're counting on veterans like you four."

A month later, he started counting them out. Musselman dealt Natt to Wyoming, used Moore infrequently, permanently rooted the overweight Grissom to the bench, and hounded Rowland into nearly breaking. Musselman began talking contemptuously of the "old Patroons" who had accepted losing the previous season. He'd make them winners his way or follow through on increasingly frequent threats to "trade their asses" out of Albany.

"It was probably the hardest year I've ever had in my life, as far as basketball goes," Grissom said. "The worst was the 11th or 12th game. I'd been in the game, and I'd made one mistake. I made a foul and he took me out. Then about five minutes later, he walks down to the end of the bench and just yells at me, 'You're out of here. You're, you're not only...you're gonna be gone from the team tomorrow!'

"When a coach does that during the middle of a game, and he just turns around and gets right back to coaching...he had no rhyme or reason for doing that. That was probably as low as it got. But, of course, during the course of the year, he did that about 10 times. After about the third one, I kind of knew he wasn't going to do it."

Such stormy developments couldn't be forecast from Musselman's first-night platitudes about those same players. Musselman, however, was perfectly blunt as he began an unending monologue about CBA players.

"Hey, listen, you know..."

Musselman began droning. A litany of stories about CBA players followed. Moore, Natt, and Rowland were familiar with the names. Roth, Scott Brooks, and the other rookies didn't have a clue. It didn't matter to Musselman. That was an inherent advantage of being the only counselor in Camp Musselman.

Anyway, most of Musselman's CBA stories had a happy ending, with a former player getting the call to the NBA.

The CBA had changed dramatically during Musselman's reign. Players were called up routinely. As Musselman addressed his troops that night, 39 former CBA players were in the NBA, 18 sent up by Musselman himself. More would follow. And who better to lead them to the promised land?

Musselman laid out the team rules succinctly: no curfews, no problems. "I'll treat you like men," he said. "If you're out drinking or partying all night, I'll know. I'll know the next day in practice."

The message was implicit: don't screw up. "I don't care about a player's past," Musselman said many times. So he invited any player he thought was useful, including ex-Knicks forward Sly Williams and NBA drug abusers Richardson and Mitchell Wiggins.

Williams never came. The former New York Knick spoke twice with Patroons General Manager Gary Holle about coming to camp. Twice, Holle made plane reservations for Williams to fly to Albany from New Orleans. The second time, Holle spoke with Williams on the phone 90 minutes before his scheduled departure.

"You're sure you really want to come to camp?" Holle asked.

Williams said he was sure. He said to ignore his first missed flight because he had to take care of some important personal business. This time, Williams told Holle, he'll be there.

When the flight from New Orleans arrived in Albany that evening, Williams wasn't aboard.

"Screw him," Musselman said the next day.

The case of Wiggins was much more complicated. Wiggins and former Houston Rockets teammate Lewis Lloyd were banned by the NBA January 13, 1987, for drug abuse. Wiggins wound up playing briefly in the CBA in the winter of '88 for Mississippi. He averaged 21 points in six regular-season games and 18 points in the first round of the playoffs, when Albany eliminated the Jets in a four-game sweep.

Albany traded three players to Mississippi to get the rights to Wiggins, a player who was certainly capable of dominating CBA competition. He had done so in college, after he transferred from Truett-McConnell College in Cleveland, Georgia, where he didn't play; to

Clemson, where he averaged just 5.5 points playing behind Larry Nance and Horace Wyatt; to Florida State, where he averaged 23.2 points in two seasons.

A first-round draft pick by Indiana in 1983, Wiggins was traded to Chicago for the draft rights to Sidney Lowe. Wiggins averaged 12.4 points for the Bulls in one season before they traded him to Houston. There he averaged 9.9, 6.8, and 11.1 points in 2½ seasons before being booted out of the league under the NBA's Anti-Drug Program.

Wiggins applied for admission to the CBA and was allowed to play after interviewing with CBA Commissioner Carl Scheer. Wiggins told Musselman he'd drive from Tallahassee, Florida, to Albany.

That was the last Musselman heard from him as the first week of training camp came to an end. Then a positively bizarre story appeared in the Albany paper, the *Times Union*, Friday, November 13.

Under a headline "Wiggins in, but doesn't call Patroons," Patroons beat writer Tim Wilkin reported that the receptionist at Howard Johnson's said Wiggins had registered November 11. Wilkin's story also said Wiggins had been seen by at least one other player. "I saw him in the hallway after the morning practice and said, 'Hi,' but that was it," Michael Brooks said. "It was definitely him."

Musselman fired this memorable salvo when asked by Wilkin if Wiggins had showed up at practice: "I don't know where he is. I haven't seen him. If it took him five days to drive to Albany, how can you expect him to find the Armory?"

Ten days later, after Albany had won its first two games on the road and was preparing for its home opener, Wiggins arrived in Albany again, citing personal problems in Champaign, Illinois, where his wife lived. Wiggins said it was his fault for not contacting the Patroons, but that "family comes first."

Not quite. Musselman had already traded him to Quad City (Illinois) for 6–8 center Kèn Johnson. "This is the strangest situation I have ever had to deal with," Musselman said. "What did he think, I would just put him on the club without any training camp, without any practice? I understand he had some problems."

They weren't over. Wiggins flunked a drug test in Quad City and was kicked out of the CBA. The season went on without him.

————————●

Training camp in the CBA was limited to two weeks, precious little time to construct a team. Musselman and other CBA coaches had to work around the continually changing status of fringe NBA players.

Each CBA club was affiliated with two NBA teams and would inherit those teams' cuts, provided another CBA squad didn't have previous rights. Albany's NBA affiliates were the Knicks and Boston. When the Celtics jettisoned Carlisle, Musselman was ready. He had already talked to Carlisle that summer about coming to Albany if he didn't stick with the Celtics.

"I said, 'Rick, I'm Bill Musselman. If you get cut—now I don't think you should get cut because I think you're good enough to play somewhere in the NBA—but you know it's a numbers game. And if you get cut, I want you to know that I want you to come in right away, so you stay in shape. Don't break stride. Don't lose any conditioning. Pick it up right where you are.

'And I say if you come and play for us, we're going to win. And when we win, we're going to dominate. And you're going to be playing and moving right back up. You're not going to be with me very long anyhow. But I'd like to coach you for a short period of time. I mean I'll guarantee if you come, I'll do everything I can to get you back 'cause I think you should be in the NBA. If I don't think that, I wouldn't be talking to you. I only talk to guys who should be in the NBA.'

"And he looked at me and says, 'Here's my phone number. Call me if I get cut.'

"He got cut. I called him: 'Rick, are you ready?'

"Do you realize how many hours away from coaching you have to spend to do that? That's what I mean, when guys are cut, they're ready. When Carlisle got cut, I didn't wait and say, 'Hey, hey, hey, come on,' then sell the CBA. I already sold the CBA. I already sold him. They're cut; they're ready to come in. I couldn't wait two weeks, three weeks for Carlisle to decide. He already knew where he was going."

When Carlisle showed after being cut by Boston, he ran the gamut of Musselman's opinions. After a particularly dreadful first day in camp, the coach said, "I can't believe how bad he is."

Carlisle quickly learned of Musselman's disapproval: "It was like the third day I was there. What happened was I went in for a straight layup, and instead of just laying it in, I tried to go up and fake and make a reverse layup. I missed it, and he said, 'Come on. Make the damn layup.' I said. 'Oh, sure.'

"The next time I get the ball, I kind of lollygagged it. I was supposed to cut the middle, turn, and pass. I kind of tried to catch the ball and fling it backwards over my head in one motion, and he said, 'Jesus fucking Christ. What the fuck do you think this is? This isn't Boston. You don't have Larry Bird to bail you out anymore. When we go over something, dammit, you execute it.' From that point on, I was kind of tuned in to what he was trying to do. I've never had a coach like that, and probably never will unless I play for him again.''

Carlisle quickly improved in camp, and Musselman had a shooting guard.

But there were lots of guards in camp and too few spots available on a 10-man roster. Lowe was certainly going to be the point guard, but Moore, Natt, Scott Brooks, and rookie Rod Martin were all playing well. And Richardson would arrive the final day of camp.

Up front, Musselman was clearly delighted with Roth. Musselman felt he was versatile enough to play four positions: center, both forward spots, and, if necessary, off guard.

Michael Brooks arrived for the second day of camp after flying all night on the red-eye from San Diego, where he played $3^1/2$ years with the Clippers before a knee injury changed his life. Understandably, Brooks was a tad sluggish his first afternoon in Albany. Musselman, of course, was all over him. Brooks apologized for his poor practice, told Musselman he'd be better the next day, and eventually fashioned a much-deserved MVP season.

Musselman loved his work ethic. Brooks treated each practice as if it was Game 7 of the NBA Finals. Still, Musselman rode him, especially for the unlikeliest of reasons, over-passing. Brooks was such an unselfish player that he gave the ball up on breaks. Too many times, Musselman thought. Too many times, Musselman reasoned, Brooks should have finished the play himself.

One of Musselman's favorite preseason drills was one-on-one full court with no out-of-bounds and no fouls called. "He loved to see guys diving around," Wilkin said. "You could almost see that little smirk come up when somebody even came close to drawing blood."

Early in training camp, it became apparent that the players with a lock on making the 10-man roster were Lowe, Rowland, Michael Brooks, Roth. and Carlisle. The status of other players in camp fluctuated as Musselman waited to see if four players Albany held the rights to would stick in the NBA: John Stroeder (Milwaukee), Milt Wagner (Lakers), Tod Murphy (Clippers), and David Henderson (Washington). Each of the four teetered on the bubble. They'd either be the last to make their NBA team's 12-man roster or the final cut.

While he waited, Musselman complicated his situation by adding Ozell Jones, a 7-footer, to the mix. Albany got him from Quad City for a player to be named.

Jones' first practice with the team, just six days before the season opener, began with Musselman extolling Jones' virtues in front of the entire team: "Ozell Jones, you're going to be a star in this league. You're going to dominate in the CBA. You're going to go to the NBA. I wish I was your agent."

Travel agent, maybe. Musselman cut him before the opener when one of the old Patroons, Grissom, thoroughly outplayed Jones in full-court scrimmages.

Richardson received clearance from CBA Commissioner Mike Storen and rolled into Camp Musselman November 16. Final cuts were due by 5 p.m. that day, and Richardson's presence increased the Albany roster to 13, three over the limit. If Richardson, a four-time NBA All-Star who had been banned by the NBA for two years for repeated drug use, didn't make a quick impression, he'd be gone. "Okay, Micheal Ray, you got 20 minutes to show me you can play basketball or you're out of here," Musselman said.

In those 20 minutes, Sugar shined. Musselman was impressed, but there was another hurdle Richardson had to clear before joining the Patroons. Richardson's agent, Eileen Murdinger, told him he could make $900 a week in the CBA. The Patroons, however, couldn't pay him more than $500 a week because of the team salary cap of $80,000.

Richardson huddled with Musselman. Musselman told him what his salary would be. Richardson told Musselman he had offers from other CBA teams. "I tested Micheal Ray the first day," Musselman said. "In our league, we don't pay that much. He said he was going to go somewhere else to play unless we gave him more money. Well, if that money meant more than the things he told me, I didn't want him around. He was shocked when I said, 'Go ahead, go,' because he knew he had a great practice. He went on the phone with his agent. He said, 'I'm staying here. This is where I want to play. Forget about asking for more money.' "

Conceding Richardson a roster spot on the last day of camp made Musselman's decision on final cuts more difficult. At 4 p.m. he still hadn't made up his mind. As the 5 p.m. deadline neared, Musselman commandeered his two trusted players from the Thrillers, Lowe and Michael Brooks, and placed them in one office in the Armory. Gary Holle waited in another. Musselman paced back and forth between the two offices, repeating "This is an important decision." At 5:30, Musselman called Storen's office in Denver. Arguing that Richardson's arrival had required Storen's dispensation and that Richardson hadn't arrived until that afternoon, Musselman asked for and received a one-day extension for one roster spot.

Musselman had two more to take care of, immediately. He continued pacing, intermittently talking to Lowe and Brooks. "I asked their opinion because they're pros," Musselman said. "A lot of times, guys don't want to play with certain guys. Wantin' to play with your teammates is very important. And I always ask my point guard's opinion—or any veteran I respect."

Did Musselman pay attention to what he heard? "We really didn't talk about much," Lowe said. "I think his way of dealing with it was to go in there and talk to us and try to clear his mind. I think that shows some of the sensitivity of Coach. He doesn't want to get rid of guys. He likes all the guys, and he thought he wanted to keep them all. What eventually happened was he was trying to find positions on other teams for the guys he was going to release. That's pretty rare. You don't find too many coaches that are going to release a guy and at the same time try to find somewhere for him to go before he released him. He did that with Ozell Jones."

Ten minutes before 7 p.m., nearly three hours after practice ended, Musselman cut rookies Mark Ridlen and Percy Eddie. The following day he waived Jones, who wound up playing all 54 games of the season with the Quad City Thunder. "Believe me, I've never seen a guy so happy to be cut," Carlisle said. "Usually somebody gets cut and they're kind of embarrassed. Ozell was going around slapping hands with everybody. He knew he didn't want any part of playing for Bill."

Stroeder earned a roster spot with the Bucks. Murphy played one game with the Clippers, was waived, and then was sidelined for several weeks by mono. Wagner made the Lakers. Henderson was cut by Washington but didn't contact Musselman immediately.

Richardson and Musselman would have a volatile year together in Albany, but Richardson remained drug free. He was randomly tested two times a week, and visited an Albany halfway house to speak with teenagers about the misuse of drugs, specifically cocaine. Richardson appreciated Musselman giving him the opportunity to play in the CBA, yet their frequent verbal battles took a toll. All season long, Richardson told his teammates what he'd say to Musselman when the season was over: "Bill, thank you and fuck you."

Richardson and Musselman also shared some light moments. On the road in an airport one morning on a typically endless day of travel, Richardson performed. "When Coach Musselman's at a game, everybody'd say, 'This man's nuts. This guy's crazy,' " Lowes Moore said. "And then, when he's in the airport, he's just like the nicest guy in the world. He's sitting there like he's all drained out because he coached his whole heart out the night before. He probably stayed up all night on the phone trying to figure out if he can make another trade, if he can get rid of somebody or bring somebody in. He's sitting there, and Micheal Ray starts imitating what he says about us during the game. Everybody joined in:

'Lowes, you're too slow.'

'Micheal Ray, you're terrible. Get out of here.'

'Scott Brooks, will you play some fuckin' defense?'

'Rowland, that's your man.'

'I'm going to trade you. You're out of here.' "

Moore described Musselman's reaction: "He just cracks up. He said, 'Naw, that ain't me.' Micheal Ray said, 'Coach, don't fool yourself.' "

Musselman's opening night roster at Savannah was: Natt, Moore, Richardson, Scott Brooks, Michael Brooks, Rowland, Carlisle, Roth, Lowe, and Grissom.

Albany took the opener 118–94, and the next night won in Charleston 117–109. The Patroons kept winning. The home opener was a 119–97 rout of Pensacola. Before the game began, Moore and Natt offered a prayer for Marquese Koonce, a 9-year-old Patroons fan who drowned the previous summer. "How will a 9-year-old boy be missed?" Moore asked the SRO crowd of 3,518 at the Armory. "Wherever we heard the laughter of a child. Any time his smile would brighten your day. We're all a bit sadder with him not here to root for his favorite team." Natt dedicated his season to Koonce.

Game by game, the Patroons began dominating: Lowe running the team, Michael Brooks powering his way inside, Rowland, Carlisle, and the versatile Roth backed up by Moore, Scott Brooks, Natt, and Richardson. After the Patroons reached 6–0 with a 119–108 win at Topeka, the Knicks took Carlisle. He made a quick impact, scoring an NBA career-high 21 points in a loss to Seattle.

Without Carlisle, the Patroons kept winning. Mississippi gave Albany its closest game to date, but the Patroons prevailed in Biloxi 97–94 to reach 7–0. On deck was a four-game home stand that Albany could use to surpass Musselman's own CBA record for the best start, 9–0 with the Thrillers.

Albany moved to 11–0 with easy wins over Charleston, Mississippi (twice) and Rochester (Minnesota). Roth provided two monster games, making a CBA-record 18 straight free throws and 20 of 21 overall for 42 points in the first game versus Mississippi. Against Rochester, he scored 30 and hit 13 of 14 at the line.

Eight of the Patroons' next nine games were on the road. Back in Biloxi December 8, Albany took a 67–66 lead into the fourth quarter. But Mississippi rallied behind guard Ricky Wilson's 26 points for a 91–85 win. The streak was over, and Musselman exploded.

"After the game, I walk in the locker room and say, 'How in the hell could you guys do this to yourself?' " Musselman said. " 'I can't believe it. Shit, you just blew a chance to go 54 and 0.' I mean, I was screaming and raving."

Said Lowe: "I think that was the most I've ever seen him upset. He went absolutely berserk. We weren't sure how to take it. I guess we thought to ourselves, We just lost one game. We were disappointed, definitely, but at that time, I don't think all the guys thought we should be reprimanded the way we were. I think he was just really letting off steam, getting the frustration out. He really wanted 54 and 0. I thought he was kidding around, but then I realized he wasn't."

Musselman's histrionics didn't seem to help his team. In Pensacola two nights later, Albany lost again, 102–95 to a team coached by Gary Youmans, Musselman's former Ashland player and Thrillers GM.

Youmans' team handed Albany three of its six defeats in 1987–88. Naturally, Musselman didn't take any of the losses well.

Youmans first coached against Musselman December 26, 1986, when Pensacola hosted the Thrillers in a game televised by ESPN. "That was crazy," Youmans said. "I'm thinking, Holy shit, I'm going against my mentor. He's probably going to kick my ass, plus it's going to be on national TV. But we just played out of our gourd, and they played horrible. We just, we crushed 'em (109–94).

"He didn't talk after the game. I never saw him. But he was furious. He came back and pounded us after that. It was funny 'cause the first year, we had traded and I picked up Eric Laird. We played him like three days later in Tampa, and we beat Muss by 10 and Laird had 26 points. He called me up and he reamed me. He really gave me hell. He says, 'Damn you, you take that player from me. You hustle that player out of me. I'm telling you right now, I'm going to kick your ass.' I mean, he was madder than a hornet. Then he hung up the phone.

"He came up to Pensacola three days after we had beaten him. He called me up again and gave me all this shit. I was trying to be nice, saying, 'Oh, I've been loyal to you,' and all this. That night we walk on the floor for the national anthem and I turned to look at the flag and I looked at him and I could read his lips. He's going, 'Fuck you.' Like that. I'm easy-going but when I blow, I blow. So I grabbed my nuts like, 'Screw you.'

"We beat him again (100–96), and he was just nuts. But we didn't beat him after that. Then we went into the playoffs that year and that's when we had all the trouble. Dale Blaney got his jaw smashed by one of my players and there was a big fight with Laird and Clint Wheeler. Muss and I took off on each other in the papers. We didn't talk and we never shook hands or nothing that whole series. I saw him that summer and I didn't say nothing. He came over. He was standing like four feet away from me, and he says, 'Gary,' in that low voice of his. I say, 'Hey, Coach, how are you doing?' Like that. So we got talking. That was like a make-up deal."

In 1987–88, Youmans bested Musselman in the first of their six meetings. "He came running down after the game and I go, 'Holy shit. Here we go again,' " Youmans said. "He goes running by. He says, 'Nice game,' and he takes off after the referee. The whole year, no matter if we won or lost, he would talk to me. After the third loss, he said, 'It looks bad when you beat me and you don't beat these other teams. That's not good for your reputation. I can accept losing to you, but dammit, you beat me and then you go lose to Savannah. That looks terrible.' "

A year later, Musselman was still fuming about the Pensacola losses. He was still mad at Youmans: "Anybody can get a team ready to play the Lakers. Getting 'em ready to play somebody who's not winning, that takes effort and work. That's what I told Youmans: 'Why do you get beat by Savannah twice in a row after beating us?' " (After beating Albany 102–95 December 10, Pensacola lost at Savannah on successive nights by 16 and 6).

"Gary just looked at me, sayin', 'I'm trying, Coach. I'm trying.'

"I said, 'No you aren't. You beat us; you think it's great. I don't care if you beat me, you're a former player. I get irritated 'cause you beat me and turn around and lost to Savannah twice in a row. In fact, it nauseates me, because you're resting on beating me. You should be embarrassed to get beat by a team like Savannah. Now we'll see if you can coach. We'll see if you can motivate 'em, if you can drive your guys. Let's see if you make 'em hungry after patting them on the back for beating us in a big game. That's coaching.' ''

Physically, Musselman was in a hotel room in New York City 15 months after Youmans' transgressions against Albany and Savannah. Mentally, he was talking directly to Youmans rather than a visitor to his room. The anger was still in Musselman's voice. The emotion. The feeling of frustration. And Youmans didn't even have top billing. That spot was clearly held by Charley Rosen, Phil Jackson's former assistant at Albany. Rosen's Rockford Lightning had the audacity to score the final eight points of the game to inflict Albany's only home loss in 27 regular-season games, 108–107 on January 30. Unbelievably, the night before, Rockford had lost at La Crosse 139–90.

Losing has never agreed with Musselman. Losing a home game by one point to a team which lost by 49 the night before galled Musselman, and he said so to reporters after the game. He accused Rosen of pointing to the game in Albany and not trying to win the night before in La Crosse. That a team would naturally point 'to Albany, a team destined to be the greatest in CBA history, was a school of thought Musselman never attended. Alone after the press had left that Saturday evening, Musselman tried dealing with the defeat.

"He'd take losses very hard," Laverty said. "It usually took him two to three hours to settle down after a loss. It wasn't uncommon for him after a loss to drive to Lake George and back, taking two or three hours, just thinking about the game and how he could've done things differently. He blamed himself for many of the losses that he had."

During games at the Armory, Musselman was frequently a bubbling volcano ready to erupt. He perceived anyone, be it his players, opposing players, or referees, as being in his way, interfering with his team performing to his rigorous standards. The Armory was a perfect setting for him.

In the 1950s through the early '70s, the Armory was the home court for Siena College. Dormant for years after Siena opened an on-campus arena in 1974, the Armory was refurbished when Coyne organized a group of local businessmen to purchase a CBA franchise in 1982. Operating as a not-for-profit organization, the franchise chose a nickname to reflect the Dutch heritage of New York State's capital city, 150 miles up the Hudson River from New York City. Patroons were early Dutch landowners.

The 100-year-old Armory, a cavernous dungeon with a Gothic facade and iron-barred windows, was bereft of typical amenities a pro basketball player might expect. Basement locker rooms were the size of a closet. A large, public bathroom downstairs doubled as a shower room for both teams.

"The Armory's got this certain mystique," Eric Musselman said. "I think that my Dad. . .he used that. You know, a shitty locker room and that type of situation. He used to make the guys think that it was the Albany Patroons against the world. Even a home game, it was Hey, we are against everybody. We're against all odds. Nothing's going our way. We don't have a new arena.' Derrick Rowland's hanging his stuff up on a hanger from a pipe. In a way, he loved that arena no matter what he says. That's like a perfect home for him.''

Musselman stalked the boundary of his home, the sideline, as a crazed tiger, his eyes locked in an icy, frightening glare. As a Patroons' home game proceeded, Musselman slowly worked his way further and further up the sideline away from the bench.

Inevitably, he'd see a play develop that he didn't like, or an opponent scoring or getting a rebound way too easily. He'd scream at the culprit, then wheel halfway around facing the working press, his fist cocked in anger ready to slam something, anything on the press table. Veteran sportswriters learned quickly to keep cups of soda out of Musselman's range of rage. A sea of arms withdrew the cups or took them off the table before Musselman invariably found something to slam: the press table, a reporter's briefcase, a radio man's amplifier, even a box of Freihofer's chocolate chip cookies that had unwisely been left on the table. Patroons radio play-by-play man Joe Hennessy made a habit of bringing a bowl of M & M's and leaving them on the press table where players, other members of the press, and Musselman could grab a handful while they lasted. Usually when he raided the bowl, Musselman would swipe a few in a quick motion. Enraged one night, he swiped a handful so hard the M & M's flew into the stands 10 feet behind press row.

There were much more dangerous Musselman moments in the Armory. One game, he punched out Hennessy's amplifier. Three other times, he nearly got into fights with opposing players when his constant woofing hit a raw nerve. Andre Patterson and Tony Karasek of Charleston and Walker D. Russell of Savannah all had to be restrained by teammates after Musselman taunts. Each time, Musselman stepped closer to that opposing player as if he'd like nothing better than to mix it up with an athlete twice his size. Musselman told Patterson, "Fuck you Andre." He said to Karasek, "Eat me." With Russell, Richardson urged Musselman into combat, yelling, "Go on. Go kick his ass." Intervention by other players prevented the confrontation.

Musselman didn't confine his raving to opposing players. He literally picked Scott Brooks off the bench at one home game and threw him onto the court as a substitution.

As a member of the team's board of directors, Ken Lyons frequently helped out during Musselman's reign. The 6–4 Lyons was asked to pick up Brooks when he flew into Albany in preseason. "When Scotty arrived, I think he saw me looking at him a little funny since he looked to be about 5–10 and had just come in off the beach," Lyons related. "He said, 'Don't let my looks fool you. I'm as tough as nails.' "

Playing for Musselman, he had to be. "I think my Dad sees a lot of himself in Scotty Brooks," Eric Musselman said. "He was very hard on Scotty verbally. One night when I was talking to Scott Roth, he said that I'd better talk to Scotty Brooks. Scotty was in tears because Dad had really verbally attacked him after the game."

Musselman wasn't adverse to verbally attacking referees. He got 17 technical fouls in the regular season, though he was thrown out of just one game. He did it with gusto, screaming "Fuck you, asshole" at the official as Patroons Manager Rich Sill escorted him off the court. As he exited, Musselman kept turning his head back to scream more obscenities.

Thirty-two games into the season, Albany was 30–2. Including the Thrillers' regular season and playoffs the prior year, Musselman had won 49 of his last 53 games. Yet there was no peace of mind for the Patroons and their coach.

Carlisle, called up to the Knicks, was the first to leave. Musselman filled the roster spot with 6–8 Ken Johnson, who had played 64 games with Portland in 1985–86. Johnson reported woefully out of shape. After his first Patroons practice, Musselman shouted, "We'll get you in shape."

He told Grissom to work with Johnson on a drill that Musselman timed. Johnson and Grissom lined up on opposite sides of the lane and were instructed to bank the ball off the backboard so it wouldn't hit the rim and the player on the opposite side could catch it and throw it back. Musselman kept peppering encouraging remarks to Johnson, who looked none too good as Musselman continued to repeat the drill while he timed 30-second segments. An exhausted Johnson said, "Give me a couple weeks, and I'll be in shape." Musselman gave him three home games in four nights. Johnson had one point and seven re- bounds in the three games. When asked about Johnson's status after the third game, Musselman said, "He's out of here. Adios, amigo."

Next up was Clint Smith, a 6–6 swingman signed the day after Johnson left. He had played 41 games with Golden State in 1986–87. Smith stayed seven games with Musselman, averaging 2.7 points. He had some good minutes, and might have lasted with a less-talented team. In 1988–89 season, Smith and Johnson played the entire season for the Patroons and Coach George Karl. With Musselman's Pa- troons, both were victims of the numbers game. TMT—too much tal- ent.

In the span of three weeks, Musselman added 6–7 forward Tony Campbell and 6–9 center Tod Murphy. Someone had to go in addition to Smith. Kenny Natt was the someone.

A soft-spoken 6–3 guard from Monroe, Louisiana, Natt is a pro- lific scorer, the second highest in CBA history. Natt's brother, Calvin, is a 10-year NBA veteran who averaged 23.3 points for Denver in 1984–85 and has scored more than 10,000 points. Kenny Natt played bits and pieces of three NBA seasons with Indiana, Utah, and the Kansas City Kings.

In Albany, Natt had seasons of scoring 20.1 and 23.0 points per game. He'd also settled into a comfortable life in Albany with his wife, Jolene, and their infant daughter, KiEssence.

Natt and Moore had teamed to open the innovative Hoop School, exposing kids of all ages to basketball in the context of its relative worth to their lives: the importance of an education; the reality that 99 percent of them weren't going to be pro players, and dealing with peer pressure to avoid taking drugs. Those are the issues of the Hoop School that Moore and Natt (and occasionally Rowland, when he was in the mood) brought into the community. Before it began in May of 1987, the three Patroons had done dozens of free clinics and speeches to high school classes and other groups. The feeling of community ran deep in Natt and Moore, and the fans who routinely crammed the Armory embraced them.

Natt knew Musselman only from the typical abuse Musselman gave him as an opposing player. "I like it," Natt said. "I like it a lot when I play on the road. There's something about the fans for the other team or the coach of the other team getting on you. You know you're a good player. If you weren't a good player, then he (Musselman) wouldn't say anything. Some players got mad at him. They got off their game and they got into a confrontation with him, and that's what he wants. Me, I never said anything back to him even though I always heard it. I took it as a compliment."

Musselman started Natt in Albany's first two games, but by the second week of December, Natt was playing less and less. When he didn't get to play at all one game and got a cumulative 19 minutes in four others, Natt decided to talk to Musselman. He asked the coach to trade him to an Eastern Division team, because it would result in more trips home to be with his wife and daughter. Instead, Musselman shipped him to Wyoming.

"Bill Musselman had one thing on his mind, and that was winning another championship," Natt said. "He lived and died to get back to the NBA. He didn't really care about anybody. I was real disappointed because I explained to him, and he understood about my family being here. He betrayed me. He had me thinking that he was going to really look out for my interests. That showed me this man doesn't really care anything about me and my family. I wanted to play, so I went to Wyoming."

Good thing Tokyo didn't have a CBA franchise.

Natt thrived in Wyoming playing for Cazzie Russell, whose Wildcatters made the playoffs despite finishing 3–20. They wound up going seven games with Albany in the championship series. "It had to be as much of a shock to him as it was to me," Natt said.

Despite his personal bitterness with Musselman, Natt recognized Musselman's knack for coaching: "In training camp, I've never been that much in shape. It was so intense, and you had to concentrate. He wanted every quarter. He wanted every game. He wanted you to make every shot. He wants every ball that comes off the board. He gets the best out of his players.

"After you get away from it, you realize, 'Hey, this is how the guy is winning and other teams are not. It's because this guy wants everything.'"

Musselman said, "Think about how good we were. We didn't need Kenny Natt. Nothing against Kenny. We just didn't need him, and he's a pretty good player. There was no place for him."

There was for Tony Campbell. A sleek 6–7 forward from Ohio State, Campbell was taken in the first round of the 1984 NBA draft by Detroit as the 20th pick overall. In the second of three seasons with the Pistons, Campbell played in all 82 games for a winning club (46–36). The following season, he played in half as many games and roughly a quarter as many minutes.

The Washington Bullets signed him as a veteran free agent, but Campbell didn't make the Bullets' roster. La Crosse (Wisc.) had his CBA rights, and Campbell had no desire to play there. He was home, playing pick-up games in Teaneck, New Jersey, when Musselman dealt for his rights December 19.

"The first day he came, I called a team meeting," Musselman said. "I talked to Jack McClosky and Will Robinson (GM and assistant to the GM of the Pistons). I had it on intercom. They said he can score 30 points a game in this league, but he's not going to go back up to the NBA until he plays defense. And I let him know. The whole team had the impact of why he wasn't in the NBA. I said to Tony, 'When you come out of the ball game, it'll probably be because of that. Tony, I'll be up front with you. Right away, you know exactly why you're not in the NBA.' His teammates know it, and everybody can hear. He told me to get on him when he didn't play defense."

Campbell joined Richardson on the Patroons' bench. Both players were used to the NBA. In the CBA, they were reserves. "Tony handled it like a champ," Musselman said. "I respected him for it. The kid really tried to play defense. Every place he'd been, they tried to make him an offensive player. He wants to play defense, but he has to be schooled in it. He has to be reminded over and over. He's not a selfish player. He loves to win. That's why he accepted coming off the bench."

Campbell made his CBA debut Christmas night, ironically in La Crosse. The Catbirds had started their season almost as well as the Patroons, winning their first 10 games. They were 11–3 when Albany came to town for a showdown between the leaders of the Eastern and Western divisions. A crowd of 6,072 gathered for the game, which Albany won 100–96 as Campbell scored 10. The next night both teams played in different cities, Albany winning at Rochester 114–101, while La Crosse lost at Quad City 91–90. On December 27, Albany played the Catbirds again in La Crosse. The Patroons won again, this time 97–91. Musselman's Patroons had made a statement that their incredible start was not an aberration. If anything, Albany was getting better as new teammates learned to play together and Campbell blossomed.

Musselman made the Patroons even stronger on January 5. He waived Smith and signed Murphy, finally recovered from a lengthy bout with mono but still lacking conditioning. As Murphy got stronger, Musselman's lineup began looking more and more invincible. There was Murphy, Michael Brooks, Roth, Campbell, and Rowland up front, and Lowe, Scott Brooks, Moore, and Richardson in the backcourt. Only three developments could slow the Patroons: 1) injuries, 2) NBA call-ups, and 3) lack of motivation to keep pounding teams they had already beaten. The injuries were minor and infrequent, the NBA didn't call again for nearly two months, and the coach manufactured the motivation. Lowe recounted Musselman's message after the home loss to Rockford: "Coach was screaming and yelling, and he looked at us and said, 'You guys. Who the hell have you beat? You haven't beaten anyone. Who'd you beat?'

"We just looked at each other and kind of smiled. We were 30–3."

19

All-Star Interlude

The CBA's eighth annual All-Star Game, January 23 in Topeka, Kansas, matches a team chosen by the league's coaches against the Topeka Sizzlers. The logic was to increase attendance by having the All-Stars play a home team instead of each other. Topeka was chosen the year before, and that's why a national TV audience is treated to a matchup of the league's best players against a 13–15 Topeka Sizzlers club.

Neither All-Stars Coach Bill Musselman nor Sizzlers Coach John "Killer" Killilea are thrilled about the game. Musselman is angry about a league rule that mandates each of the 11 other CBA clubs have an All-Star. "They could have picked a whole team of guards," he reasons.

In practice the night before the game, he tees off on Wyoming center Brad Wright. Musselman can't believe Wright goes to three different spots to set a pick on the same play. "Brad Wright, will you please go to the same spot?" Musselman asks. The coach is only warming up. Displeased with the lack of enthusiasm some of the All-Stars are showing during a near two-hour practice, Musselman calls the team to the mid-court circle and gets directly to the point: "Some of you guys aren't executing. If you don't execute, you're not going to play tomorrow."

Wright asks Musselman after practice what parts of his game he needs to work on. Except, he calls Musselman "Coachy." Musselman nearly gags.

Killilea's club had to interrupt a Southern road trip for the All-Star Game. The Sizzlers were at Pensacola, Florida, Thursday night, will play the All-Stars Saturday in Topeka, and then play Monday night in Savannah. "I'd rather have stayed in Florida," Killilea says at practice Friday night.

Musselman doesn't get back to the hotel until 8:30 that night. He summons his former trainer and confidant from Tampa Bay, Pensacola trainer Guy Hill (the trainer for the All-Star Team) and hails a cab. "Let's go to Bennigan's," Musselman said. "I know the owner, Ron Washington. We'll eat for nothing. Guaranteed."

Topeka doesn't seem to be hopping this Friday night in January, but Bennigan's is crowded. No matter. Musselman bursts through the front door. He asks the hostess:

" 'Where's Ron Washington?'

'I'm not sure if he's in tonight.'

'Well, I'm Bill Musselman, coach of the Albany Patroons, and I'm in town to coach the All-Star Team tomorrow against Topeka, and Ron and I are good friends and he said whenever I'm in town to come over and...'

'Have a seat; I'll get the manager.' "

Musselman detests smoking. There's one table open—in the smoking section. He walks over, inspects it, circles it, inspects it again, and finally, grudgingly, gives in to his hunger. Musselman orders and is halfway through dinner when the manager arrives at the table:

" 'Can I help you?'

'I'm Bill Musselman, coach of the Albany Patroons, and I'm in town to coach the All-Star Team tomorrow. Look, Ron Washington and I are good friends, and he said the next time I'm in town to come over to Bennigan's and have dinner on him.'

'Ron Washington isn't in tonight.'

'Why don't you call him at home?'

'Well, he's sick with bronchitis and I don't want to bother him.'

'He's got bronchitis? Gee, I didn't know that. But he said the next time I'm in Topeka to come to Bennigan's and he'd take care of it.' "

Full-court press.

"Of course, Mr. Musselman, we'd be delighted to have you as our guest tonight."

Musselman isn't finished just yet. He enters a cab for the ride back to the hotel and asks the driver: "Hey, you want to go to the All-Star Game tomorrow?"

"Yeah."

"I'm Bill Musselman and I'm coaching the All-Star Team tomorrow. Why don't you forget the fare and I'll leave you two tickets at the gate tomorrow."

"Great."

Sauntering through the lobby, whittling a toothpick, Musselman tells Hill, "I told you we'd eat for nothing. And then we got a free cab ride, too."

Musselman is smiling ear to ear. Hill has seen it many times. "Thanks, Coachy," he says getting on the elevator. "Coachy," Musselman says, shaking his head. They both laugh.

ESPN's live broadcast is planned for 3:35 Saturday afternoon. But the college basketball game the network is showing runs 20 minutes late. The CBA All-Star Game waits for ESPN.

The players congregate in a corner of the Landon Arena in the Expocentre, quite possibly the ugliest sports arena in America. It's a steel barn well-suited for tractor pulls and little else.

Before the game, five players participate in the first—and hopefully the last—CBA Slam-Dunk Championship. A sixth contestant, Micheal "Sugar" Ray Richardson of the Patroons, is on hand but not competing. The 6-5 Richardson rarely dunks but was asked by league officials to participate in the Slam-Dunk for his marquee value. He arrives in Topeka late after missing his original flight, then decides to drop out of the Slam-Dunk because he doesn't want to risk injury. So he's a spectator at practice Friday and the game Saturday. But he has a good time, especially at the practice when he crowns All-Star guard Jamie Waller "Young Mike Tyson."

Waller, a 6-5 rookie guard, does indeed bear a facial resemblance to Tyson. The judges, a panel of five local media members, give Topeka guard Lloyd Daniels two extra dunks, but Waller wins first prize, $150 and airfare for two anywhere in the continental United States. This is good, because after the game he's traded to Charleston for Ray Hall, another All-Star in the Slam-Dunk Contest.

Rockford's Pete Myers loses the contest by a single point. However, he forever endears himself to the judges by asking several times if he can fly to Hawaii if he wins. That's okay. One of the other All-Stars, before a game at Rapid City, asked if Mount Rushmore was created naturally.

On the plus side, McDonald's donates $10,000 in Waller's name to the Topeka Ronald McDonald House.

Killilea is less than charitable with the officials. After an All-Star takes an extra step before scoring on a drive, Killilea yells to referee Tommie Wood, "Tommie, why don't you buy him a suitcase?"

Killilea fails to notice a large disparity in foul shots, 24–8 in his favor, which keeps his team in the game for the first half. But the Sizzlers are destroyed in the second half and wind up losing 115–94. Worse yet for Killilea, he loses starting forward Bill Martin because of a sprained ankle. A month after the game, Killilea is fired and replaced by Bob Hill.

Cruising with a 20-point lead doesn't mollify Musselman, although he does leave intact the microphone he's wearing for ESPN. In the fourth quarter, he calls a timeout and goes off on Pensacola guard Tommy Davis. "Dammit, Tommy Davis, you're not playing for Pensacola; you're playing for me," Musselman tells him and the national TV audience enduring the rout. Earlier in the game, Musselman barked at Wright into the ESPN mike, "If your guy gets off one more shot, you're not going to play another minute." All-Star guard Kelvin Upshaw marvels at Musselman's deportment: "He took the All-Star Game like it was no joke. He said, 'Get the fuck out of here if you don't want to win.' I never heard anybody like that."

Musselman is gentler in his postgame comments, spreading praise among his guards, Albany's Sidney Lowe, who had an All-Star-record 13 assists while not taking a shot from the floor, Ricky Wilson of Mississippi, and Upshaw of Rapid City. Musselman credits Michael Brooks, the MVP with 15 points and six rebounds, for "playing an outstanding game."

The Killer gives some of the world's greatest minds food for thought by observing, "It was just a game."

20

Chasing Another Championship

Life on the road with Musselman was never dull.

At 31–3 following an easy win against Charleston, Albany began an eventful three-game road trip in early February. At Pensacola, Albany blew a seven-point lead in the fourth quarter and lost 114–108. The Patroons almost lost Scott Roth, too. He was knocked to the floor while going for a rebound and banged his forehead, requiring several stitches. Roth wasn't expected to play the next night when the Pats visited Mississippi. He did.

Musselman needed every point he could get that night and the next as Albany edged Mississippi in back-to-back overtime games, 117–110 and 126–124. Besides being close, both games were physical. Kenny Siler of Mississippi got ejected for two unsportsmanlike conduct fouls despite playing just two minutes the first night. The second night, Ken "The Animal" Bannister got ejected for a flagrant foul when he broke Roth's nose. Coach Tom Schneeman and Musselman came close to exchanging blows. Musselman wasn't just upset about the Roth incident. Before the game, Schneeman's wife had harangued Richardson from the stands, yelling "Just Say Yes."

When Roth got hit in the face by Bannister, Musselman erupted. "Coach Musselman went running over to see if he was all right," Lowes Moore said. "He said, 'I can't take it anymore.' There was a speaker on the press table, and he just pounded it. Boom. The guy at the table jumped back. Coach went crazy."

Attack one of Musselman's players, and you'd have to fight the coach, too. He may scream at his own players, curse them, ride them, and bench them, but they were always *his* players. His family in basketball.

Joe Hennessy's involvement with the Albany Patroons seemed over at the outset of the 1987–88 season. He began with the Patroons as their PR man, then switched to a successful radio career that included three seasons of doing the Patroons' play-by-play.

Hennessy then declined an offer from Patroons General Manager Gary Holle to do another season. Holle didn't find a replacement until the morning the Patroons flew to Savannah for the season opener. Hennessy's replacement hadn't spent any time with the team in preseason, and his debut left much to be desired. He misnamed Patroons Scott Lowe and Steve Roth and even managed to botch Richardson's first name. But his lowest moment came at the start of the second half. He introduced Savannah's lineup: Walker D. Russell, Tico Brown, Steve Burtt, and "two other guys."

Back in Albany, Holle's phone didn't stop ringing. Other members of the Patroons organization couldn't believe what they were hearing on the radio. Instead of fouls, the broadcaster called them penalties. It was enough for Holle to call Hennessy and beg him to reconsider. Hennessy came in the next morning, worked out a new contract, and caught an early afternoon flight that got him into Charleston, West Virginia, in time to do the Patroons–Gunners game that night.

Hennessy spent most of his time on the road by himself. He felt getting too close to the players or the coach would hinder his objectivity. If he did socialize, it was usually to get a pizza or go to a movie with a player, usually Lowes Moore. Other than that, Hennessy checked home with his wife, Virginia, spoke to their son, Joe, Jr., and watched TV. He hadn't planned on spending another season away from home. Nor had he ever done obstacle broadcasting.

The 5-5 Hennessy grew increasingly frustrated trying to do play-by-play behind the 5-9 moving object that was Musselman. Cavs broadcaster Joe Tait had the same problem when Musselman was in Cleveland. "He'd stand in front of me," Tait said. "Toward the end when things really got very strained, I've often felt that he did it on purpose."

Hennessy literally had to do stand-up play-by-play: "No matter where I sat, he was always right in front of me. Everywhere. I'd move two seats down. I'd move two seats up. I don't think it was conscious on his part, but I had to do the entire 54-game schedule up and down, up and down. It was generally a difficult way to call a ball game."

Not as difficult as working without an amplifier or control box. "He used to run up and down the (press) table and bang his fists," Hennessy said. "And I've got my machine there. I'm plugged into the world. All it takes is one little knock on that machine, and I'm off. So whenever he'd get up from his chair and start to slide down the sideline, all of us at press row would reach out and protect our things. That was the thing: were you going to survive the night on the air with this maniac who was running up and down the table banging things?"

Before one road game, Hennessy's station decided to tape delay his live broadcast to air a two-hour opera. This wasn't a case of the game not being over until that fat lady sings. Rather, the game didn't start until the fat lady stopped singing.

As his relationship with Musselman deteriorated, Hennessy arranged his priorities in life. No. 1 became avoiding Musselman on the road, a strategy that seldom seemed to work.

The Patroons lost at Savannah 111–103 March 2. Before the game, Musselman learned the Denver Nuggets wanted to sign Michael Brooks to a 10-day contract. As he had done with Roth, Musselman advised Brooks to hold out for a contract for the rest of the season. The Nuggets called CBA Commissioner Mike Storen to find out why the NBA/CBA Development Contract wasn't being observed. Storen called Coyne, then Musselman. Neither budged. Coyne backed Musselman completely, even when the threat of a lawsuit against the Patroons became a real possibility. If the CBA couldn't deliver Brooks to the Nuggets, the whole $1.8 million, three-year NBA/CBA contract was in jeopardy. To avoid that, the CBA threatened to sue the Patroons. Coyne told the league to go ahead; he was backing Musselman.

The lawsuit never materialized, because the next day the Nuggets decided to sign Brooks for the rest of the season. Once again Musselman had accomplished the absolute best for his player. The night before, he was trying to cope with the loss to Savannah, the loss of Roth (signed by Utah a week earlier), the upcoming loss of Brooks, and increasingly frequent rumors that the Lakers were going to sign Campbell.

Hennessy gives the play-by-play after the game: ''He said to me, 'Let's go out and eat.' I said, 'Oh, God, no. No. I got to go back to my room. I'm waiting for a phone call. I'm not eating tonight. I've got to lose weight.'

''In the past, I'd order a pizza and sneak it into my room. That night, Lowes calls me up and says, 'Hey, you want to get something to eat? Want to get a pizza?'

'Oh, yeah. I was going to order one anyway.'

'All right. We'll order one. I'll come down to your room.'

''Musselman's room is right next to me. So now I'm worried about him seeing that I'm with one of his players. I said I was going to make it an early night, and I'm ordering pizzas. So, of course, I'm waiting for the pizza to come, and I'm looking out the door to make sure that he doesn't see the pizza guy come. God forbid, he's going to come in and eat pizza with me. That would be the real killer.

''Lowes comes in and we're waiting for the pizza. I hear a knock on the door. I think it's the pizza. Lowes gives me 10 bucks. I go over to the door with a $20 bill. I open the door, and there stands Bill Musselman. My pizza hadn't come yet. And Bill Musselman's standing in the doorway with his undershorts, no top, no shoes, and no socks, clutching his chest. At the same time he clutches his chest, the pizza guy shows up and he says, 'Eleven dollars.' So I got the coach of the team out there clutching his chest like he's in severe trauma, maybe having a heart attack at my door.

''My No. 1 priority at that point was to pay for my pizza. I said, 'Hold on, Bill. Just one second. Lowes, look after Bill. If he falls down, take care of him until I get the change.' I paid for my pizza. Now I see he sees I'm eating a pizza but then I realize this isn't really his priority anymore, eating dinner with me, because I think this man may be having a heart attack. This is at the time Michael Brooks was being courted by Denver. He was on the phone with the CBA and Denver for 24 straight hours, I think. He's so pumped up with this whole thing, it's taken over. He's holding his heart at the door, and he said, 'I'm having some chest pains.'

'Why don't you come in for a second and sit down. Would you like a piece of pizza?'

'No, I don't want a piece of pizza. I'm feeling some aching and numbness in my left arm.'

''My wife's a nurse. When you get the numbness and aching in your left arm and you're having chest pains, to me it's a sign of a heart

attack. He was ashen. He was white. We had him come in and sit down for a few minutes. We had to literally almost tie him to the chair to keep him seated. I just told him to relax and that he's just got to stop going crazy. He's got to calm down. He's got to realize he's got a life; that he's got a son (and daughter); that there are other things more important in life than basketball; that he could be dead tomorrow.

'Wouldn't you rather be able to live another 20 to 25 years and see your son (sic) grow and mature?'

'You're right. You're right. You're right.'

'You've got to give this Brooks thing a rest. You've got to take a couple of deep breaths and realize all you've accomplished. You've been working so hard. Take some enjoyment out of what you accomplished the last four years. Instead of making it such an obsession, relax and enjoy what you've accomplished. Enjoy coaching today. Take some of the stress and pressure off.'

'You're right. You're right. You're right.'

'Don't make any more phone calls tonight. Let's call the paramedics.'

''He had called the trainer from Savannah. The paramedics didn't come. The trainer, Doc, did. And, of course, Doc was good at taping ankles and shaving calluses, but Doc knew very little about cardiac arrest. Doc's response was, 'Hey, you want to go to the hospital?'

'Bill, why don't we go to the hospital. I'll go with you to the hospital.'

'Nope. Nope. Nope. No, I'm all right.'

'Why don't you stay with me and Lowes for a little while, and we'll just watch you and make sure everything's okay?'

'No. Nope. No. I want to go back to my room. I'll be all right. Be all right.'

'Now, you're not going to do anything? You're going to calm down?'

'I'm going to lie down. I'm going to lie down. I'll be all right. I'll leave my door open a crack. I'll call you if there's any problems.'

'Why don't you just stay here? You could lie on that bed right there. Lowes and I are just going to eat the pizza and watch TV, Bill. Why don't you just relax with us?'

'No. No. No. I want to be by myself.'

''Bill leaves. Like five minutes later, my phone rings. I pick it up real quick because I think maybe the guy's dying. Whoever it was on the other line hung up. So now I'm thinking the man just died. I run out of my room, I bust open his door and run into his room, and he's standing there on the phone, yelling to Pete Babcock from Denver, saying, 'This kid deserves more than a 10-day contract.'

"He went from the throes of having a heart attack and being scared as shit, and in five minutes, no exaggeration, five minutes, he was back in his room yelling on the phone. That's how hard that man worked.

"By the way, the pizza was cold."

The overtime victories at Mississippi kicked off a 14-game win streak as the Patroons moved to 45-4, hiking their level of play to a level never seen before in the CBA. In 12 games, Albany's average margin of victory was 29.0. In one six-game segment, the margin was 40.3. "He played his cards perfect every time," Lowes Moore said. "He just had the right chemistry."

Musselman said, "The chemistry was incredible. You'll never see a CBA team that good again. Ever. You'll never find a team that was that close."

Nor one that played better defense. The popular image of the CBA is one of nonstop, run-and-gun play. Musselman's Patroons shredded that image, becoming the first team to allow less than 100 points per game for a season, 97.5. "I always got people that cared about defense," Musselman said.

At Wyoming December 15, Albany had established a record for fewest points allowed in an 80-68 win. The mark lasted only two months. February 19 in Albany, against the same Wildcatters team, Albany won 104-60, setting records for least points allowed in a game, half (26), and quarter (8).

Cazzie Russell's Wyoming club was in the midst of a 14-game losing streak and was playing its third game in a different city in three nights. The Wildcatters made just 21 of 71 shots and committed 33 turnovers. "What's amazing is that they got eight points in one quarter," Musselman said. "Our defensive intensity just picked up another level."

In its two previous games, Albany had routed Charleston 131-103 and 148-97. Both games were in Charleston as Musselman faced his former assistant, Gerald Oliver. With 30 seconds left in the second game, which produced the Patroons' largest winning margin ever, Musselman called a timeout. Asked why he would do that against a long-time friend, Musselman scowled. "We weren't executing," he said.

Funny, everybody considered Musselman the ultimate executioner, one who wouldn't even think about pausing before he let the guillotine go with a lifelong friend's head on the block. "All I do is, each time up and down the court, I expect my players to execute defensively and offensively," Musselman said. "Everybody thinks I'm hard. Everybody says I'm a Hubie Brown clone. That's bullshit. I don't want to be compared to that guy. Everybody has their own individuality. My players respond."

Musselman was pushing as hard as he knew how, trying to get back to the NBA. "It's the only challenge I have left in coaching," he said in a radio interview.

There were other challenges confronting Musselman: how to deal with the unending media invasion and how to win despite losing his best players to the NBA.

A focal point of national media attention was February 25, 1988, the two-year anniversary of Richardson's NBA ban due to repeated drug abuse. The two years were up. The NBA would be setting precedent with its decision on whether to reinstate Richardson, whose twice-weekly random drug tests indicated he had stayed clean in Albany. "People said he's disruptive," Musselman said. "That's totally false. In fact, he was a plus. His attitude was phenomenal."

Two months later, Musselman nearly threw him off the team.

Albany was home against Charleston February 24. Two film crews flew to Albany from Atlanta, one for TBS and the other to work on an anti-drug movie for high schools. Two of the networks had their Albany affiliates interview Richardson before the game.

But there was no breaking news. The NBA hadn't completed an investigation of Richardson's conduct in Albany and postponed its decision for nearly three months, when Richardson was allowed back in the NBA. (It didn't matter. He played in Italy in 1988–89 for former Knicks coach Bob Hill.)

There were other stories besides Richardson. Most of them were about Musselman. One gem went unreported because it happened at a practice closed to the press. Former Providence College star and NBA guard Ernie DiGregorio, widely regarded as one of the greatest passers in the history of basketball, called Musselman several times seeking a tryout. At the age of 37, DiGregorio desperately wanted one more shot. He had tried officiating the previous season in the CBA and wasn't satisfied.

Finally, Musselman relented and invited DiGregorio to come to the Armory and scrimmage with the Patroons for an afternoon. He showed up with his former Providence teammate, Kevin Stacom, and proceeded to demonstrate two points: 1) You can tell a great player was still a great player at age 37, and 2) 37-year-old legs can't keep up with ones 10 to 15 years younger. "Ernie D." went back to Providence, his family, and a life without pro basketball.

Stories about the Patroons ran in the *Los Angeles Times*, the *Boston Globe*, the *Dallas Morning News*, *USA Today*, the *New York Daily News*, the *St. Petersburg Times*, the *Sporting News*, *Basketball Weekly* and the *Bergen Record*. The *New York Times* featured a story on the first page of its sports section.

There were unknown writers and conspicuous ones who came to Albany to write about Bill Musselman. One out-of-town writer, Paul Franklin from the *Courier News* in New Jersey, set up an afternoon interview. Musselman already had planned to go to Troy to have a picture taken for an ad. Ken Lyons drove, and Musselman agreed to let Franklin tag along and do the interview in the car. They talked, Musselman had the picture taken, and Lyons drove everybody back to the Armory so Musselman could get his car. "The reporter thanked Bill very much, got out, and left," Lyons said. "Bill turned to me and said, 'Who was that guy?' "

At the other end of the spectrum, Musselman went out of his way to manufacture a new image when *Sports Illustrated* sent William Nack to Albany. Think the *SI* jinx isn't true? Nack spent three games with the Patroons, and they went 1–2. Plus, after Nack had spent mammoth interview sessions with Musselman for four days, *SI* decided to not run Nack's story, a crushing blow to Musselman.

"When *Sports Illustrated* was there, he was trying to get rid of the image of madness," More said. "He wanted to erase what had happened in the past with the college fight and Cleveland. We lost two games because *Sports Illustrated* was there. One game, we were playing just terrible, kicking the ball out of bounds. And 'cause the guy from *Sports Illustrated* was in the locker room at halftime, he said, 'All right, fellows, look. You gotta want to win this game. Okay? We didn't have a good first half. Let's go out and play together and have a good game. Come on. Let's go.' "

No screaming. No cursing. In essence, no Musselman.

After the game, the one-point home loss to Rockford, the players huddled. "We all got together and said, 'Sidney, go talk to Coach and tell him to go back to normal,' " Moore related. "Sidney said, 'Coach, what are you doing?' He said, 'The man from *Sports Illustrated* is here. I can't. . .they blow everything out of proportion that I do.' "

If Nack could have secretly video-taped the postgame locker room the game after he left, he would have found a different Musselman. "My man went nuts," Moore said. "We were sitting in the locker room, and on the VCR Musselman's going over the Mississippi game we had lost. He took off his coat, looked at it, and threw it down. He grabbed a chair and slammed it against the wall, saying, 'Arrgh. You guys, you make me sick. I work so hard.'

"He just kept flipping the video back and forth. Fifteen minutes. 'You look like a bunch of fools out there, a bunch of clowns.'

"Then he stands up. He flips off the VCR and hits the television. The television's on a stand. He hits the top of the VCR, and then, Boom! The whole thing just crumbled. He goes, 'Oh.' He's trying to fix it, then all of a sudden, he just stopped and went nuts. You could see it in his eyes. Then he was talking about his Mom: 'My mother worked so hard. I never smoked.' We went back through his life story. We were in there a long time."

Roth was signed by the Jazz February 25. Michael Brooks went to the Nuggets March 3. Musselman found the best replacements he could, 34-year-old center Eric Fernsten, working as a carpenter in Boston, and swingman Reid Gettys, playing for Athletes In Action in San Diego.

"He'd been touching base with me all that year," Fernsten said. "I said, 'You're sticking your neck on the line, really, pal.' I came to Albany and met the guys and they started busting on me immediately. I was a fossil. 'Tell me, was it George Mikan or you that started the hook shot? Jeez, did Bob Cousy really make such great passes all the time?' I said, 'Now wait a minute, I'm not that old, guys.' " He wasn't too old to help, averaging 7.5 points and 6.1 rebounds and getting a team-high 14 blocks in the playoffs.

Gettys (5.9 points) would help, too, but with rumors constantly circulating about more NBA call-ups for Campbell, Murphy, and Lowe (Campbell did go; Murphy and Lowe didn't), Musselman was faced with the frightening prospect of assembling the best CBA team ever and not winning a championship. "It would have ruined the season,"

Lowe said. "What's the use of having the best record in the league if you turn around and lose the championship?"

Musselman didn't want to find out. Albany blew away Savannah 4–1 in the opening round of the playoffs. Musselman, however, didn't like the way his players practiced in preparation for the next round. "We were going through the motions," Musselman said. "Practice was about over. I had 15 more minutes to go. They weren't hustling. Sidney looked at me and whispered in my ear, 'This is the worst practice I've ever seen you have. We're not doing anything.'

"I started screaming, 'Here we are getting ready for the playoffs a couple days away, and you guys don't want to win at all. I'm through putting everything I've got into it today. I'll see you guys later. To hell with you, I'm leaving.' "

Only he forgot his clipboard. Musselman re-entered the Armory. "Campbell says, 'You can't leave us, Coach. You can't leave.'

'Screw you, Tony. I've had enough for today. You had your chance. I'm leaving.' "

So did Campbell the next day, to the Lakers. Suddenly, the Patroons didn't seem so invincible. Campbell had led the CBA in both field goal and free throw percentage and topped the team in scoring (23.7). Michael Brooks led the league in rebounding (11.9), but he, Campbell, and Roth (19.5 points per game) were gone.

The Eastern Division finals matched Albany against Pensacola, which had done better against the Patroons (3–5) than any other team. Musselman caught a huge break when Pensacola's point guard Mark Wade, who led the CBA in assists (11.3), was signed by the Golden State Warriors. Without him, Pensacola fell apart.

Albany swept Pensacola 4–0, taking each game by five points. Moore had outstanding performances in Games 1 and 2, 24 points in 21 minutes and then a season-high 30 points in 33 minutes. He shot a combined 24 of 32 from the floor and 6 of 6 at the line. Murphy had finally found his game, averaging 17.3 points and 13.3 rebounds.

Lowe and Gettys watched a preview show of the NCAA national championship on a TV in the Pensacola airport. The highlights included the 1983 title game between North Carolina State and Houston. "I guarded him," Gettys said. "We never talked about it until that night in the airport. The air ball (the shot by Dereck Whittenburg that Lorenzo Charles converted into the winning basket as time ran out), I'm saying to myself, 'Don't look over at him. Don't look.' But I did. He was sitting there with the biggest grin. Then we cracked up."

Albany moved into the finals against Wyoming, maybe the biggest longshot in pro basketball history to reach a championship series. Once a vibrant franchise, Wyoming had sputtered along with the local economy in Casper. Team owner John O'Donnell bailed out at the end of February, forcing the CBA to operate the franchise. The task seemed a brief one: Wyoming limped into fourth place in the Western Division, gaining the final playoff spot despite losing 20 of its 23 final games. Then Wyoming dropped the first two games of its opening-round series with first-place La Crosse.

At that point, Wyoming's record in its last 25 games was 3-22. Stir in the fact the team lost forward Richard Rellford to the NBA (San Antonio), and marvel at the results. Wyoming won four straight against La Crosse, then polished off Rockford 4-2, ending the Western Division final with a 137-134, four-overtime victory on the road.

Kenny Natt was coming home after all.

Having beaten Wyoming in three regular-season games by 12, 44, and 24 points, the Patroons headed into the series as huge favorites despite the NBA call-ups. Musselman asked Fernsten, Gettys, and 6-7 forward Bob Davis, who would score but two points in a limited performance, to fill the talent gap left by Brooks, Roth, and Campbell.

Games 1, 4, 5, 6, and 7 were to be televised live by ESPN. Fans around the nation would see if Musselman could get his fourth consecutive championship.

The common assumption was that Albany would blow away Wyoming in Games 1 and 2 in the Armory, where the Patroons were 30-1. The first three quarters followed that script, with Albany increasing a three-point halftime lead to 86-70 heading into the fourth quarter.

But the Wildcatters outscored Albany 37-21 to force overtime, and they eventually won 116-113. That wasn't the only bad news for Musselman, who took on Micheal Ray Richardson, then columnist Tim Layden and sports editor Al Vieira of the *Times Union*.

Richardson, extremely teed off about playing just 15 minutes despite scoring 11 points on 5-of-8 shooting, was handed a cup of water during a timeout in overtime. Whether he dropped it or threw it down was incidental to the result—water spilled on Musselman's clipboard. "Coach had to wipe the board off, and he looked up at Micheal like he was a little pissed," Lowe said.

Musselman was major-league mad, telling reporters after the game that Richardson might be kicked off the team before Game 2 the following night.

If losing Game 1 and Richardson's antics weren't enough, Musselman was leveled in Layden's Sunday morning *Times Union* column. Layden, who since has moved on to *Newsday*, criticized Musselman for his brutal, dehumanizing treatment of his own players. Musselman went absolutely nuts when he read the column. "He wanted a lawyer to sue Layden," Laverty said.

Musselman didn't sue Layden, and he didn't kick Richardson off the team. Instead, Richardson scored 20 and Rowland had 27 in Game 2 as Albany evened the series.

After the game, Musselman raged. The entire season, he routinely came out of the locker room five to 15 minutes after the game to talk to reporters. This night, he walked into a room full of reporters, said, "We played well," then called Layden's column "the worst piece of journalism" he'd ever seen. Musselman wheeled and went back inside the locker room slightly ahead of the media pack shadowing him. When Musselman slammed the door behind him, the locker room became off-limits to the press as it had been during the rest of the season. Layden wasn't at the game (he was out of town covering the Boston Marathon) but his boss, Vieira, was. Infuriated by Musselman's attack of Layden, Vieira tried to push his way past a Patroon official blocking the locker-room door. Vieira demanded:

'I'm going in there.'

'No you're not. Just back off.'

'All right. You tell Musselman I'm out here.'

Musselman's reaction? "Fuck Al Vieira."

Musselman then opened the door and walked into the public bathroom downstairs in the Armory with Vieira in hot pursuit. Standing in the front entrance of the bathroom, Musselman and Vieira engaged in a heated argument while a local TV station filmed the exchange. Actually, it was closer to a soliloquy than a discussion as Musselman did virtually all the talking. Vieira wrote a kissy-face column the following day in the *Times Union* ostensibly to appease Musselman.

Games 3, 4, and 5 were in Casper. Wyoming beat Albany 83–80 in Game 3. Afterwards, Musselman held a film review of the game at the hotel. The session went on past midnight. "All he did was sit there flipping the video," Moore said. "Every time somebody made a mistake, he'd just run it back, flip it and run it back."

Apparently it helped. Game 4 was tied 59–59 after three quarters. Albany then outscored Wyoming, 45–26, evening the series at

2–2 and ensuring a trip back home for Game 6. That contest meant survival for the Patroons, because the Wildcatters embarrassed them in Game 5. Wyoming built an 83–59 lead and coasted to a 109–90 win.

Murphy was playing hurt (Achilles tendon). The fact he was still playing in Albany was amazing in itself. Golden State had asked Murphy to sign a 10-day contract, and he declined. "A sign of unusual character," said Golden State interim Coach Ed Gregory.

A gap of six days between Games 5 and 6 gave the Patroons plenty of time to prepare for their final stand, one started without Musselman, who flew to Sarasota while the Patroons returned to New York.

Beth Harbour, the Patroons' director of public relations, drove a van down to Newark Airport to pick up the players. On the way home, they dined extravagantly thanks to Holle, who loaned Harbour his credit card. The bill came to more than $800. Holle lost about five years from his life expectancy when he read about the dinner in the paper the next morning.

But the excursion had a healing effect on the players, whom Musselman had pushed to the limit. The Patroons were merely one loss away from a rotten ending to a remarkable season. Meanwhile, in Florida, Musselman ran on the beach trying to clear his mind and figure out a solution to revive his club from its only lopsided loss of the season.

Musselman may have won the championship when he decided to give his players time off before Game 6. "For three days we didn't practice," Musselman said. "I wanted to make them hungry. I was worried about winning Game 7. I knew we'd win Game 6. I figured the way we'd win Game 7 was by letting Wyoming practice all week. Our emotion will win Game 6, and our rest will win Game 7. We saved their legs."

Saved a championship. An overflow crowd of 5,231 and ESPN's TV audience watched Albany pull away from the Wildcatters in Game 6 for a 102–81 victory. Rowland scored 28 points, while Fernsten had 14 rebounds and 7 points.

As he did in Game 6, Musselman started the forgotten man, center Greg Grissom, in Game 7. Grissom responded with the game of his life, 14 points and 13 rebounds. Rowland scored 20. Murphy, named the playoff MVP, had 21 points and 14 rebounds. The man of the hour, however, was clearly Lowes Moore, who came off the bench to score 23.

Wyoming led 33–19 in the second quarter when the Patroons began their rally. With the final seconds of the first half ticking away, Wyoming led 49–47 and had one last possession. Guard Boot Bond brought the ball upcourt.

Moore swiped it cleanly, had the presence of mind to realize he was crossing halfcourt with two seconds left, pulled up, and deposited a 30-foot 3-pointer as time expired. The Patroons ran off the court with a 50–49 lead and all the momentum they would need.

"To me, that shot made the whole season because of all the things that happened to me," Moore said. "I think that shot showed what kind of person I was. When there's pressure, I like to say I come through. At the end, Coach realized I could still play basketball."

Near the end of Game 7, Wyoming wouldn't wilt. Fittingly, with Albany nursing a 90–88 lead with five minutes left, the "old Patroons" finally finished off their gutty opponents.

A basket by Moore made it 92–88. After Natt missed a three-pointer, Grissom's long pass to Murphy resulted in an easy dunk for a 94–88 lead. An off-balance 15-footer by Grissom with 50 seconds left made it 100–92. The final was 105–96.

Musselman had done it again. The following morning, he and his players took off for Puerto Rico. They returned to Albany five days later, disbanded and scattered quickly to pursue their separate basketball careers.

The next season, Campbell played intermittently for the Lakers, coming up big in the NBA Finals. Scott Brooks played well as point guard Maurice Cheeks' backup with the Philadelphia 76ers.

Lowe, traded to Rapid City for Kelvin Upshaw, sat part of the season out, joined the Thrillers briefly, and was called up to the NBA, where he played extremely well for the Charlotte Hornets.

Richardson played in Italy, Michael Brooks and Tod Murphy in Spain. Rowland played half a season in the Philippines before rejoining Greg Grissom and the Patroons.

Moore became head coach at Hudson Valley Community College in nearby Troy, and played for the Patroons in the playoffs.

Carlisle hurt his shoulder in training camp with the Knicks and missed the entire year.

Musselman waited to hear from the Minnesota Timberwolves.

21

Return to the NBA

"I spent a lot of time calling Bill in the summer," Jim Laverty said. "I'd call him maybe two, three times a week, and he was real down because Minnesota was really giving him the run-around. It was his dream, and they were dangling him. He went through a lot of stress.

"I remember I called him one day, and I says, 'How are you doing?' He says, 'Listen, I don't care what happens. If they offer me that job, I'm not going to take it.' I says, 'You're a damn liar. I know you got the job now.' And he started laughing. They announced it that next week. He was absolutely thrilled. He'd worked like hell."

Professional basketball in the Twin Cities of St. Paul and Minneapolis has a glorious past—one of five championships in six years, one forever linked to the dominating presence of George Mikan, Jr.

As much as NBA play in the 1970s and '80s showcased the center with goggles, Kareem Abdul-Jabbar, the early NBA days spotlighted the center with glasses, George Lawrence Mikan, Jr. He was 6-10 in an era of 6-6 centers. He was 245 pounds, strong yet graceful enough in his movement to make spectators wonder, 'Did he actually do that?'

He did, year after year, season after season. A first-team NBA All-Star six times. Mikan led the Minneapolis Lakers to NBA championships in 1949, 1950, 1952, 1953 and 1954 as he fashioned his Hall of Fame career.

One of Mikan's Laker teammates was homegrown Arild Verner Agerskov Mikkelsen. Mikkelsen played high school ball in Askov, Minnesota, and then matriculated at Hamline University in St. Paul. Thus he was a popular selection when the Lakers tabbed him in the first round of the 1949 draft.

Mikkelsen (6-7, 230) and Mikan combined to give the Lakers an inside game few opponents could contain. In Mikan's prime years, 1948-54, the Lakers were 275-131. In Mikkelsen's rookie season, 1949-50, they went 51-17. Their only playoff defeat in Mikan's first six years was administered by Rochester, three games to one in the 1951 Western Division finals. Rochester went on to beat the Knicks for the NBA title.

Minneapolis bounced back to take three more championships before slipping to a 40-32 record in 1954-55. Mikan returned from a one-year retirement in 1955-56, but couldn't prevent the Lakers' first losing season (33-39). After Mikan retired for good, the Lakers endured losing campaigns of 34-38, 19-53, 33-39, and 25-50.

Owner Ben Berger sold the team for $150,000 in 1957 to a group of Minneapolis businessmen headed by Bob Short. Short relocated the franchise to Los Angeles following the 1959-60 season. "Ben was always sorry he sold the Lakers," Berger's widow, Midge, said in an April 1989, interview. "They were so successful."

Professional basketball would not return to Minneapolis for three decades, although Musselman tried to revive the sport in a little-known episode a decade earlier. He envisioned three scenarios that would bring professional basketball back to the Twin Cities in 1976: 1) an NBA expansion franchise, 2) an existing ABA team looking to relocate, or 3) an existing NBA franchise looking to relocate.

Musselman discussed his ideas with Ben Berger, who expressed initial interest. A Minneapolis newspaper account delineated the roadblocks:

"The NBA has several good reasons for not wanting to expand or move an existing NBA team here. The majority of its teams are losing money and reportedly two of them are being carried by the league.

"Most of the cities, which are losing money, would be judged superior basketball cities to Minneapolis. They have larger populations and have stronger basketball cultures.

"Minneapolis has lost three pro teams in the last 16 years. There has been no public outcry to bring a team to town.

"The local CBS affiliate, Channel 4, will not even carry the NBA playoff telecasts and All-Star Game when they're scheduled on a week night. A station spokesman said that 4,000 local viewers tuned in the NBA All-Star Game when Channel 4 carried it two years ago.

"Another obstacle to bringing a team here next year is the continual talk of a merger between the NBA and the rival American Basketball Association (ABA). The NBA might agree to take some of the ABA teams into its membership. Some of the ABA cities are superior to existing NBA ones and absolutely preferable to this area.

"Musselman suggests that the Virginia team of the ABA might be transferred here. The franchise has had a series of financial problems and reportedly neither NBA or ABA officials want it around much longer."

The following season four ABA teams, San Antonio, the Nets, Denver, and Indiana, were absorbed by the NBA. Musselman's dream of coaching an NBA team in the Twin Cities was forgotten for a dozen years.

On April 22, 1987, the National Basketball Association awarded expansion franchises to the cities of Charlotte, North Carolina, Miami and Orlando, Florida, and Minneapolis/St. Paul. The purchase price was $32.5 million for each franchise. Miami and Charlotte played last season; Orlando and Minnesota begin in November.

Paying the freight for the Minnesota Timberwolves are Marv Wolfenson and Harvey Ratner, who own Northwest Racquet Swim and Health Clubs, a chain of 11 clubs around the state.

Musselman was interviewed by Wolfenson and left encouraged: "Marv Wolfenson asked me why I wanted the job. I said:

'Because this is the best job for me. Certain coaches are good for certain NBA jobs. This is the best job.'

'I agree. Why do you think you haven't been back in the NBA before?'

'Because it's political.'

"He stood up behind his desk and said, 'I agree. It is political. Now you've got politics on your side,' " Musselman related.

Bob Stein, Wolfenson's 41-year-old son-in-law, was hired as president and chief executive officer of the Timberwolves. Stein was an All-State football lineman at St. Louis Park (Minn.) High School. At the University of Minnesota, he became an All-American defensive end.

Stein played seven seasons of pro football before a knee injury finished his career. As an agent with a law degree, Stein represented NBA players Randy Breuer, Craig Hodges, and Jim Petersen. He dropped all three to avoid a conflict of interest.

Having met the NBA's December 31, 1988, deadline to have $13 million of the franchise fee paid and a minimum of 10,000 season tickets sold, the Timberwolves front office focused on building a team and continuing construction of an 18,000-seat arena scheduled to open next year. They will play their initial NBA season in the Metrodome.

They'll be playing for Musselman. "I knew I'd get an NBA job," he said. "They couldn't keep me out."

First he had to get in. Stein said he delayed bringing Musselman to Minnesota until his season with the Patroons was over. In the first week of May, he summoned Musselman to Minneapolis for an extensive two-day set of interviews.

Before May, Musselman thought he was a viable candidate. He felt even better when Stein asked him to come to Minneapolis. When he got there, though, he wasn't quite sure what to make of Stein's request that Musselman take psychological tests. "At first I thought I was the only guy taking them," Musselman said. "I thought, 'Man, they've heard all kinds of stories about me.' I got to go to a psychologist. My God, they don't know if I'm normal. I thought I was an enigma or something."

Musselman was relieved to learn the tests were administered to all candidates for key positions in the Timberwolves organization. "It's a very thorough organization," he said. "They check and triple check."

Stein had been checking out Musselman extensively. "It was just a critical decision, and if I ever overdid one, I wanted to overdo this one," Stein said. "I talked to Bill on the phone. I started following Albany's team and taking their newspapers. I had someone in Cleveland go to the library and get every clipping on the Cavaliers during the time he was there. I went through everything that was written about him during the time he was with the University of Minnesota here. I talked to the athletic director (Paul Giel) who had been here when he was here. I talked to every owner that he's worked for, with the exception of the Albany owners because I didn't think that was really appropriate at a time they were trying to keep him."

By the end of January 1988, Stein deemed Musselman a serious candidate. The 48–6 season he was compiling with the Patroons impressed Stein: "It reinforced that he's an excellent coach. To take four separate teams and just about start from scratch each year and win four straight championships anyplace is real tough and it's real impressive. Two Coach of the Year awards. Then the record Albany had that year was unbelievable. And I thought he handled the players real well. He won the championship (in Albany) after losing his four top players. There were just a lot of elements that were real impressive to me.

"Then I talked to people who had been assistant coaches for him. I talked to agents who had dealt with him about how he handled their players when he coached them and in terms of being unselfish and helping them move up to the NBA. I talked to players. I talked to players' wives. What I saw was just a totally different impression than the one I started out with."

Stein called Sidney Lowe and spoke with his wife: "Her comment was that he was real good with players, that he treated everybody the same, and that he was color-blind. He didn't treat star players different than backups; he was considerate of his players' families. She said their son called him 'Coach' and knew him real well. And it was very coincidental that I called her, because the day before she had gotten a letter from Bill just writing to inquire as to whether she and the baby were doing okay with Sidney out of town (playing for Calgary in the World Basketball League) and them home alone. You just never see things like that.

"I was a professional athlete, and I know how rare it is for a guy to take an interest even in one or two players when they're done playing for him. And here I started hearing a lot of times where he'd call a guy once a month, even if he's overseas, to see how he's doing. He really made an investment in the player. That impressed me. Not because I wanted a saint to coach the team. It impressed me because I'm convinced that in the close confines of a team, you can't fool people. A player, academically or intellectually, is more than smart enough to know whether you have any interest in him as a person and whether you know what you're talking about. So here I saw two key elements that were critical: the guy knows how to coach and he knows how to handle people. Plus they respect him."

Stein labeled Musselman's tenure at the University of Minnesota a "little plus" despite the fight and 128 NCAA violations: "He turned the whole state around as far as interest in basketball. He just revived the Minnesota basketball program from nothing. They hadn't won a

Big Ten championship in 53 years. I saw, also, unanimity as far as people's observations of his work habits; that he was completely dedicated to having the best basketball team that he could."

The names bandied about in the Twin Cities newspapers as candidates besides Musselman were Bob Weiss, Bill Fitch, and George Karl. A former NBA head coach who asked anonymity said Weiss was the only other serious candidate Stein considered. Stein said, "I interviewed a lot of coaches. Most of the names did not become public because I wasn't comfortable turning the selection process into a publicity vehicle for the team at the expense of a coach who wouldn't be hired. When names came out some other way, I didn't deny it when it was true, but there were a lot of people I talked to whose names were never published at all."

The name he chose was Musselman. At the August 23, 1988, press conference announcing he had signed a four- year contract with the Timberwolves, Musselman described what his team will be like: "Visualize a cold, dark night in the state of Minnesota. A pack of timberwolves stalking and waiting for its prey. And the prey—the opposition—is fearful what might happen. World War III will take place. In lighter terms, the prey is in for a tough night and the battle of its life."

Reflecting back, Musselman said, "It was a good feeling to be announced coach of the Minnesota team, their first coach ever. I felt fortunate they gave me the opportunity."

Others felt differently. Columnist Joe Menzer of the Willoughby, Ohio, *News-Herald* cited Musselman's press conference description of the Timberwolves, and asked, "Do these sound like the ramblings of a sane man?" In his column, covered by the headline "Madman Musselman didn't deserve the chance," Menzer told his readers, "Don't be fooled like the Timberwolves were. Musselman won in the CBA because he went where the owners had money and scruples that matched his. He scrounged up every outlaw no one else wanted and ended up with more talent than the opponents." In closing, Menzer wrote, "And I bet Musselman won't survive the length of his contract. Any takers out there?"

A blast from the Cleveland *Plain Dealer* didn't surprise Musselman. The inaccurate factual information did. Columnist Bill Livingston began a spiteful attack on Musselman: "Such as shame, really, that Bill Musselman ever escaped the minor leagues. He belonged in the Continental Basketball Association. Specifically, he belonged in

Rapid City, South Dakota, where he toiled for three of the past four years. South Dakota, where the mountains look like Presidents, is accustomed to stone heads, you see.'' Musselman coached in Rapid City for one month during the 1987 playoffs, after the Thrillers relocated from Tampa Bay.

In his column, Livingston called Musselman ''Ted Stepien's right-hand Bozo'' and continually referred to him as Musclehead. Livingston concluded: ''Perhaps Musclehead has learned something, about the league, about how to deal with people. God knows he had plenty of room for improvement.

''Certainly, he will be given the benefit of the doubt in Minnesota, which is the only place in the country outside the granite of Teddy Roosevelt's nose on Mt. Rushmore that you could say that.

''Still, the bet here is that next season (1988–89), when he is paid not to coach, will be his most successful. Incredibly, the Timberwolves, who begin play in 1989, gave him a four-year contract, only three of them to be actively spent on the bench.

''My question is: Why did they so honor the guy? Did they run out of human beings, or what?''

A month into the 1988–89 NBA season, the 33 staff members of the Timberwolves front office engaged in a two-week contest selling season tickets. ''As soon as we said it was competition, Bill Musselman's eyes lit up,'' Stein said. ''I'd say it lit a fire.''

Musselman sold 22 the first day, missed seven days on a scouting trip, and won the contest anyway by selling 14 more. ''I like to sell, because it's numbers, like wins,'' Musselman said. ''It's concrete. You can show the work you accomplished.''

Less tangible results arose from the work Musselman poured into scouting nearly 150 NBA, college, and CBA games during his season without players last winter. He and Director of Player Personnel Billy McKinney scouted separately, came back to Minneapolis regularly, and went over their notes together with Stein.

Musselman focused his scouting on searching for his type of players. ''No. 1, you want people that know how to play the game,'' he said. ''Game intelligence is very important. A lot of people play the game; very few know how to play it. I think intelligence and character are important. You also have to get players that other people like to play with, and you have to find competitors. We want good people with character and work habits who'll be playing in the league for eight to 10 years, providing they don't get hurt.''

Eric Musselman was with his father when he scouted point guard Tim Hardaway of Texas–El Paso in January. "Dad said to me, 'He's my point guard. He's just like Sidney Lowe. I can see it in his eyes. He wants to win,' " Eric related. "That's what Dad was watching—how bad the guy hated to lose."

Musselman's life on the road began with NBA preseason games in October. His ever-hectic itinerary took him forth and back across the country. He recounted the specifics of one slice of his season on the road: "October 6, I went to the San Antonio–Cleveland game. October 12, I flew to the Air Force Academy to watch Dallas play Denver. The next night, I fly into Vegas. Drive 110 miles to St. George, Utah, to watch Indiana play the Jazz. Next night I fly to Milwauk...I mean Phoenix. Took Sunday off and ran. Monday night, I watched the Suns play the 76ers. The next night I went to Santa Clara, California, and saw the Warriors–Clippers. Next night I saw the Lakers against the Jazz. Next night I fly to Sacramento, see a Kings game. A night later, I fly into Portland. I drive 200 miles to watch an exhibition game. I got a 6:50 flight to Florida the next morning. I get in about 4 o'clock. Game at 7:30 between Miami and Indiana. Next night, I go to, I think it's Houston. Then to Cincinnati. To Baltimore. Then to Sarasota for a day and a half of rest. Then back to Minnesota for two days of speaking engagements. Then I head for the Celtics–Knickerbockers opener in Boston. Then a speaking engagement the next day in Maine and a coaching clinic. Next day, I head back to Minneapolis. Take a couple of days off and start all over again.

"It's, it's wearin' me out," he said last January. "You wouldn't believe how many games I've seen. When I'm not at a game, I run. I run on campus at SMU doing my sprints. I run in a football stadium at Vanderbilt. I run the mountains in Phoenix. I run in Sacramento, in the desert. You know, I run every place I go to stay in shape. And if not, I stay where there's a health club and work out. Eat, sleep, work out, watch games...on the road, pack, unpack, lie awake, evaluate player against player. So I know the personnel. When I was in the NBA before, I didn't know the personnel like I know 'em now."

Musselman was in Albany January 24, watching his son and Flip Saunders' Rapid City Thrillers beat George Karl's Albany Patroons 113–110. His original itinerary for the week had him in Syracuse to watch a Big East game. Instead he came to Albany. He showed up at the Armory about an hour before game time and immediately was greeted by a bevy of fans congratulating him about the Minnesota job or just welcoming him back. He headed for the concession stand to get a box of popcorn. He never made it. The small pocket of people circling him kept growing. Some wished him luck next season; others asked for an autograph or the opportunity to pose with him on the court for a picture.

Just seconds before tip-off, Musselman took his seat at press row, just two seats from Saunders. During the game he fidgeted nervously with a pen in his hand. The pen became a metronome, keeping an eerie rhythm that documented his discomfort in seeing a game and not coaching in it. Rowland stopped briefly in front of Musselman. They shook hands quickly as Rowland made his way downcourt, trailing a play way ahead of him.

Late in the first half, Albany was up by 12 and Musselman gave advice to Saunders. Incredibly, Musselman had signed a $5,000 consultant's contract with the Patroons for the 1988–89 season. Of course, Musselman shepherded prospects to his son's team, not the Patroons.

When he intermittently passed on suggestions to Saunders, Musselman publicly displayed his sentiment, one he'd told friends: blood's thicker than water. And when Musselman failed to return the $5,000, the Patroons held his championship ring hostage.

After the game, Musselman was again greeted by an array of fans, players, and an agent who happened to be at the Armory. As the conversations dragged on, Eric and Saunders were waiting for him. They had agreed to go out to dinner after the game, if Eric could ever pry his father out of the building.

Bill Musselman was still at the press table, talking this time to Patroons center John Stroeder, who had recently spent two weeks in the NBA with the Golden State Warriors. Musselman asked a question and Stroeder took a pen and started diagramming a play. By this time, Musselman's voice was hoarse. He was croaking out sentences.

"He just asked about some defensive schemes that Golden State ran," Stroeder said a couple days later. "He couldn't understand how they could be winning when the tallest guy in the lineup was 6–8. He wanted to know how we guarded 7-footers. All that stuff I learned up there, I keep in my head. I always have, so that when I become a coach some day, I'll be able to use it."

It was nearly 11 p.m., 45 minutes after the game ended, when Eric and Saunders finally corralled Musselman. They got into Musselman's rented car outside the Armory.

"It's all experience," Musselman began. The subject is Saunders.

Eric said, "Well, he's not doing a bad job."

"No, he's doing a good job," Musselman said. "I'm gonna make him a great coach. Hell, he's got the potential. He just doesn't have the years of pro ball." Musselman looked into the rear-view mirror at Saunders. "You do a great job. You're going to become a great coach. Soon as something happens on the court, you've got to read it quick. I knew the moment they put in (Wayne) Engelstad at center what was going to happen."

Saunders, who played for Musselman at the University of Minnesota, said, "Yeah, they're just going to clear out and go."

Musselman continued his dialogue with Saunders:

'Yeah, you got to read that quick, and relay it to the players because the whole game is matchups. It's like when both teams are going down to take perimeter shots. You look out there and say, Now they got all those slow guys. They got no lateral individual defensive skills. And really, your club doesn't have a lot of great individual defensive players. It's pathetic really, for as much as you've won (Rapid City was 22–8 and in first place in the Western Division). I'm not saying they can't be a good team defensively, but, who have you got that just goes out and stops 'em?'

'Jimmy Thomas and Keith Smart.'

'But Flip, Thomas is not quick.'

'He relies on technique. Everything's technique.'

'And position.'

'Milt Wagner couldn't play D, Bill. He couldn't stop you.'

'Thomas can't create anything. All he can do is contain a scorer.' "

Eric, noticing his father had made a wrong turn leaving the Armory, said:

'We're staying at the Hilton, not your old apartment.'

'OK, Eric. In your face.'

Musselman resumed his conversation with Saunders:

'So the thing is, a kid like Thomas, as good as he is and how hard he works, he only stops players as the information is given to him. Like here, knowing that Derrick Rowland, on the left side, goes into the lane all the time. Does he ever shoot? It's into the lane, and he goes to get fouled. He doesn't go to finish the play.'

'Here's the thing, okay, Bill? Jimmy Thomas. You know how many times we went over that? Five different times on Derrick Rowland. Jimmy Thomas, right now, he didn't play well. I mean, he's in a funk. That's how he is. He's the type of guy who's got to have the whole scouting report. He's got to know exactly what his guy does, where we want him to go.' "

The conversation shifted as they drove to the Parc V for a late dinner. Saunders told a story from his college days playing for Musselman at Minnesota: "When I talked to Mark Olberding, he says it was probably one of the classics of all time, after we got beat at Ohio State. First of all, Bill didn't invite Dennis Shaffer to the team meeting 'cause he played shitty at Ohio State. We were at Indiana the next game, and they had won like 36 straight in the Big Ten over two years. We get into Indiana, we all get taped up and everything. So we go out there and grab the balls and Bill says, 'Take away the fucking balls.' So the manager, he kind of moves the balls to the end of the court, and Bill goes, 'Hear what I said? I said take away the fucking balls.' So he takes the balls, and Olberding's looking at me like, 'What the hell's going on?' Bill says, 'Follow me.'

"He marches us all the way up to Indiana's top row in their arena. You're so fucking high up there you couldn't even see the nets, you know, being so steep. And he says, 'You guys sit down.' We sat down and he talked to us for a few minutes. He said, 'I'll tell you right now: 18,500 people, they're going to be here tomorrow. They're going to want to kick your ass. All a sea of red (Indiana's color). All a sea of red.' "

"Then we were done. So we went down, cut off our tape and come out the next day. I mean, we played a great game. Even though we lost, we only lost by three. (Saunders' memory had gone the route of all ex-players. Indiana won by 20, 79–59.) Mychal Thompson had 29 (actually 23) and Olberding 20-something. And they were freshmen."

Musselman said, "They were too quick for us."

"But those two guys, I mean that was an unbelievable game," Saunders said. "I remember, in fact, Olberding went up, got the ball on the baseline, pump-faked (Kent) Benson, and shot through him for a three-point play. Benson's looking at the ref like it's not a foul, and Olberding grabs the ball and shoves it into his stomach. Benson doubles over."

Musselman wasn't doubling over with laughter about the story. After all, it was a loss to Bobby Knight.

The stories dragged on through dinner. Musselman tried to eat, continue conversations even though his voice was almost too hoarse to be heard, and watch the Knicks–Lakers game on a giant TV set near the bar.

It was after 1 a.m. when Musselman got back to his hotel. The following night (Wednesday), Musselman was watching Tennessee at Alabama. Thursday night, he was in Tulsa, Oklahoma, to see Oral Roberts play Cincinnati. Saturday afternoon he was in Las Vegas for UNLV's game against Oklahoma. Saturday night he made it to Reno for another game, Nevada–Reno against Boise State.

Musselman had seen five games in five cities in five nights, crossing the continent along the way. There were plenty of other games left to see, games he felt he had to see. Monday started another week of scouting.

During the '88–89 season, Musselman, Stein, and McKinney gauged the mixed results of the initial seasons unfolding in Charlotte and Miami. Charlotte led the NBA in attendance with an average of 23,172, second highest in league history. Miami got much notoriety by starting 0–17, but also did well at the gate, averaging 14,945 in its 15,008-seat arena. Charlotte had a better record (20–62) than Miami (15–67), relying more on veterans. Only one rookie, Rex Chapman, was among the Hornets' top five scorers. Conversely, three of Miami's top four scorers were rookies.

"I think there's a fine line," Musselman said. "You don't want a bunch of veterans, but at the same time you want some veterans around who'll give your young people a chance to develop."

Musselman had developed enough frequent-flier points to last a lifetime. Wednesday night, March 8, Musselman watched Illinois pound Iowa. "I was impressed with the whole Illinois team," he said. "They have enough talent to win it all. I like (Kenny) Battle and (Lowell) Hamilton, but I don't know how good they'll do in the pros. Their most valuable players are undergraduates."

Musselman left Champaign, Illinois, Thursday morning and arrived in New York City at 5:30 p.m., two hours late because of an airline strike and heavy traffic in Manhattan. He came to New York to see the Big East Tournament.

He checked into his room on the 12th floor at the Marriott Marquis, a lavish midtown hotel with 48 floors, see-through elevators, and prices in one of its restaurants that were eminently reasonable: glass of orange juice, $3.50; cup of soup, $4.50. The price for a room for a night: $245. Musselman got a weekend rate of $179.

There was only one tournament game Thursday night at Madison Square Garden at 7 o'clock, so Musselman had little time to change. Among the items he unpacked was his black binder notebook, filled with roughly 1,250 players' names, addresses, phone numbers, agents' names and phone numbers, and the players' various family members. There were 50 pages of names with about 25 players on each page, except an occasional page which had names on both sides. A sample under the *M*s: Kevin Mackey (coach at Cleveland State; Musselman helped him get the job), Tom Meehan, Wayne Mello, Scott Meents, Fred Miller, Bertha and Jim Miller (Musselman's mother and stepfather), Loren Miller, Ralph Miller (Oregon State coach), Richard Mills, Sam Mitchell (former Thriller), Larry Moffett, Bill Moore, Curtis Moore, (Lowes's younger brother), and Lowes Moore.

A player has to turn at least 40 years old before Musselman will stop keeping tabs. Thus, Coby Dietrick's name is still in the book.

Is Musselman thorough? How about eight different phone numbers for Steve Rambadt, a 6–8 forward who averaged 8.0 points and 5.3 rebounds in two CBA seasons for four different teams, none of them Musselman's. Listed in Musselman's notebook are Rambadt's number at home and work; friend, Alma; girlfriend, Karen; girlfriend's parents; father, Stanley; and home and work number for Rambadt's mother. "He's tough to get a hold of," Musselman explained.

Musselman didn't take time to eat, hailing a cab for the Garden. His principal interest Thursday was Boston College guard Dana Barros, the Big East's leading scorer the last two seasons. Before the tournament, Musselman had the 5–10 Barros ranked tentatively as the second-best senior point guard in the country, behind Hardaway and ahead of Georgetown's Charles Smith. None of the trio come close to Musselman's evaluation of LSU's sensational freshman, Chris Jackson: "I couldn't believe what I saw. If I had to design a point guard, he'd be it. He's too good for college basketball. There's no question I'd pay admission to see him play."

Lower on Musselman's point guard list were Syracuse senior Sherman Douglas, the all-time NCAA career assist leader, and Mookie Blaylock of Oklahoma, who was suspended for one game in March for public intoxication. "He didn't show good judgment getting intoxicated at this key time (just before the Big Eight and NCAA tournaments)," Musselman said.

Of Smith, Musselman said, "I like his defense. He's a tough kid mentally. I wouldn't discount him. They're not as effective without him, which is a credit to him."

Musselman's tickets for the Big East Tournament were in the upper loge. The Garden was nearly half-empty because not many fans were interested in watching the lowest two seeds of the Big East, St. John's and Boston College, battle for the right to be in Friday's quarterfinal against top seed Georgetown. Musselman found a better spot, then settled into the mid-court mezzanine seat and went to work.

Using mimeographed scouting sheets, Musselman tracked Barros's shots and how each was taken: off the dribble; off a screen; did he use a drop step; did he have lateral movement; was there contact when he shot?

On a separate sheet of paper, Musselman wrote down significant comments about Barros: "What I look for is how does he read picks; were his feet under him when he took his shots; did he show patience coming off picks; does he set his man up to use a pick; does he look at the other guard; is he alert for coaching?"

Barros kept Musselman busy, scoring a Big East Tournament-record 38 points in a narrow BC win. Musselman had focused so sharply on Barros, he said after the game, "I couldn't even tell you who was playing for St. John's."

Musselman looked forward to Friday's games because Seton Hall was one of the few strong teams in college basketball he hadn't yet seen in person. Seton Hall was matched against Connecticut, which had two pro prospects, center Cliff Robinson and guard Phil Gamble.

The other quarterfinal Friday afternoon was Syracuse against Providence. A doubleheader Friday evening had BC–Georgetown and Pittsburgh against Villanova.

The cab driver who took Musselman to the games Friday protested as soon as Musselman said, "Madison Square Garden."

"The Garden? I was just at the Garden. It was 20 minutes every block," she said. Musselman wasn't budging. Waiting in a line for a taxi had squandered 10 of the 20 minutes he left to get to the Garden. "Twenty minutes every block?" he asked, the panic apparent in his voice.

"Twenty minutes," she said, but then she tried an alternate route and sped down Ninth Avenue. It was a brilliant move that avoided whatever traffic tie-up she had encountered before.

Musselman wasted little time to engage in conversation and learned she was: 1) married; 2) not married—she only says she's married to inquiring males; 3) had a father who was Portuguese and a mother who was Puerto Rican; 4) had a 9-year-old child; 5) owned the cab she drove; and 6) wasn't particularly fond of driving it in New York City. Musselman then asked her why she did it.

" 'To make a buck.'

'Why don't you move out of New York?'

'My parents are here. My brother is here. I have family.'

'Take them with you. Hey, you should move to Pensacola, Florida. Move your entire family there.'

'I bet there's a huge demand for cab drivers in Pensacola.'

'There is. Hey, I can tell you're a nice person. I'm looking for somebody to take care of me. I live in Sarasota. You'd love Florida.'

'Can't do it. Are you going to the airport tonight?'

'I'm not sure. I might be going tomorrow.'

'I'll take you. Here's my phone number. Call me and I'll take you.' "

The ride was over. The cab had found the traffic snarl half a block from the Garden.

"You're better off walking," she said.

Musselman paid the fare, didn't say a word about his status as a basketball celebrity, said again he would call her if he went to the airport the next day, and left her cab. As Musselman re-entered his world of basketball, he left a New York City cabdriver who was facing gridlock with the unlikeliest of tools: a smile. Maybe it lasted for only a few seconds, but she was definitely smiling after her conversation with Musselman.

Settling in his seat before the Seton Hall–UConn game, Musselman said, "I look for certain skills. Michael Smith at BYU. He's a pro shooter and pro passer."

Robinson played as if he was neither a pro scorer nor a pro rebounder and certainly not a potential member of the Timberwolves. In one of the most miserable performances of his collegiate career, he shot three for 17 from the field and had just six rebounds. Gamble was unimpressive, too, as Seton Hall pulled away late for a 74–66 victory.

Of Robinson, Musselman wrote, "Poor shooting. Never gets the tough rebound."

Musselman had a kinder appraisal for two seniors from Seton

Hall, center-forward Ramon Ramos, who played in the 1988 Olympics for the Puerto Rican National Team, and forward Daryll Walker.

Musselman wrote 10 comments about Ramos, a muscular, polished player with an NBA body: 6–8 and 250 pounds: "1) went for the loose ball on the floor; 2) tough reaction to ball off boards; 3) strong, good competitor; 4) garbage player; 5) reads ball well, knows how to position to get shot; 6) can get a guy on his ass (and score); 7) will body up on low post people; leans on people; tires them out; 8) reacts to boards; 9) excellent knowledge; 10) rebounds in a crowd."

Walker, who mostly toiled in the obscurity one would expect from a 5.2-point scoring average, also drew kind words from Musselman, who wrote: "Quick jumper." Then, the 6–8 Walker grabbed a rather ordinary defensive rebound. "Look at that kid," Musselman yelled as if he'd discovered an elixir for expansion teams. Then he screamed even louder: "Sleeper." In a hushed tone, Musselman said, "Hey, he's not a bad player. How tall is he?"

During Syracuse's second possession in its game against Providence, Musselman noted the play of Sherman Douglas: "Doesn't like to catch and shoot." He added, "running, one-hand jump shot, defense at mid-court—didn't try to recover when guy went by him, will set a good pick, not shy of contact."

Disdaining a cab, Musselman walked the 15 blocks back to the hotel. The sidewalks were crowded. "Look at these women," he said many times. Frequently he said, "How are you?" One out of 20 muttered hello, a pattern that puzzled Musselman. "Do I look tired?" he asked twice.

He concluded that he probably looked just fine and that strangers in New York City aren't overly friendly. Musselman thought a few seconds about walking to a demonstration one block away—Albanians protesting their status in Yugoslavia—and finally found someone, a male policeman on horseback, who returned a response:

" 'Hey, what's going on down there with those people?'
'What people?'
'Two blocks away. There's a demonstration. What are they protesting?'
'I don't know. They don't tell me.' "

Musselman resumed walking. Back at the hotel, he returned to his room and phoned his two children. Nicole, a freshman at Southern Methodist University, would be getting a visit. Musselman's itinerary included scouting a Dallas Mavs' home game that Monday night. Nicole wasn't in her room, so Musselman left a message on her answering machine: "Nicole, I'm coming in Sunday or Monday. I love you. I miss you. Love, Dad."

Eric was next, and Musselman again had to settle for leaving a message: "Your phone machine doesn't work too well, Eric. Hope everything's fine. Good luck in your next game. Love, Dad."

Dinner was next, but there was little time with Friday night's first game starting at 7. Musselman again decided to walk to the Garden and wound up eating in Nathan's. He probably was the only person there who had never heard of the famous establishment.

Then, he further betrayed his tourist status by having soup instead of a hot dog.

Go figure.

22

A Team Comes to Life

Warm, splendid sunshine bathed the Twin Cities May 23, 1989. Inside the 98th Street Swim, Racquet, and Health Club, at 9 a.m., Bill Musselman was a coach once again.

As he surveyed 23 free agents in the first of four Timberwolves tryout camps, Musselman relished the pure thrill of being on the sidelines with a whistle around his neck. "This is the happiest I've been in months," he said. "It seems like I've been out of coaching 10 years. It was a relief to get onto the floor."

It had been nearly 13 months since Musselman's Patroons won the 1988 CBA championship and exactly nine months since he was hired as coach of the Timberwolves, beginning an odyssey of scouting, organizing, hiring staff, and speaking engagements. "It was a funny year," Musselman said. "One moment I felt like a public relations man. The next day I was a salesman. The day after that I felt like a clerk, and the day after that I was a recruiter. I felt anything but a coach."

How excited was he to get that feeling again? "I blew my whistle at home once a day just for practice," he said. When he blew the whistle for real, he faced an anxious group of players hoping to play well enough in three days to earn an appearance in training camp—and the opportunity to compete for one of the Timberwolves' 12 roster spots.

The coach wasted no time in setting the tone of Camp Musselman. "Practice is at 9 o'clock. Not one minute after, not two minutes after. Nine o'clock."

Musselman divided the players into four teams. Before he began an hour of scrimmaging, he advised the campers: "We keep score. You play to win."

Most knew that. Sixteen of the 23 had been in the CBA. Four had played for him: Derrick Rowland and Rick Carlisle in Albany; John Stroeder and Sam Mitchell in Tampa Bay.

Rowland had split the 1988–89 season, playing in the Philippines through December before rejoining the Patroons under George Karl. "There's just something inside me that keeps telling me not to give up," he said. "When it's time to step away, I'll know. It's not time yet. I'm here because I feel I can play in this league. I've seen a lot of guys I've played with and against become successful in the NBA, and between them and me, there's not a lot of difference."

Carlisle missed the entire '88–89 season when he injured his shoulder during the third day of the New York Knicks training camp. "It's been a long year," he said. "I want to prove to people I can still play."

Carlisle showed Musselman he can still shoot, twice making 72 of 80 in a spot-shooting drill from four locations marked around the basket. "It's hard to believe a four-time NBA All-Star had never done spot shooting, but Micheal Ray Richardson hadn't done it until he came to Albany," Musselman told the troops.

A dozen free agents earned admission into the Wolves' second tryout camp starting June 13. The competition grew increasingly demanding. Eighteen new players included NBA veteran Gene Banks and 7-footer Wallace Bryant, who played last season in Spain.

Musselman, though, was more impressed with Mitchell and another arrival from Spain, Tod Murphy. "They played as well as anybody in the first two free-agent camps we had," Musselman said. "We had 23 guys the first camp, 30 the second. Sam Mitchell was the best player. He's got a chance to make the club. But he's got a good contract offer in Europe, so I don't know. I don't know how much money he's going to want."

From the summer free-agent camps, Musselman wanted to build a foundation "so that everybody knows what you want. We started with the guys at the first camp, and we started to put in a system. Then we took the top guys from there and added more guys. Then we take the top guys there, and we add players from the expansion draft and players from the college draft and some other free agents. You keep subtracting and adding players until you get what you want.''

What Musselman desperately wanted was a chance to select players he and McKinney had evaluated from their months of scouting NBA and college games last winter. Here, Musselman got an unexpected assist from one of his compatriot former Cavs head coaches, Chuck Daly.

The expansion draft had been set for June 22 as long as the NBA Championship Series went more than four games. But when Daly's Detroit Pistons completed a four-game sweep of the Los Angeles Lakers June 13, Musselman, McKinney, Minnesota, and the Magic of Orlando were suddenly center stage. The expansion draft was June 15.

A coin toss at noon June 12 at the Airport Marriott Hotel in Los Angeles would decide the order in the expansion and college drafts for Minnesota and Orlando. Three minutes before the toss, an earthquake measuring 4.5 on the Richter Scale shook the room. Musselman seemed oblivious as he continued to answer a question from a reporter.

The tremor passed. Precisely at noon, NBA Commissioner David Stern, flanked by Musselman and Orlando coach Matt Guokas, officially brought the NBA's two newest teams into the league.

A specially designed coin, with ''Timberwolves'' on one side and ''Magic'' on the other, came up Magic.

Musselman was 0–1.

Guokas announced the Magic would take the first pick in the expansion draft.

That gave the Timberwolves the 10th and 38th selections in the two-round college draft. Orlando would pick 11th and 37th.

Musselman told reporters the Timberwolves probably would have opted for the higher pick in the college draft even had they won the coin toss. ''We're happy with the way it is,'' he said.

At 12:20, Musselman was not happy. This time, he felt the floor quiver from an earthquake aftershock that measured 4.3 on the Richter Scale.

A reporter said, ''It's an earthquake.''

Musselman said, ''Earthquake? I don't like to hear about that stuff. I got to get on a plane and get back to Minnesota." A leery flier, Musselman couldn't get to the airport fast enough.

Only Miami and Charlotte were excluded from the expansion draft, which allowed each NBA team to protect eight players on its roster. The draft's early date and the threat of a $250,000 fine for any club leaking names on protected lists combined to make Musselman's first personnel move a dazzling one.

Orlando's initial choice was Sidney Green, a power forward for the New York Knicks. That freed the Timberwolves to pounce on Rick Mahorn, the starting power forward for the new NBA champion Pistons. "We thought he'd be the first person to go," Musselman said.

Green, unhappy with his playing time with the Knicks, said he was pleased to relocate in Orlando as a starter. Mahorn, the NBA's king of enforcers or the league's leading thug, depending on your point of view, was stunned. So was Daly.

Both were at a celebration party at the Pistons' home court, the Palace. At the party, Mahorn referred to himself as "the baddest Bad Boy you've ever seen." Less than an hour after the party ended, Mahorn learned he was no longer a Piston. He hurriedly gathered his belongings from his locker and left the building, declining to comment to a horde of reporters following him.

Daly expressed shock: "This is the happiest day of my life because of the celebration, but this is also the most devastating moment. We took a calculated risk." Pistons General Manager Jack McCloskey added, "It was lousy timing."

The Pistons reportedly made an unsuccessful last-minute offer to keep Mahorn, trying to induce a three-way deal with the Timberwolves and the Indiana Pacers involving Detroit guard Michael Williams and an exchange of draft picks.

McKinney, an expansion pick himself when Dallas took him from the Kings in 1980, said he wasn't surprised at Mahorn's reticence: "I'm sure I'd have the same reaction. In fact, I did."

Later that night, Mahorn shared his sentiments: "Of course there were tears. It's been an up-and-down day—but it's part of basketball. A champion one day, someplace else the next. I've had the one highlight of my career. Now it's time to push on to someplace else."

Mahorn's mother, Alice, told of the phone conversation she had with her son: "He cried and I cried. It was a shock. Here he is on top of the world one minute, then somebody pulls the rug out from under him a little. He's bouncing back, though. He's ready to go.''

Mahorn is one of the most controversial players in the NBA: an excellent defender whose age (31), back problems (he underwent surgery in 1988), and penchant for fighting induced the Pistons to leave him unprotected. Mahorn, 6–10 and 255 pounds, averaged 7.3 points and 6.9 rebounds in 1988–89 while leading the NBA in fines ($11,000) but fouling out just once. Most of the 66 times he's fouled out were early in his nine-year NBA career, 50 of them in four seasons. Stein described Mahorn as ''one of those guys nobody likes unless he's on your team.''

After Orlando took Atlanta guard Reggie Theus, Minnesota plucked Tyrone Corbin, a 6–6 forward who started 30 games for another highly successful team last season, Phoenix. In his fourth NBA season, Corbin averaged 8.2 points and 5.2 rebounds while shooting 54.0 percent from the floor and 78.8 percent at the line. He also led the Suns in offensive rebounding. ''We got a guy who was a starting small forward on a team that won 55 games,'' Musselman said. ''He's the epitome of a tremendous role player. We're looking for overachievers. To be the leading offensive rebounder at 6–6 on a great team, that tells you something.''

McKinney said, ''We went in hoping we would get either Mahorn or Corbin, and we got both. Getting good big people is always the hardest thing.''

In its ensuing picks, Minnesota selected center Steve Johnson of Portland, center Brad Lohaus of Sacramento, point guard David Rivers of the Lakers, guard Mark Davis of Milwaukee, forward Scott Roth of San Antonio, forward Shelton Jones of the 76ers, forward Eric White of the Clippers, guard Maurice Martin of Denver, and 7–4 West German Gunther Behnke, who has never played in the U.S.

In addition, the Timberwolves picked up a second-round college draft pick (34th overall) from Milwaukee for not selecting Larry Krystkowiak or Tito Horford.

''We had a helluva expansion draft,'' Musselman said. ''Hey, we got a starter off a world championship team and a starter off a team that won 55 games. We got everybody we wanted but Otis Smith.'' Smith, a 6–5 guard from Golden State, was Orlando's fifth pick.

When the draft ended, Musselman was ecstatic and exhausted. But with the college draft demanding immediate attention, there was little time to rest.

Reports of trade offers were everywhere as teams postured for better position. Chicago offered Minnesota its No. 6 overall pick for Mahorn and the Timberwolves' No. 10. Indiana offered its No. 7 for Corbin and Minnesota's No. 10. Chicago tried again, offering its No. 25 pick for Mahorn (Chicago had three picks in the first round thanks to previous trades). "We had 11 teams call up and ask about Corbin," Musselman said.

The Timberwolves stayed pat, hoping their three picks, 10th, 34th, and 38th, would yield long-range players so vital to an expansion team's future. Musselman figured more help could be obtained later by signing veteran free agents such as Tony Campbell of the Lakers and/or the Knicks' Trent Tucker, who played at the University of Minnesota.

At every level and place Musselman has coached, he's made a point guard a top priority. The Timberwolves weren't an exception.

While TBS gave the June 27 NBA Draft in New York City unprecedented prime-time, live TV coverage, Musselman, McKinney, and Stein waited through the first nine picks. They had reached their consensus decision just one hour before the draft started.

Pre-draft analyses appearing in *Sports Illustrated* and *The Sporting News* predicted Musselman would take either a shooting guard or point guard.

When only one guard, Florida State's George McCloud (taken by Indiana with the No. 7 pick) went before Minnesota's selection, the Timberwolves were free to take Stanford's Todd Lichti, pegged as the nation's best shooting guard, or point guards Tim Hardaway of UTEP or B.J. Armstrong of Iowa.

Before Minnesota's selection was announced, TBS switched to a live remote at the Minneapolis Convention Center, where an estimated 12,000 had gathered for what was billed as the NBA's largest Draft Day party. Timberwolves co-owner Harvey Ratner said, "I didn't invite many people to this because I figured, 'Who'd want to come?' But it turned out to be the biggest non-event in the history of Minnesota." Even Mahorn made it, sending out positive feedback about his transition from the Pistons to the Timberwolves when interviewed by TBS: "We have a good nucleus coming in right now. Everybody's looking forward to working hard and making sure that we can get the winning spirit back here in Minnesota." TBS flashed a couple of George Mikan film highlights from Minneapolis Lakers games 36 years earlier.

The network switched back to NBA Commissioner David Stern, who announced each first-round pick. "Minnesota's 10th pick in the 1989 NBA Draft is Jerome "Pooh" Richardson of UCLA," Stern said.

Bad Boy Mahorn and a guy named Pooh on the same team?

Richardson, a 6–1 point guard, watched the draft from his agent's home in Los Angeles. "I felt I was going to go in the top 15," he said. "I didn't know exactly with who."

TBS commentators Rick Barry and Steve Jones expressed surprise, as did most NBA observers. Indeed, the Timberwolves came up with one of the most talked about selections of the entire draft. *The Sporting News* had Pooh pegged No. 3 at point guard behind Armstrong and Hardaway. Two well-known color commentators had opposing views: Billy Packer sounded shocked; Bucky Waters called Pooh Richardson a steal.

With their second-round picks, the Timberwolves drafted 7–1 center Gary Leonard from Missouri and 6–6½ swingman Doug West from Villanova.

The following morning, the *Star Tribune* carried a Page 1 story of the draft party. Writer Steve Aschburner described the reaction to the selection of Richardson:

"It was one part 'Pooh!.'

"One part 'Boo!'

"And one very large part 'Who?' "

A huge headline in the sports section said, "Pooh (Who?) a Timberwolf."

In a postdraft analysis by United Press International, teams were graded on their selections. Writer Keith Drum gave the Timberwolves a B+. Only four of the other 25 NBA teams (Houston traded away its draft picks) got higher grades: Chicago, San Antonio, the Lakers, and Sacramento.

The Sporting News had a decidedly different evaluation in its review: "The Timberwolves passed up numerous deals, and took UCLA guard Pooh Richardson (10th) as their first choice. It's difficult to fathom how the Timberwolves elected to take Richardson when they could have traded Rick Mahorn and that 10th pick to Chicago for the sixth pick, which the Bulls used to land Stacey King. Grade: C-."

In a separate article under *The Sporting News'* "NBA Notebook", the same salvo was fired again: "The expansion Minnesota Timberwolves made several baffling decisions on draft day. Besides taking UCLA guard Pooh Richardson with the 10th pick, which was about 10 spots higher than most scouts had him rated, the Wolves also turned down a deal that would have sent Rick Mahorn and that 10th pick to the Bulls for the sixth pick. With the sixth pick, the Wolves could have had Stacey King, who probably would have led them in scoring for 10 years and probably would have scored more points than Mahorn and Richardson combined.''

Criticism closer to home came from *Star Tribune* columnist Patrick Reusse two days after the draft: ''The Timberwolves scored a clear victory over the Orlando Magic when Round One (the expansion draft) was held 12 days earlier. Tuesday, the victory went to the gentlemen from Florida. It says here that the Woofies made the first serious mistake of their brief existence when they selected UCLA guard Pooh Richardson with the 10th choice, leaving Orlando to take Illinois forward Nick Anderson with the 11th.'' Reusse concluded, ''The Woofies blew it when they handed Anderson to Orlando.''

Jan Hubbard of *Newsday* said, ''Richardson may be the best pure point guard, but the Timberwolves needed a scorer.''

McKinney disagreed with Reusse and Hubbard: ''People say 'You have no scoring; you should have taken Nick Anderson.' But we're an expansion ball club, and we're not going to have all the pieces the first year. Talk about having one big scorer, Charlotte had one (Kelly Tripucka) last season, and they won five more games than Miami, who didn't have a scorer. What's five games if you're looking at it long-term? You build year by year and you get some of the pieces now, and you add a little each year.''

Star Tribune columnist Sid Hartman told of the response he got after the draft from Univeristy of Minnesota Coach Clem Haskins: ''They picked the right guy. He will give Musselman the leadership in the backcourt he needs with all those big guys he got in the expansion draft.''

NBA Director of Scouting Marty Blake said Richardson ''knows how to finish a play, and that's the sign of a true point guard.''

Musselman said, ''It was a tough decision taking a point guard No. 10. That was Billy McKinney's pick, and I agreed with him. Bobby Knight called me the day after the draft. He said we did a good thing taking a point guard. He said, 'You got no shot at all in the NBA without a point guard. I'm glad you took a guard.' ''

Why wasn't it Hardaway or Armstrong? McKinney said, ''People were looking for a name point guard, but we're going to go with players who fit our philosophy. We want players who understand their roles, who play hard, who are unselfish. You look at his track record, and you'll see those things.''

In his senior season, Richardson had an excellent 3-to-1 assists-to-turnovers ratio (averaging 7.6 assists and 2.5 turnovers), and averaged 15.2 points as the Bruins went 21–10. Richardson, named All–Pac-10 for the third time, had bizarre shooting statistics. He made 49.5 percent of his 3-pointers and shot 55.5 percent from the floor, yet was miserable (56.2 percent) at the foul line.

Richardson's nickname was a term of endearment from a doting grandmother watching her grandson in his crib. To her, he was as cute as Winnie The Pooh.

To Musselman, he's a ticket to credibility, an unselfish point guard with a widely respected court sense cultivated during his schoolboy years at Benjamin Franklin High School in Philadelphia. ''I had good competition all the time,'' Richardson said. ''I played with guys like Nate Blackwell, Hank Gathers, and Howard Evans.''

Walt Hazzard, a Philly high school legend who was captain of John Wooden's first national championship team at UCLA in 1964, recruited Richardson. ''He's the guy I wanted to play for,'' Richardson said.

Hazzard was the fifth coach who attempted to solidify the Bruins' program after Wooden retired in 1975. In his first season, 1984–85, Hazzard led the Bruins to a 21–12 record and the NIT championship. In his second season, he handed the ball to Richardson, his freshman point guard who would eventually set a UCLA and conference record with 833 career assists.

Richardson had a dynamic freshman season, earning conference Co-Freshman of the Year honors with Sean Elliott of Arizona. A third outstanding freshman guard in the Pac-10 was Stanford's Lichti. Richardson's conference-high 179 assists and a 10.6 scoring average were inconspicuous in UCLA's mediocre (15–14) season.

The next season Richardson excelled, and the Bruins did, too, going 25–7. Setting a school record with 208 assists and averaging 10.5 points, 5.1 rebounds, and 1.5 steals, Richardson teamed with Reggie Miller, Montel Hatcher, and Jack Haley to take the Bruins to the Pac-10 title and into the NCAA Tournament for the first time in seven years.

In 1987–88 UCLA slumped to 16–14, and Hazzard was forced to exit. Richardson had a solid season, breaking his own UCLA record for assists with 210 and averaging 11.6 points, 5.1 rebounds, and 1.8 steals. But a noticeable flaw had developed in Richardson's game.

While the 3-pointer became routine among college guards, Richardson made just four treys in his sophomore and junior seasons—combined.

With a new coach, Jim Harrick, Richardson worked on that deficiency and turned his outside shooting into a strength. In UCLA's first 10 games, Richardson made 12 of 15 to temporarily lead the nation in 3-point accuracy. Though his 3-point percentage leveled off, his positive impact didn't. Richardson's 18-footer with 11 seconds left gave UCLA a one-point win against USC.

"People wanted to see if I could shoot the basketball," Richardson said. "I want to be depended on. I like the challenge. There's a fine line between looking for the pass and being an aggressive point guard and looking for the shot."

The ability Richardson displayed after the regular season sold Musselman and McKinney. In the NCAA Southeast Regional in Atlanta, UCLA beat Iowa State 84–74, then lost to North Carolina 88–81. In the first game, Richardson had 19 points (8 for 14 from the field), 14 assists, five rebounds, and just one turnover while playing the entire 40 minutes. Against North Carolina, he had 14 points, five assists, four rebounds, and four turnovers.

Richardson's best performance came in the Orlando Classic in April, when he went head-to-head against Hardaway, Charles Smith of Georgetown, and Boston College's Barros in three heavily scouted all-star games.

"He played great down there," Musselman said. "Everybody was waiting to see him against Tim Hardaway. Well, he outplayed Hardaway. Billy McKinney liked him, too. Everybody was impressed with him. Armstrong may be a better shooter. Hardaway gets into the paint better. But as a true point guard, Pooh is the best. He likes to lead. He makes decisions on the court as well as anybody. He showed that in Orlando."

Musselman especially liked Richardson's progress in his senior year: "He improved this year from the first game to the last because Jim Harrick did an unbelievable job with him. Defensively, he has tremendous leg strength and lateral movement. He's very good covering the ball, and he plays good position defense. He's cocky, an extremely confident kid. He has an attitude about him that just reeks confidence. And he knows the game. You sit down and talk to him, and he talks the game much beyond his age. Magic Johnson's worked with him. Magic's his tutor."

At a press conference in Minneapolis the day after the draft, Richardson tried to be nonchalant about his association with Magic. But then he admitted: "As a freshman, I was pretty anxious to meet him. We met. We played against each other. He took me to lunch. Then to dinner. Then to his house. I had a chance to sit right next to Magic Johnson at his house. Wow! Nice house!"

Besides introducing Richardson to the local media, the Timberwolves used the press conference to unveil their uniforms: white with green trim at home and blue with green trim on the road.

Star Tribune columnist Dan Barreiro called the uniforms bland, but they looked good to Richardson, who is more than happy to make his NBA debut with the Timberwolves: "It's a great opportunity. You get to learn a lot by playing a lot. I feel great about going there."

Gary Leonard was touted as a first-round selection; in fact, he was one of 15 players invited to attend the draft at the Felt Forum in Madison Square Garden. He brought along his parents. The three agonized as team after team passed on Leonard. Finally, he left.

"My parents first decided to get up and leave," Leonard said. "That didn't rest real easy with me, them leaving and me staying."

So he followed them out. "It was just too hard to sit there, with the TV cameras on you the whole time playing up everything, playing on agony," Leonard said.

The Sporting News rated Leonard the second-best center in the draft, behind Vlade Divac of Yugoslavia, yet called him a project. *Sports Illustrated* pegged Leonard as the 11th pick in the draft while using that same word: project.

Leonard, though, was a central figure in Missouri's success, averaging 10.4 points and 5.5 rebounds while shooting 59.3 percent from the floor. Missouri finished 29–8 and captured the Big Eight championship.

"We took him because he was there, a center who was available," Musselman said. "I thought he'd go in the first round."

West is a talented scorer, versatile, and plays hard. He didn't get as much media attention last season in the Big East because Georgetown, Syracuse, Seton Hall, and Pitt had better seasons that Villanova (18–16).

"I saw Doug play seven, eight times last season," Musselman said. "His outside shot was not as consistent as I thought it would be for an off guard, but he's 6–6½ and he's a great athlete. The guy has a quick first step. Villanova played a matchup zone and didn't run with the ball, so he's going to be a better pro than he was in college. He was a steal.''

West averaged a team-high 18.4 points and finished as Villanova's third all-time leading scorer. His durability is a decided plus: he averaged 34.5 minutes as a senior.

''In my heart, I'd like to play pro basketball,'' West said. ''I'd like to get that chance.''

He's got it. And so does Musselman.

When the Charlotte Hornets and Miami Heat ended their initial seasons in the NBA with 20 and 15 wins, respectively, the Timberwolves front office had gauges to measure the team's debut this season.

Stein was asked how his Timberwolves will fare in their maiden voyage in the Midwest Division against Utah, Denver, Dallas, Houston, San Antonio, and Charlotte. ''How many wins do I expect our first season?'' Stein asked. ''If we were somewhere around 15, I suppose that would be okay. I guess 13 would be a reasonable downside.

''An expansion team, I guess, is a mixed blessing,'' Stein added. ''On the one hand, you don't lose players in the expansion draft. On the other hand, you don't get to play just expansion teams. I don't know. I would guess 20, 22, would be doing very, very good, but again, I'd consider that a false step if it was done at the expense of developing a team the third, fourth, and fifth years. That's when you're really starting to be competitive.''

Asked how he expects Musselman and himself to handle the growing pains an expansion team accrues, Stein said, ''Bill knows what it is to win. That's one of the reason he's been able to motivate a lot of teams to play well and consistently play hard. Winners compete to win even when they don't win, though that doesn't mean being unprofessional or going to pieces or anything like that. It means he's not going to like it. I'm not going to like it. None of us are going to like it, but we are going to be realistic. We're not going to try to fix something that we can't fix immediately.''

Stein was asked how a man as obsessed as Musselman is with winning would react if the Timberwolves were to challenge Miami's 0–17 start. ''Somebody said you'd be able to jump start a car from Bill's neck,'' Stein said. ''I honestly think he'd handle it in a very professional manner on the outside, but inside he'd be driving himself crazy.''

It's a trip Musselman has made many times. The pressure, as well as the drive, comes from within. There are always games to be won, wars to be fought. In his mind, he is a Don Quixote of basketball, not realizing the windmills he spars with are born of his own unceasing imagination.

"I pour my guts into coaching every second," Bill Musselman says. He is a man obsessed. Truly a man never at peace.